Eyewitness Accounts of the American Revolution

Military Journal of Major Ebenezer Denny

The New York Times & Arno Press

Reprint Edition 1971 by Arno Press Inc.

*

LC# 70-140860
ISBN 0-405-01214-4

*

Eyewitness Accounts of the American Revolution, Series III
ISBN for complete set: 0-405-01187-3

*

Manufactured in the United States of America

Military Journal of Major Ebenezer Denny

Your faithful E Denny

MILITARY JOURNAL

OF

MAJOR EBENEZER DENNY,

An Officer in the Revolutionary and Indian Wars.

WITH AN

INTRODUCTORY MEMOIR.

Mirror of ancient faith!
Undaunted worth! inviolable truth!

DRYDEN'S ÆNEID.

PHILADELPHIA:
J. B. LIPPINCOTT & CO.
FOR THE
HISTORICAL SOCIETY OF PENNSYLVANIA.
1859.

STEREOTYPED BY W. S. HAVEN, PITTSBURGH, PA.

MEMOIR.

Ebenezer Denny was born in Carlisle, Cumberland County, Pennsylvania, on the 11th of March, 1761. He was the eldest child of William Denny and Agnes Parker. William, and his brother Walter, came to Cumberland from Chester County, in 1745. Walter Denny settled two or three miles south of Carlisle, where he owned a large tract of land, now divided into five farms. He raised a company for the Revolutionary struggle, was killed at the battle of the Crooked Billet; and his son taken, and kept three months on board a Jersey prison-ship. David Denny, for many years pastor of the Presbyterian church at Chambersburg, was a son of Walter. William lived in Carlisle. He was the first Coroner west of the Susquehanna, and a Commissary in the war.

The mother of Ebenezer Denny, Agnes, was the daughter of John Parker, and grand-daughter of Richard Parker. Richard, as early as 1730, acquired lands on the Cannadaguinnet, three miles west of Carlisle. These lands continued for two or three generations afterward in possession of his descendants. It was there that his grandsons, in the intervals of their military service, turned their swords into plowshares. All three—Alexander, Richard and Andrew—were actively engaged in the war. Alexander furnished two teams, at his own expense, when the army was at the White Plains. He was commissioned in Colonel Irvine's regiment, Second Lieutenant in Company No. 1, Captain Hay, January 9th, 1776. Marched in April following, from Carlisle to New York and Canada—promoted a First Lieutenant in Company No. 4, Captain Rippey, June 9th, 1776, and Captain, 31st July, 1777, in Colonel Irvine's regiment. In the first campaign against Quebec, he and his cousin, John Parker, who was one of his sergeants, suffered great hardships, and narrowly escaped being taken prisoners. At the close of the Revolutionary War, whilst Richard and Andrew emigrated to Kentucky, Alexander Parker settled in Western Virginia, on lands which he acquired by settlement and purchase, at the mouth of the Little Kanahwa, on which is now the town of Parkersburg. His only surviving child, Mary, whilst on a visit to her relative in Pittsburgh, was married to William Robinson, Jr., of Allegheny. On that occasion her cousin from Kentucky, a grandchild of Richard Parker, afterward Mrs. T. Crittenden, was her bridesmaid.

Agnes, the mother of Ebenezer Denny, was an uncommon woman, of great energy and intelligence. She was of middle height, fair complexion, blue eyes, bright sandy hair; beautiful in her younger days, attractive at all times, and prepossessing in her old age. Her numerous friends and relatives approached her always with confidence in her affection, her sympathy, her good temper and sound judgment. A devout Christian—with her Bible, in every sense, by heart. She never failed to ascribe the many deliverances of her son Ebenezer, to a particular providence—as other pious persons did to the prayers of herself, his good mother.

Her father left his large estate to his sons; as was the custom in those days. Agnes inherited nothing. Her husband, a highminded and gentlemanly man, fell away in his habits and circumstances. Ebenezer, therefore, felt that he ought to endeavor to assist them, as well as to support himself. At the age of thirteen, he obtained employment as a bearer of dispatches to the commandant at Fort Pitt. He crossed the Allegheny mountains alone, lying out in the woods with any party of pack-horsemen whom he overtook at nightfall. His friend in after years, Samuel Murphy, of "Murphy's Bend," on his first visit from Bullskins to Fort Pitt in 1774, met him at Turtle Creek, on his return from the fort: "a slender, fair, blue-eyed, red-haired boy, two or three years younger than himself, between eleven and thirteen years old." Murphy expressed, at the time, his surprise that the public authorities would intrust a mere lad to carry important dispatches through a wilderness infested with savage enemies. Twenty years afterward, Murphy was a lieutenant in a military expedition to Presqu' Isle, commanded by the person who was that night at Turtle Creek his camp-mate and bed-fellow. Once during that expedition, whilst suppressing a mutiny, and again, when returning, he fell out of his perogue, the life of the commander was saved by that brave and athletic soldier. "When I met him at Turtle Creek," said Murphy, "he must have been on his return from the fort. I know him too well to suppose that he would have disclosed to me the nature of his business, until after it was executed." On two of these missions to Fort Pitt, at the Loyalhanna and at Turkey-foot, he was chased into Fort Loudon by the Indians.

He was afterward employed in his father's store in Carlisle. Fresh from his bridle path on Chestnut Ridge and Laurel Hill, and familiar with its danger, it was hardly to be expected that he would be content at home behind a counter, whilst his uncles, of whom he was justly proud, risked everything in the war.

A letter of marque and reprisal was about to sail to the West Indies. He repaired to Philadelphia and shipped as a volunteer. The captain intended to intercept a British merchantman, with a valuable cargo, bound from the Bahamas to Halifax. But entertaining a party of friends who accompanied him down the Delaware, was unable to command his ship when, outside the capes, the expected prize came in sight. He made amends for this disappointment afterward by a vigilant, daring and successful cruise. His ship became noted in the Gulf. On one occasion, off Martinique, he had a running fight with three armed British cruisers. In that chase and action, Ebenezer attracted the notice of the captain by his alacrity and intrepidity, as he had throughout the voyage by his modesty and fidelity. Observing that in every emergency he was not less brave than any of the crew, whilst he was always reliable and trustworthy, the captain, on the voyage home, promoted him to the command of the quarter deck.

To overcome his scruples and aversion to what seemed so much like highway robbery, that even the love of adventure could not gloss it over, he was offered the privilege of supercargo, to induce him to embark again in another cruise. This tempting offer reached him in the family cabin at Carlisle, surrounded by his mother and sisters, whose affectionate endeavors to dissuade him from its acceptance only increased his desire to earn something for himself and them. He decided to go back to sea. He invested his share of the prize money in whiskey and flour, and had crossed the Susquehanna with his wagon on his way to Philadelphia, when he received a commission of Ensign in the First Pennsylvania regiment. He gladly disposed of his produce at Harrisburg, and joined the army at Little York. This was shortly after the mutiny in the Pennsylvania line. In his military journal, which then commences, he describes the pain he felt at being obliged to witness the execution.

Then followed Wayne's forced marches into Virginia, and the first action of the Pennsylvania troops, under Lieutenant-Colonel Richard Butler, near Williamsburg, where they had a desperate encounter with Simcoe; the British partisan and his rangers being very much emboldened by their recent success at the junction of the Rivanna and Fluvanna rivers, at which point, with a detachment of yagers, infantry and hussars, they frightened the Baron Steuben into a night retreat of thirty miles, and destroyed the greater part of his stores scattered along the river bank; although he was at the head of five hundred Virginia regulars, with some militia, separated from the enemy by deep water, and the boats all on his own side. This was Steuben's first and only separate command.

Soon after, Wayne, who also was credulous, but in the opposite way, attempted to surprise Cornwallis. He expected to find his army partly crossed over and divided by the James river. Our young ensign, the extent of whose marching of late had been the length of his quarter deck, frankly confesses that he could not keep up with his company. As they were coming into action, his captain and fellow townsman, falling behind and walking by his side, quietly said to him, "Now, Eb., for the honor of old Carlisle, do not disgrace yourself." Montgomery made this rallying appeal to the memory of their native place, supposing that his young townsman was going into his first action; probably not knowing that the youngster was fresh from the perils of the sea, and familiar with the smoke of gunpowder on the deck of a privateer. The boldness of their commander advanced them into a position of great danger, from which they were extricated only by still greater daring. Cornwallis, astonished at the hardihood of the attack, sent a regiment of infantry to meet him, and cautiously deployed his whole army to the right and left. The regiment of British infantry, in front of the American line, marched up in open order, with perfect regularity; Wayne reserving his fire until they were within a distance of seventy paces, when both lines enchanged shots for a few minutes. The hero of Stony Point was in full uniform—his horse prancing in front of the Pennsylvania infantry, his face glowing with pleasure. He seemed to Ensign Denny, who stood near him, to be amused with the loss of his plume, which was cut off by a ball on the first fire. Nearly all the field officers were dismounted.

A young officer, acting in the staff, whose pantaloons were rubbed by some bleeding horse, imagining himself wounded, fainted, and was carried off the field. Being very handsome, one of the few young men of fortune in the army who could afford to dress well, he was envied by his brother officers, who made the most of the accident to laugh him out of the service. Ensign Denny was the only officer in the company who was not wounded. The captain and lieutenant were disabled at the first fire. The troops retreated by companies. Montgomery's fell to the command of the ensign. They recrossed the swamp by the narrow causeway, in good order, but with such expedition, that he could again hardly keep up with the men. But "thanks to the veteran first sergeant, the most important officer," he remarked, "in a company, they were kept together."

The unexampled hardihood of Wayne, persisting to advance, and actually fighting after he must have been aware that the whole British army were at hand, perplexed Cornwallis, made him apprehend an ambuscade, and hesitate in his pursuit. Otherwise, Wayne and all his force would have been taken. The loss of the Americans in this battle, according to Mr.

Denny's account, was one hundred and eighteen killed wounded and prisoners, including ten officers.

Subsequently, at the siege of York, on the night of the 14th October, Ensign Denny was in the advance attack on the redoubts, in which the Pennsylvania troops distinguished themselves under the lead of Hamilton. In the ceremony of the surrender, Lieutenant-Colonel Richard Butler, (afterward General Butler, killed at St. Clair's defeat,) in honor of his recent services and the signal part his regiment had taken in the capture of the redoubt, was appointed to plant the first American flag upon the British parapet.

Colonel Butler, who was a short heavy person, detailed for this service his youngest ensign, in his figure and stature a contrast to himself; probably partial to him, as coming from his own town, Carlisle. The young officer mounted the parapet, in the presence of the three armies, and was in the act of planting the flag-staff, when the Baron Steuben rode out of the lines, dismounted, took the flag, and planted it himself. The disappointed and mortified subaltern had nothing to do but submit. But not so his colonel, the hero who had avenged the Baron's flight from Simcoe. He, that night, sent the arrogant foreigner a message, as every one expected, and it took all the influence of Rochambeau and Washington to prevent a hostile meeting.

Perhaps there was some excuse for the Prussian martinet, in the fact, that a dispute on a point of military etiquette had arisen among the general staff at headquarters, in which Lafayette and Rochambeau took opposite sides; the Marquis contending that he should "take the flag," and the Count claiming the right for the Baron Steuben.

In no part of his diary or correspondence does he allude to the subject of two duels, in which he was concerned as second. One of these affairs grew out of some offense given to the surgeon of the regiment, by a brother officer. The aggressor, as was his custom, when he thought he had offended an officer of lower grade, was seen in camp next day without his epaulets, to show that he waived his rank, and was ready to give satisfaction. The surgeon, like many other surgeons in the Revolutionary army, was a brave man, and expert with the pistol; nevertheless, at the hostile meeting which followed, they exchanged shots without effect, very much to the surprise of the challenged party, who at first accused his friend of having loaded the pistols only with powder; but on being shown the trees directly behind them, freshly barked by the balls, recovered his good humor, and requested him to "prime and load." Lieutenant Denny, instead of doing so, assured his friend that he was in the wrong, and succeeded in reconciling the combatants before they left the field. They walked back to the camp, arm in arm, the officer congratulating himself that he had not killed his doctor.

It will be recollected that they were officers of the army—at a time when dueling was more than now the fashion—were on the soil of Virginia, where the custom was indigenous—and in the presence of our allies, the French chivalry.

Ensign Denny, as appears from his journal, was afterward with Lieutenant-Colonel Josiah Harmar, and the First Pennsylvania regiment, in the Carolinas—under the command of General St. Clair, and at Charleston, during its investment, and after its evacuation.

In the order book of Lieutenant-Colonel Harmar, dated Philadelphia, August 27th, 1784, we find him arranged as ensign in Captain M'Curdy's company of infantry. From that time, throughout the campaigns of Harmar and St. Clair, and his own expedition to Presqu' Isle, his diary is a sufficient sketch of his life for that period. The Adjutant of Harmar and the Aid-de-camp of St. Clair, no one had better opportunities of obtaining authentic information.

When the United States Commissioners were at Fort Finney, waiting for the Shawanees to come in to the treaty, General Clark kept aloof from his colleagues. There appeared to be some jealousy and coolness between them. But to the young commandant, Lieutenant Denny, he was like a father. He invited him to pass his evenings at his tent; threw off his reserve, and talked about his own adventures. He told him that frequently, at night, when his soldiers lay upon their arms, he has crept, on all fours, to the neighboring lick, with only his tomahawk, for fear of alarming the Indians, watched for the deer to pass, and selecting a young one, killed it, and carried it back to the bivouac for the supper of his men. He was a stout, rather short, square man, with a high, broad forehead, sandy hair, blue eyes, and heavy, shaggy eye-brows. With his personal prowess, hardihood and capacity for detail, there was always comprehensive wisdom in his plan and purpose. He raised his force and supplies promptly. He knew exactly, and therefore never overrated the dangers in the way. He marched quietly to his distant object and took it by surprise. There was no martial pageant, no ostentatious and pompous parade. He threaded the forest silently—or on his Chickasaw ponies galloped across the prairies, and gave the first notice of his presence to the savages by his flag supplanting that of their great allies. Hence that prestige, that renown amongst them which was of such value to carry on hostilities or dictate a peace. When he was present, the great warriors never noticed any other General.

The night on which his little party from Kentucky reached the Kaskaskia river at Menard's Gap, they saw on the opposite bank the Jesuits' seminary lighted up, and heard issuing from it the sounds of the violin. Clark, leaving his horses and most of his men on the eastern side, waded across at the warm ford. It was a ball given by the British officers to the French inhabitants. He placed one of his men quietly at each door, outside, with orders to let none pass. He himself, wrapped in his blanket capot, his arms folded, leaning against the door-cheek, looked in upon the dance. An Indian who lay on the floor of the entry, intently gazing at his features in the light reflected from the room, suddenly sprang to his feet and gave the war-whoop. The dancing ceased, the ladies screamed, and the Frenchmen rushed to the door. Clark, without moving from his position, or changing his grave expression, desired them to go on with the dance. "The only difference is," said he, "you now dance under Virginia, instead of Great Britain." At day-light he and his mounted men were opposite to Fort Chartiers, on the crest of the bluff, and by marching along its profile so as to be seen from the fort, countermarching out of sight and again showing themselves in a continuous file, his force appeared so large that the much more numerous enemy capitulated without a shot.

The massacre of the Blue Licks recalled him to Kentucky. He described to Lieutenant Denny the panic in the settlements, in the face of which he beat up for volunteers; and what no other man could have done, he promptly raised a party and hung on the bloody flanks of the enemy. His masterly march on the Wabash and capture of Post St. Vincent, he related somewhat different from, and without the flourish of history.

After his conquest of Illinois, he was voted a sword by the State of Virginia. The bearer of it met the grave and discontented hero on the bank of the Wabash. He was anxiously waiting for news that the House of Delegates had passed his accounts, and had voted money to pay them, to enable him to make good his engagements, on sudden emergencies, for supplies to his men. He was disappointed. He took the sword—drew it from its scabbard, and placing the point to the ground, thrust it deep in the soil he had conquered, and broke it off by the hilt. Throwing away the glittering handle, he said, "I asked Virginia for bread, and she sent me a sword!"

During the campaign of 1790, and at the battle of the

Maumee towns, the Journal and letters of Major Denny, who was in fact the acting Adjutant-General of the army, state so fully every military occurrence, and his deposition before the court of inquiry, on the conduct of the commander, is so clear a summary, that it is only necessary to refer to them.

The reader will see that there runs through the whole a vein of loyal attachment to the gallant and accomplished Harmar, which has the ring and lustre of the pure metal, and does honor to them both.

On the 14th December, 1790, President Washington communicated to Congress a military dispatch from the Governor of the North-Western Territory, dated November 6th, in which General St. Clair says: "Mr. Denny, the gentleman who takes General Harmar's dispatches, I beg leave to mention to you in a particular manner; and if you will be pleased to do so to the President in his favor, you may be assured he will not disappoint any expectations that may be formed. He has every quality that I could wish a young man to possess, who meant to make the army his profession. There are, however, some other traits in his character as a man, that are not generally known, that would endear him. Out of the little pittance he receives, he has maintained two aged parents for a long time."[1]

In Brigadier-General Harmar's dispatch to the Secretary of War, dated November 4, 1790, after giving an account of the battle, he says: "The bearer, Lieutenant Denny, is my Adjutant. It will afford me great satisfac-

[1] American State Papers, vol. iv. on Indian Affairs, page 104.

tion to know that some mark of honor will be shown him. His long and faithful services merit it. There is a vast deal of business in this western country. If there is no impropriety in giving me an aid-de-camp, I wish him to be the person." At the foot of the General's letter he says: "N. B. My Adjutant is really and truly an officer."[1]

Major Denny's habitual reserve on the events of his military life, was by no means lessened on the subject of the melancholy scenes of the 4th of November, 1791. As he says in his Journal, he recurred to them with pain and reluctance.

The unfortunate commander himself, modest and dignified as he was, more frequently conversed on the subject, in his retirement at Chestnut Ridge. To his neighbor, still living, the venerable Alexander Johnston, he said that nothing had ever given him more concern than his having dispatched his aid-de-camp, Major Denny, whose worth, and the value of whose life, no one more appreciated, upon a most desperate mission, from which, on reflection, he had no hope of ever seeing him return alive. This was probably at the commencement of the attack on the 4th of November, when with Colonel Oldham he rode forward to the creek, where the Indians had driven in the militia, and vainly endeavoring to arrest their flight, that brave Kentuckian was shot by his side and fell from his horse, execrating the cowardice of his men.

---

[1] Documents, Legislative and Executive, Congress United States, 1st to 3d Session of the 13th Congress.

In the confusion of the battle, when the officers were nearly all killed or wounded, John Morgan, the aid of the disabled Butler, rode up to Major Denny and asked for orders. His horse, covered with blood, rubbed his wounded face on the Major's pantaloons. This was not noticed at the time; and afterward General St. Clair observing the blood, said to his aid-de-camp, "Major, you are wounded." The latter dismounted, drew off his boot, but finding no wound, recollected Morgan's horse. The General smiled and said, "Don't you remember the Irish beauty?"—alluding to the young officer at the battle of James River, who perceiving his pantaloon stained in the same way, supposed himself wounded, and was carried off the field. This was told to the writer by his father, as an instance of General St. Clair's coolness and self-possession in the midst of the panic.

After General Butler had received his first wound, he continued to walk in front close along the line, with his coat off and his arm in a sling, encouraging the men, and retired only after receiving a second wound in the side. The Commander-in-chief sent Major Denny, with his compliments, to inquire how he was. He found him in the middle of the camp, in a sitting posture, supported by knapsacks — the rifle balls of the Indians, who now surrounded closely the whole camp, concentrated upon that point. One of the wounded General's servants and two of his horses were shot there. He seemed, however, to have no anxiety, and to the inquiry of the aid-de-camp, he answered that he felt well. Whilst making this reply, a young cadet from Virginia, who stood at his side, was hit on the cap of the knee by a spent ball, and cried so loudly with the pain and alarm, that General Butler actually shook his wounded side with laughter. This satisfied Major Denny that the second wound was not mortal, that the General being very fleshy, the ball might not have penetrated a vital part. He always believed that he might have been brought away and his life saved. Probably his own aid-de-camp, Major John Morgan, may have offered to bring him off, as was his duty, and the wounded General declined, conscious that his weight and helplessness would only encumber his brave young friend for no use, and hinder him from saving himself.

It is among the traditions of the family at Carlisle, that as their relative rode in the rear of the retreating army, a woman caught his horse by its long tail, and held on, although threatened with hoof and sword. She was rewarded for her confidence in his generosity by being taken up behind, and carried in safety to Fort Jefferson.

The first intelligence of the disastrous termination of St. Clair's campaign was brought to Philadelphia by his aid-de-camp, who rode down Market street on the gallant little horse which had borne his tired rider night and day from Fort Pitt, and now reined up, bespattered with mud, at the President's mansion. General Washington had a party at dinner that evening. A servant came up stairs, and said that a young officer from the army had a letter for the President. The private secretary, Mr. Tobias Lear, was sent down to receive it.

The officer said that his orders were to give the dispatch to the President only, which being told to Washington, he came down to the ante-room and received it. He had not read more than a few lines, until he perceived its import, and broke out in expressions, which the young officer did not set down in his diary, but which Mr. Tobias Lear, the private secretary, recorded in his private journal, to be published at this late day, and cited in confirmation of the probable truth of the allegation, that Washington swore profanely at that traitor, Lee, in the battle of Monmouth.

In a most violent passion, says the secretary, he exclaimed, "Did I not in the last words I said to him, warn him against a *surprise?*" As if a *surprise* was the only thing to be feared, the only advantage needed by an enemy, brave by nature, and trained to war from childhood, to enable them to vanquish an equal number of undisciplined troops, raw from the jails of the cities, poorly equipped, hurried off, late in the season, to fight them, united in their forest home—and to be "surprised"—as indeed they were—only because the second in command, the officer of the day, would not permit the information, regularly had, that the enemy were near the camp in unusual numbers, "to go beyond his own tent." His bravery, his exertions during the day to redeem it from the consequences of his fault, and his fate, made some atonement.

But there was no excuse for the President attaching to the expedition an officer of his high rank and pretensions, without giving him the command-in-chief. There was no excuse for his sending against the Indians, all united under Brant, a force not more numerous than them, and so irregular and mutinous that it took the best regiment to protect the convoys of provisions from the deserters.

After Major Denny's resignation and retirement to civil life, he married, on the first of July, 1793, Nancy Wilkins, also a native of Carlisle; the youngest daughter, by the first wife, of John Wilkins, Sr., formerly of that place, who was a captain of a volunteer company in the Revolution and at the battle of Brandywine. Before removing to Pittsburgh, Captain Wilkins resided for some time at Bedford, and represented Bedford county in the Convention of 1777, which formed the first Constitution of Pennsylvania. Mrs. Denny was the sister, by the same mother, of John Wilkins, Jr., a surgeon's mate in the Revolutionary army, afterward Quarter-master General; of Charles Wilkins, of Lexington, Kentucky; and of the Hon. William Wilkins, of Homewood.

In 1794, Ebenezer Denny was again commissioned a captain, and commanded the expedition to Le Bœuf, the ostensible object of which was to protect the commissioners in laying out a town at Presqu' Isle — but the real and important purpose, to prevent the Six Nations uniting with the Miami Indians against Wayne.

Major Denny, as instructed by Governor Mifflin, kept a journal, in which he entered minutely every occurrence on the expedition. In transcribing his original diary, he thought many of the details not worth preserving. But it is believed that even the daily entries of the weather on French Creek, sixty years ago, are not without interest at present.

In the years 1795 and 1796, Major Denny resided with his young family at his farm and mill, about six miles from Pittsburgh, near the Monongahela, about half a mile from the river, where the road to M'Keesport crosses Street's Run. Whilst residing there he was taken up as a candidate for the State Legislature. His opponent was John B. C. Lucas, a native of France, only recently an emigrant from that country. The result shows the force at that time of party spirit. On one side was a native of the State, a Revolutionary officer, who but lately served with credit in three expeditions against the Indians; the last one of which he himself commanded. Many of the early settlers in the election district, and most of the influential men amongst them, had served under him. On the other hand, a foreigner, speaking the English language with difficulty—but a short time from Europe—his family not attempting to conciliate the prejudices of their puritanical neighbors—having himself the reputation of being an "avowed Atheist"—his wife "plowing on Sunday."

Lucas' farm was about half a mile lower down the Monongahela, on the brow of Coal Hill, the high bluff which flanks that river on the south side. They were near neighbors. On the morning of the election, Lucas, on his way to the polls, passing the mill, exchanged friendly salutations with his rival. "Your father," (I shall give Judge Lucas' own words,) "your father asked me to wait until he got his horse; he supposed I was going to the election, and said he would go along. We rode together to the place in Mifflin township where the election was held. Arriving on the ground, the country people shook hands with him, inquired about his health and his family, but spoke not a word to me — no man spoke to Lucas — not one. Your father, being a modest man, said to me, 'Lucas, we have no business here; let us vote and go home.' We did so. On my return, Mrs. Lucas said, 'Well, Lucas, how goes on the election?' I replied, 'Oh! they are all for Major Denny. They greeted him in the kindest manner — no one spoke to Lucas.' She agreed with me that my chance was bad. However, next morning the return judges calling with us on their way to town, stated that I had a majority in the township — in fact I was elected. Next year, or year after, your father was a candidate for Commissioner of the county, and received nearly every vote — that not being then considered a party question." This was about three or four years after the meeting of the insurgents at Braddock's Field, to which convention no small delegation went from Mifflin township. The greater part of the voters had indeed been "Whiskey Boys." "Your father," said Lucas, "was the 'family candidate' — the brother-in-law of General John Wilkins, the obnoxious Quarter-master who would not buy the illicit whiskey." Calumnies circulated on the ground to the prejudice of Lucas were promptly and warmly contradicted by Major Denny, to whom a few confidently referred those who believed that he killed his son in a fit of passion, and that his wife, during his absence in France, had "plowed on Sunday."

It was well known that Lucas, as well as Gallatin, was identified with the popular cause. No one knew better how to avail himself of rural political prejudices. At the same time neither he nor Gallatin were in favor of extreme measures. Mr. Gallatin, on his way to and from Pittsburgh, on the road home to New Geneva, was accustomed to stop and spend the night with Lucas. After the convention at Pittsburgh, he called as usual and remained all night. He had with him a fresh proof of the resolutions adopted by the meeting. He showed them to Lucas, and asked what he thought of them. "In my opinion," he replied, "they are too strong." "I think so too," said Gallatin; "it was not my fault that they are so."

The next year Major Denny being elected Commissioner of the county, returned to his residence in town. Lucas and he sold their farms — Lucas to go to the newly acquired territory of Louisiana as a Territorial Judge. The five thousand dollars which he got for his Monongahela farm, he laid out in a Spanish grant, then adjacent to St. Louis—now the finest part of that city—and worth nearly as many millions of dollars. Whilst sitting as a judge in the territorial court, there came on for trial a case in which his old neighbor, Ebenezer Denny, was plaintiff, and Alexander M'Nair defendant. M'Nair was one of the first settlers, was married to a lady who belonged to one of the most influential French families. He was well known, very popular, and was elected the first Governor of the State of Missouri, beating General William Clark. On the other hand, Ebenezer Denny was a non-resident, not present at the trial, and personally unknown to the jurors. Seeing, therefore, such odds against him, Judge Lucas undertook to charge the jury, which he did in French and English: "When I lived," said he, "in Pennsylvania, I was the next neighbor to the plaintiff; we differed in politics—we were opposing candidates for office, but there never was a more honest man. It is impossible that he could set up any claim that was not just and true." The jury, without leaving the box, found a verdict for the plaintiff for the amount he claimed.

Although it appears from his correspondence, that he was an applicant for office at the organization of the new counties in Western Pennsylvania, it is very certain that he never received any civil appointment whatever from the government, State or Federal. This may have been owing to a diffidence which kept him in the background, or a soldierly stiffness which made him a bad courtier. In his letter of the 14th December, 1796, to General Harmar, the intimate personal friend of Governor Mifflin, he says quite as much for his competitor, George Thompson, as he does for himself.

About the beginning of the present century, he entered into partnership in business, with Anthony Beelen, a Belgian, introduced to him by his father, the Austrian Minister, Francis, Baron de Belen Bartholf. Denny and Beelen were concerned with Lafleur, or "Falure," a Frenchman, in a glass works, probably the second or third factory of the kind established at Pittsburgh. It was on the north bank of the Ohio, opposite the ripple at the head of Brunot's, the first island; hence the name—"*Glass-house Riffle.*"

In 1803, he was Treasurer of Allegheny county. He appears first on the list of the County Treasurers—and was again Treasurer in 1808.

In 1804, Ebenezer Denny was appointed a Director of the Branch of the Bank of Pennsylvania, established that year at Pittsburgh. This was the first bank west of the mountains. "The Miami Exporting Company" was not then a bank, and did not become so until afterward. Three years subsequently a bank was started in Kentucky, under the name of "The Kentucky Insurance Company." It was, in reality, an institution for banking purposes. Like the bank established the same year in Nashville, it failed, as did the Bank of Kentucky and its branches, some years after.

The Branch of the Bank of Pennsylvania at Pittsburgh was subsequently transferred to and merged in the office of the Bank of the United States. Thomas Wilson, who had been a Teller in the Bank of Pennsylvania, subsequently, through the influence of Langdon Cheves, was made principal Cashier of the Bank of the United States in Philadelphia. In this capacity Wilson again visited Pittsburgh during the great money pressure and general insolvency of 1819. He came out with full powers to settle with the debtors of the western offices. Major Denny, then a Director of the Branch of the Bank of the United States, was engaged by several of the principal debtors of the Branch, to endeavor to induce Wilson to accept of property in settlement. He was selected for this purpose, from his own perfect solvency and freedom from debt to the bank, and from the confidence which Mr. Wilson had, when in the office here, reposed in his judgment and integrity. Notwithstanding that the property of the Pittsburgh debtors was offered at a low valuation, it was refused. Similar offers in Cincinnati were, fortunately for the bank, accepted.

In the first Board of Directors of the Branch of the Bank of Pennsylvania at Pittsburgh, five of Major Denny's associates had been officers in the army of the Revolution: Presley Neville, Abraham Kirkpatrick, Adamson Tannehill, George Stevenson and John Wilkins, Jr. James O'Hara, who succeeded John Wilkins, the first President, was the President when the Branch Bank of Pennsylvania was transferred to, and merged in the office of the Bank of the United States. Although not an officer in the Revolutionary war, he was a Commissary and Quarter-master General during the subsequent Indian hostilities, and at least a coadjutor with the army in the Indian prolongation of the War of Independence. James O'Hara was a man of foresight and enterprise. In partnership with Major Isaac Craig, he established the first glass works, and was the pioneer in that branch of Pittsburgh manufactures; which next to, if not more than even iron, is the staple of the place.

A large proportion of the prominent citizens of Pittsburgh, at this early period, being, as it thus appears, retired officers of the army, they necessarily constituted a majority in the boards of trustees of the Church, of the Academy and the Bank. Nor does it appear that the Bank of Pennsylvania, or its successor, the Bank of the United States, had any reason to regret their confidence in these gentlemen. Only one other branch of the United States, the office at Mobile, lost less money, or was more successfully managed. If in one or two instances directors were indebted to the institution, their liabilities were fully liquidated by their estates. To these brave men the country was a debtor when they died, and continues so to the descendants of most of them. But no one lost by them.

It is remarkable how many of the original settlers at Pittsburgh had been officers in the Revolutionary army: Colonels John and Presley Neville, William Butler; Lieutenant-Colonel Stephen Bayard; Majors Isaac Craig, Ebenezer Denny, Edward Butler, Alexander Fowler; Captains Abraham Kirkpatrick, Adamson Tannehill, Uriah Springer, George M'Cully, Nathaniel Irish, John Irwin, Joseph Ashton, James Gordon Heron; Lieutenants Josiah Tannehill, William M'Millan, Gabriel Peterson, — Ward; Surgeons'-mates John Wilkins, Jr., George Stevenson, John M'Dowell. They made quite a colony of retired officers at *De-un-da-ga*.

In 1805, Major Denny made preparations to move to the Mississippi, in hopes that a southern and milder climate would agree better with the failing health of one dearer to him than life. His old military friends,

Colonel Sargent, Dr. Carmichael, and farther down the hospitable coast, the Butlers, were ready to receive them with open arms. He had a house engaged in Natchez, and built a barge for the purpose of conveying his family down the river, when the beloved person for whose benefit the removal was intended, got worse, and died on the first day of May, 1806, in her thirty-first year, leaving three sons, Harmar, William and St. Clair; and two daughters, the youngest an infant, and following its mother in a few days.

There are some old inhabitants of Pittsburgh who remember that young mother and lamented wife—her graceful manners—her delicate but elegant form—expressive and beautiful features, and mind surpassing the graces of her person; who, if they have ever read the inscription on her tomb in the old Presbyterian graveyard, written by Alexander Addison, must have felt that it was no common-place exaggeration, but like everything from his pen, worthy of his warm heart and sound judgment, and a just tribute to loveliness and virtue

For several years after this period, Major Denny obtained from the War Department the contracts for the supply of rations to the troops at Fort Fayette and at Presqu' Isle, still retaining, in connection with these engagements, his mercantile and commission business, at the north-west corner of Market and Third streets, in a house which he built of the bricks of Fort Pitt.

On the declaration of war with England, his contract obliged him to supply the rations at Erie on thirty days notice. After the surrender of Hull, large quotas of militia were suddenly ordered to certain points on the lake shore. The contractors in Ohio and Indiana claiming the benefit of that clause in their contracts which entitled them to thirty days notice, did not attempt to meet the requisition. Major Denny was the only contractor who did not claim the benefit of that provision. In Ohio and Indiana they all failed. He proceeded promptly and at all sacrifices, to forward the supplies to the post at Erie. This he did in spite of the enhanced price of provisions and cost of transportation. Of course he lost a great deal of money by his patriotic — I may say, military spirit on that emergency. However, Colonel Eustis, the Secretary of War, seeing that he was the only western army contractor who did not take advantage of the terms of his contract in that respect, directed him, in addition to his own proper posts in Pennsylvania, to furnish, also, the supplies to the North-western army; which he did, and so much to the satisfaction of General Harrison, that at the close of the campaign and successful termination of the war, he wrote a complimentary letter to Major Denny, thanking him for having discharged his commissariat duties with so much promptness, energy and ability, and ascribing much of the success in the prosecution of the war in the North-west to his assistance.

Major Denny managed this business through well chosen agents, without leaving home, unless to go to Washington for the settlement of his accounts. He paid these agents liberally — with the principal one in Ohio, John Waddel, of Chillicothe, he divided his profits.

When Pittsburgh, by an act of the Legislature, on the

18th March, 1816, was incorporated into a city, Ebenezer Denny was elected the first Mayor. He declined a re-election, and retired from all public employments, except that of Director in the Branch of the Bank of the United States, and afterward of the Bank of Pittsburgh, in which he was a large stockholder; and where, from his great experience, perfect independence, judgment and integrity, he had some influence, which he used with discrimination and liberal spirit. Latterly he spent, also, a portion of his time in the discharge of some private trusts which devolved on him by the death of personal friends; and in improving his estate at the mouth of Deer Creek. In the summer of 1822, whilst on a visit to the Falls of Niagara, in company with his only daughter, he was taken ill, and with difficulty reached home, where he died, on the 21st of July, 1822, in the sixty-first year of his age.

Last winter, his Diary, or "Military Journal," was shown for the first time, to a few friends in Philadelphia, at whose instance the Historical Society of Pennsylvania resolved to publish it. For convenience in correcting the proofs, it was agreed to stereotype it in Pittsburgh. There would have been, however, nothing inappropriate in its first seeing the light in the city of the Revolution, where his services began, and where they ended.

In prefacing the publication of the Journal with an imperfect Memoir of his life, it may be said for apology, in the words of Tully:

> Hæc scripsi non otii abundantiâ, sed amoris erga te.

Appended are several letters of General Harmar, now for the first time published. Many of them illustrate the Diary. The temptation could not be resisted of including some for their own attraction and public interest. They sustain, throughout, the General's high military reputation and character for vigilance and discipline. They show that, with similar views to those of General Clark, he continually pressed upon the government the policy and necessity of conquering the Indians by first taking the "western posts."

General Harmar was tall and well built, with a manly port, blue eyes, and keen martial glance. He was very bald, wore a cocked hat, and his powdered hair in a cue. Such was his appearance, as described to the writer by the late Harmar Denny, on his return to college from his first visit to "Harmar's Retreat," on the east bank of the Schuylkill, near Gray's Ferry. As he approached the house, before he was half way up the lawn, the General, who was standing in the porch, knew him by the likeness to his father, and hailed the young collegian, with the grace, the dignity and scholarship of the old school—thus apostrophizing the virtues of his ancient friend:

> Salve pietas! Salve prisca fides!

Jos. Harmar

MILITARY JOURNAL

OF

MAJOR EBENEZER DENNY.

CARLISLE, *May* 1*st*, 1781.—The Pennsylvania Line, after the revolt and discharge of the men, last winter, were reduced to six regiments; the officers ordered to different towns within the State to recruit. An appointment of ensign in the 7th had been obtained for me in August last; the 7th and 4th were incorporated, and under command of Lt.-Col. Comt. William Butler, rendezvoused at this place—companies now about half full. The effective men were formed into four companies, and marched to Little York; I was arranged to one of the marching companies, Samuel Montgomery, captain, and George Bluer, lieutenant. All the recruits fit for service, from the different stations, were brought to York, formed into two regiments of eight companies each, destined for the State of Virginia. A few days spent in equipping, &c., and for the trial of soldiers charged with mutiny, General Anthony Wayne, the commanding officer, influenced, no doubt, by experience of the revolt last winter, expresses a determination to punish, with the utmost rigor, every case of mutiny or disobedience. A general court martial continued sitting several days; twenty odd prisoners brought before them; seven were sentenced to die. The regiments paraded in the evening earlier than usual; orders passed to the officers along the line to put to death instantly any man who stirred from his rank. In front of the parade the ground rose and descended again, and at the distance of about three hundred yards over this rising ground, the prisoners were escorted by a captain's guard; heard the fire of one platoon and immediately a smaller one, when the regiments wheeled by companies and marched round by the place of execution. This was an awful exhibition. The seven objects were seen by the troops just as they had sunk or fell under the fire. The sight must have made an impression on the men; it was designed with that view.

York, *May* 15*th.*—Provision for transporting baggage, &c., and other necessary preparation. Commenced our march for Virginia; the weather pleasant and roads tolerably good. Passed through Frederick Town (Maryland), where were some British prisoners quartered; they turned out to see us. Next day reached the Potomac; here we were detained for want of craft—boats few and in bad condition. The artillery passed over first (a battalion of artillery accompanied the brigade). The second flat-boat had left the shore about forty yards, when the whole sunk. Several women were on board; but as hundreds of men were on the bank, relief soon reached them; none were lost—got all over. Proceeded a few miles and encamped. Struck our tents every morning before day. About eight or nine o'clock, as we found water, a short halt was made, the water-call beat; parties, six or eight from each company, conducted by a non-commissioned officer, with canteens, fetched water. Seldom allowed to eat until twelve o'clock, when the arms were stacked, knapsacks taken off, and water sent for by parties as before. Officers of a company generally messed together, sometimes more; one of their servants carried cooked provisions for the day; no cooking until night. Not acquainted with the country on our route, but understood that we were marching much about — very circuitous — keeping off the Blue Ridge close on our right. This to avoid the enemy and secure our junction with the Marquis Lafayette.

June 18th.—Joined the troops under command of Lafayette. The Marquis had marched two or three days to meet us. His men look as if they were fit for business. They are chiefly all light infantry, dressed in frocks and over-alls of linen. One day spent in washing and refreshing—in fixing arms, carriages, &c., and served out ammunition. Move toward Richmond, where Lord Cornwallis with the British army lay. Heard that his lordship was employed burning and destroying warehouses of tobacco, all the public store-houses, &c. Passed through Richmond toward Williamsburg after the enemy—joined by Baron Steuben with some new levies. Near Bacon's Bridge the British turned upon us; our advance pressed them too close. The army was formed for a fight — they did not come on. General Wayne very anxious to do something. Colonel Simcoe, who commands the British legion (horse and mounted infantry), is constantly committing some depredation abroad, and foraging for their army. Wayne hears of him — our brigade leave their tents and baggage, march at dark, with piece of white paper in each man's hat — flints taken out. At day-light reach place called the Bowling Green, where Simcoe had been the evening before. This was a severe march for me — found myself asleep more than once on the route. Returned and met the baggage. A detachment from the brigade put under command of Colonel Richard Butler. After a variety of marching and counter-marching, Butler at length intercepts Simcoe; a smart skirmish takes place; Wayne supports Butler, and Simcoe retreats. Here for the first time saw wounded men; feelings not very agreeable; endeavor to conquer this disposition or weakness; the sight sickened me. This little engagement within six miles of Williamsburg, where the enemy were encamped. Pennsylvania troops retreat — advance again. See the Marquis' light troops but seldom—know they are not far off. Kept constantly on the move. Hear that the enemy have decamped and preparing to cross James river at Jamestown. Our brigade move down; lay on arms all night about nine miles from the enemy. At day-light move on; middle of the afternoon of the 6th of July firing ahead. Our advance drove in the enemy's pickets, marching at this time by companies, in open order. My captain (Montgomery) fell behind his company where my place was, talked with me; gives me a lesson useful to me. When perhaps within one hundred and fifty yards of the enemy, we closed column and displayed; advanced in battalion until the firing commenced, and ran along the whole line. A regiment or more of the light infantry and three pieces of artillery were in the line. Saw the British light infantry, distinctly, advancing at arm's-length distance, and their second line in close order, with shouldered musket, just in front of their camp — their infantry only engaged. The main body were discovered filing off to the right and left, when orders were given us to retreat. My captain, Montgomery, received a shot in his foot and had hopped back in the rear; Lieutenant Bluer being absent, the charge of the company devolved on me; young and inexperienced, exhausted with hunger and fatigue, had like to have disgraced myself—had eat nothing all day but a few blackberries — was faint, and with difficulty kept my place; once or twice was about to throw away my arms (a very heavy espontoon). The company were almost all old soldiers. Kept compact and close to our leading company, and continued running until out of reach of the fire. The enemy advanced no farther than to the ground we left. We could not have been engaged longer than about three or four minutes, but at the distance of sixty yards only. Our loss is said to be upward of one hundred killed and wounded; among the latter twelve officers, one of whom, Lieutenant Herbert, taken prisoner; a few of the wounded not able to get off, were also taken. The artillery horses all killed; two pieces were lost.

Retreated two miles to very commanding ground, where we met the Marquis with our main body; halted and had some Indian meal served out, the wounded dressed, &c., and before day changed our ground and encamped about five miles from the field.

July 7th.—An officer, surgeon, and a few men, sent with flag to bury the dead, &c. This was done in company with an equal number of the enemy. Our wounded who were prisoners, had been properly treated. The British moved from Jamestown. About a fortnight after the action, visited the field; could trace plainly the ground occupied by both, from the tops of the cartridges which lay in a line; the distance between about sixty paces. The army marched and crossed James river at Westover, the seat of Colonel Bird, said to have been once the most wealthy planter in the State; the improvements superb, saw nothing like them before. Kept at a respectful distance from the enemy; rather between them and the route to North Carolina. Some idea of their design to return to the southward. Report going of a French fleet below. This news confirmed—great joy—army on the alert.

Sept. 1st.—Army encamped on the bank of James river—part of French fleet, with troops on board, in view. Recrossed James river and encamped at Williamsburg. Army in high spirits—reinforcements coming on.

14th.—General Washington arrived; our brigade was paraded to receive him; he rode along the line—quarters in Williamsburg.

15*th*.—Officers all pay their respects to the Commander-in-chief; go in a body; those who are not personally known, their names given by General Hand and General Wayne. He stands in the door, takes every man by the hand—the officers all pass in, receiving his salute and shake. This the first time I had seen the General. We have an elegant encampment close to town, behind William and Mary College. This building occupied as an hospital. Williamsburg a very handsome place, not so populous as Richmond, but situate on evenly, pretty ground; streets and lots spacious—does not appear to be a place of much business, rather the residence of gentlemen of fortune; formerly it was the seat of government and Dunmore's late residence. A neat public building, called the capitol, fronts the principal street; upon the first floor is a handsome marble statue of William Pitt.

The presence of so many general officers, and the arrival of new corps, seem to give additional life to everything; discipline the order of the day. In all directions troops seen exercising and manœuvring. Baron Steuben, our great military oracle. The guards attend the grand parade at an early hour, where the Baron is always found waiting with one or two aids on horseback. These men are exercised and put through various evolutions and military experiments for two hours — many officers and spectators present; excellent school, this. At length the duty of the parade comes on. The guards are told off; officers take their posts, wheel by platoons to the right; fine corps of music detailed for this duty, which strikes up; the whole march off, saluting the

Baron and field officer of the day, as they pass. Pennsylvania brigade almost all old soldiers, and well disciplined when compared with those of Maryland and Virginia. But the troops from the eastward far superior to either.

25th.—Joined by the last of the troops from the eastward. French encamped a few miles on the right; busy in getting cannon and military stores from on board the vessels.

28th.—The whole army moved in three divisions toward the enemy, who were strongly posted at York, about twelve miles distant. Their pickets and light troops retire. We encamped about three miles off—change ground and take a position within one mile of York; rising ground (covered with tall handsome pines) called Pigeon Hill, separates us from a view of the town. Enemy keep possession of Pigeon Hill. York on a high, sandy plain, on a deep navigable river of same name. Americans on the right; French on the left, extending on both sides of the river; preparations for a siege. One-third of the army on fatigue every day, engaged in various duties, making gabions, fascines, saucissons, &c., and great exertions and labor in getting on the heavy artillery. Strong covering parties (whole regiments) moved from camp as soon as dark, and lay all night upon their arms between us and the enemy. Our regiment, when on this duty, were under cover, and secured from the shot by Pigeon Hill; now and then a heavy shot from the enemy's works reached our camp. Our patrols, and those of the British, met occasionally in the dark, sometimes a few shot were exchanged—would generally retire. Colonel Schamel, adjutant-general to the army, with two or three attendants, on a party of observation, ventured rather close; they were seen and intercepted by a few smart horsemen from the British. Schamel forced his way through, and got back to camp, but received a wound, of which he died next day. His death was lamented, and noticed by the Commander-in-chief in his orders. Possession taken of Pigeon Hill, and temporary work erected. Generals and engineers, in viewing and surveying the ground, are always fired upon and sometimes pursued. Escorts and covering parties stationed at convenient distances under cover of wood, rising ground, &c., afford support. This business reminds me of a play among the boys, called Prison-base.

At length, everything in readiness, a division of the army broke ground on the night of the 6th of October, and opened the first parallel about six hundred yards from the works of the enemy. Every exertion to annoy our men, who were necessarily obliged to be exposed about the works; however, the business went on, and on the 9th our cannon and mortars began to play. The scene viewed from the camp now was grand, particularly after dark — a number of shells from the works of both parties passing high in the air, and descending in a curve, each with a long train of fire, exhibited a brilliant spectacle. Troops in three divisions manned the lines alternately. We were two nights in camp and one in the lines; relieved about ten o'clock. Passed and repassed by a covert way leading to the parallel.

Oct. 11th.—Second parallel thrown up within three hundred yards of the main works of the enemy; new batteries erected, and additional number of cannon brought forward—some twenty-four pounders and heavy mortars and howitzers. A tremendous fire now opened from all the new works, French and American. The heavy cannon directed against the embrasures and guns of the enemy. Their pieces were soon silenced, broke and dismantled. Shells from behind their works still kept up. Two redoubts advanced of their lines, and within rifle shot of our second parallel, much in the way. These forts or redoubts were well secured by a ditch and picket, sufficiently high parapet, and within were divisions made by rows of casks ranged upon end and filled with earth and sand. On tops of parapet were ranged bags filled with sand—a deep narrow ditch communicating with their main lines. On the night of the 14th, shortly after dark, these redoubts were taken by storm; the one on our right, by the Marquis, with part of his light infantry—the other, more to our left, but partly opposite the centre of the British lines, by the French. Our batteries had kept a constant fire upon the redoubts through the day. Belonged this evening to a command detailed for the purpose of supporting the Marquis. The night was dark and favorable. Our batteries had ceased—there appeared to be a dead calm; we followed the infantry and halted about half way—kept a few minutes in suspense, when we were ordered to advance. The business was over, not a gun was fired by the assailants; the bayonet only was used; ten or twelve of the infantry were killed. French had to contend with a post of more force—their loss was considerable. Colonel Hamilton led the Marquis' advance; the British sentries hailed them — no answer made. They also hailed the French, "Who comes there?" were answered, "French grenadiers." Colonel Walter Stewart commanded the regiment of reserve which accompanied the Marquis; they were immediately employed in connecting, by a ditch and parapet, the two redoubts, and completing and connecting the same with our second parallel. The British were soon alarmed; some from each of the redoubts made their escape. The whole enemy were under arms—much firing round all their lines, but particularly toward our regiment, where the men were at work: the shot passed over. In about three quarters of an hour we were under cover. Easy digging; light sandy ground.

15*th.*—Heavy fire from our batteries all day. A shell from one of the French mortars set fire to a British frigate; she burnt to the water's edge, and blew up — made the earth shake. Shot and shell raked the town in every direction. Bomb-proofs the only place of safety.

16*th.*—Just before day the enemy made a sortie, spiked the guns in two batteries and retired. Our troops in the parallel scarcely knew of their approach until they were off; the thing was done silently and in an instant. The batteries stood in advance of the lines, and none within but artillery. This day, the 16th, our division manned the lines—firing continued without intermission. Pretty strong detachments posted in each battery over night.

17*th.*—In the morning, before relief came, had the pleasure of seeing a drummer mount the enemy's parapet, and beat a parley, and immediately an officer, holding up a white handkerchief, made his appearance outside their works; the drummer accompanied him, beating. Our batteries ceased. An officer from our lines ran and met the other, and tied the handkerchief over his eyes. The drummer sent back, and the British officer conducted to a house in rear of our lines. Firing ceased totally.

18*th.*—Several flags pass and repass now even without the drum. Had we not seen the drummer in his red coat when he first mounted, he might have beat away till doomsday. The constant firing was too much for the sound of a single drum; but when the firing ceased, I thought I never heard a drum equal to it—the most delightful music to us all.

19*th.*—Our division man the lines again. All is quiet. Articles of capitulation signed; detachments of French and Americans take possession of British forts. Major Hamilton commanded a battalion which took possession of a fort immediately opposite our right and on the bank of York river. I carried the standard of our regiment on this occasion. On entering the fort, Baron Steuben, who accompanied us, took the standard from me and planted it himself. The British army parade and march out with their colors furled; drums beat as if they did not care how. Grounded their arms and returned to town. Much confusion and riot among the British through the day; many of the soldiers were intoxicated; several attempts in course of the night to break open stores; an American sentinel killed by a British soldier with a bayonet; our patrols kept busy. Glad to be relieved from this disagreeable station. Negroes lie about, sick and dying, in every stage of the small pox. Never was in so filthy a place — some handsome houses, but prodigiously shattered. Vast heaps of shot and shells lying about in every quarter, which came from our works. The shells did not burst, as was expected. Returns of British soldiers, prisoners six thousand, and seamen about one thousand. Lord Cornwallis excused himself from marching out with the troops; they were conducted by General O'Hara. Our loss said to be about three hundred; that of the enemy said not more than five hundred and fifty. Fine supply of stores and merchandise had; articles suitable for clothing were taken for the use of the army. A portion furnished each officer to the amount of sixty dollars.

20th.—Joined by a new raised regiment from Pennsylvania. Officers hastened to partake of the siege, but were too late. British troops march into the interior—to Winchester and other places. Visit Gloucester, small village opposite York; nothing seen there. Some of our officers return to Pennsylvania, others take their place. Visit Williamsburg in company with young gentlemen of the country, on horseback; spend a few days very agreeably. Militia employed leveling the lines. Our brigade prepare for a long march.

Nov. 1st.—Three regiments of Pennsylvania, a detachment of artillery, and Maryland troops, commence their march for South Carolina — General St. Clair, the commanding officer. Easy, regular marching; roads generally good, through sandy country. Pass through Richmond and Guilford, in North Carolina, where General Green and the British had a hard fight; also Camden, where Gates was defeated. Halted at least one day in the week for purpose of washing and refreshing.

Jan. 4th, 1782.—Joined the troops under General Green at Round O, in the State of South Carolina. Moved to Pond-Pond; here we lay some time. Rice farms around this neighborhood—the fields almost all under water; immense quantities of ducks; excellent sport at times. Planters return to their homes—live in style. Army change their ground; march to Ashley. Was on picket the night before we reached Ashley; got exceedingly wet—it rained all night. Marched next morning in wet clothes twelve miles, to Ashley, exposed to very hot sun; laid up with fever—carried to hospital; as soon as able, returned to camp. Hospital very disagreeable place—all sick, and some continually dying. Attendance good; surgeons very kind; furnished with some stores, sugar, tea and molasses. Continued weak and unfit for duty for some weeks. Ashley a very good position—ground high and dry; but it is now midsummer and sickly season. Men die very fast; lost several valuable officers. Ashley river low; full of alligators.

August.—Camp continued on bank of Ashley river, eighteen or twenty miles above Charleston. Enemy confine themselves to city. Their light troops and horse advanced five miles, at place called Quarter House.

Armies both seem disposed to be quiet; ours in no condition for doing much. Some talk of peace, and of the enemy evacuating Charleston. Detailed for command. Joined a captain of the Maryland line; marched with two sergeants, two corporals, and thirty men, for Georgetown, about sixty miles distant, coast-wise. Escorted a brigade of wagons loaded with rum for the army. Country appears deserted; the few people we saw looked bad enough, poor and dejected; they fled from us, and in some instances hid themselves. Farms on this route have been neglected; exposed to the incursions of the British. Negroes and stock either removed or taken. Fell in with an alligator, twelve feet in length, in the middle of the road; supposed that his pond had dried up, and that he was in search of another; soldier shot him.

September.—Our camp very thin; not more than three relieves of officers and men for the ordinary duties. Hospitals crowded, and great many sick in camp; deaths so frequent, the funeral ceremony dispensed with. Provisions scarce and very indifferent; the beef brought from the back counties of North Carolina, by the time they reach the camp, poor indeed, and must be unwholesome. Commissary's yard and slaughter place commonly short distance from camp. Soldier going there in morning about killing time, met his comrade returning in; asked how was the beef this morning? other replied, that it took two men to hold up the creature until the butcher knocked it down. Says the other, And why didn't he knock it down as it lay? Flour a rare article. Troops have lived chiefly upon rice, now and then a small allowance of Indian meal served out—rice very good for the sick, but rather washy for duty men. Governor Hamilton, of this State, himself and family, quarter at a pleasant seat, two miles in rear of camp—General Green not quite so far; each has a subaltern's guard. Very fond of getting one or other of these guards better fare than we have in camp. Officer considered and treated as one of the family.

October.—Camp at Ashley Hill. Ranks thinned very much; deaths not so frequent. Our situation as to ground, a handsome one, and, as far as I can judge, eligible, but assuredly the climate is severe upon northern constitutions. Gentlemen who can afford it, reside during summer in the city and spend the winter in the country. An unpleasant week's command. At a bridge over Ashley, six or seven miles from camp, where the great road from Charleston to the upper country crosses, a subaltern and thirty men have been stationed. It became my turn. Orders were to suffer no people to pass or repass without proper permit. It was now pretty well known that the enemy would soon evacuate the city. Many poor devils had taken protection and followed the British in; provisions scarce in town, and those people sick of their situation—they were anxious to get back to their old places of abode in the country. Some very miserable objects came out—whole families, battered and starving. Was sure, upon my representation, leave would be given to let them pass. Stated the business in writing, and dispatched a sergeant. No—ordered not to let them pass; thought this an unnecessary cruelty.

Dec. 13th.—Had been expecting, every day for a month past, to hear of the intended evacuation of Charleston. The Governor's guard was an object at this time, as the officer commanding would, of course, accompany or escort him into the city. I was so fortunate as to have the guard this day, when advice was received that the British would embark next morning. A few hours for the Governor to get ready, we set out in the evening with one tumbrel, containing books, papers, &c., and reached the city early next day. Saw the last of the enemy embark in their boats and put off to the shipping. An immense fleet lay in sight all day; found the city very quiet—houses all shut up. A detachment from the army had marched the day before to take possession as soon as the English would be off. Guards stationed at proper places, and small parties, conducted by an officer, patrolled the streets. Charleston a handsome town, situate on neck of land between the confluence of Ashley and Cooper rivers; Cooper river, however, appears to be the only harbor. Town here fronts the east; business all done on this side. Second and third day people began to open their houses and show themselves, and some shops opened. Stayed a week, and returned to our old encampment.

30*th.*—Broke up our camp. Pennsylvanians have been reduced, by deaths, desertions, &c., and were now incorporated into one regiment of six hundred men.

4

Supernumerary officers went home to their own State. Lieut.-Col. Commt. Josiah Harmar, who had acted as Adjutant-general since our junction with General Green, took command of this regiment.

Jan. 1st, 1783.—Arrived on James Island, and encamped contiguous to a very beautiful forest of pine. Had with us one complete regiment of the Maryland line, a battalion belonging to South Carolina, (which was all the troops that State had), and six companies of artillery, two of whom were from Pennsylvania, the rest from Virginia. Colonel Hamilton commandant of artillery. The woodland an elegant situation for hunting. Each company had its ground marked out, when the whole went to work, and in course of a week were completely housed. Some of the companies had more timber upon the ground they occupied than was necessary for their huts. The infantry were in a line; artillery in rear of right wing formed a park. The order and formation such as our encampment.

January.—Cantonment on James Island. Weather moderate. Troops employed finishing huts and opening the streets; not a stump left. Top of timber and brush carried to certain distance, and built up in a circular line round the cantonment. This brush barrier, or fence, could not be passed without much trouble; it served instead of sentinels round the camp. Openings left at particular places, where the guards or sentinels were stationed. Still kept a front and rear camp guard, but the usual number lessened.

February.—Very pleasant weather for working parties;

some appearance of spring. Officers and men all in comfortable quarters. Provisions good; very little occasion for fire through the winter.

March and April. — Delightful season. James Island a little paradise — the country flat, but sandy and dry. Troops healthy. Our regiment receive new clothing; officers also are furnished in Charleston with a small supply. Make a very fine appearance. Exercised often; perform the parade duties in absence of the adjutant — very fond of this. Officers go frequently to the city — police boat for that purpose; row there in half an hour. A short walk from the huts, and we have a view of Charleston, of Hadrel's Point, which is the main land east, and of Sullivan's Island, east across the channel from James Island. Visit Fort Sullivan, celebrated for the defense made against Sir Peter Parker. Curtains and embrasures faced with the cabbage tree — soft spongy wood, admirably calculated for this use. Saw where a great many shot from the British ships had entered the logs, but no damage done; holes almost closed up. From Sullivan's Island to Hadrel's Point was formerly a bridge—it was burnt by the British. Fort Sullivan still in very good condition; but Fort Johnson, upon James Island, immediately opposite (across the channel), nearly demolished. Plenty of fish and oysters all round us, and what the folks here call stone crabs, very fine; they are like the common crab, but much larger, and soft shells. Officers in rotation dine with General Green, at his house in the city. Colonel Stewart, of the Maryland regiment, on an excursion in the country, was cast from his horse into the ditch and broke his neck. Officers of the army (those on duty excepted) attended his funeral in Charleston. Preliminaries of a peace arrive. Great rejoicing—grand review—dinner—fire works, and dance at the cantonment. Ladies and gentlemen come over on this occasion from Charleston.

June 1*st*.—Preparations making to send home, by sea, the Maryland and Pennsylvania troops; transports wanting. A New England brig arrives, and contracts to carry two companies. Bond's and Irwin's companies ordered to embark. I had belonged to the latter since the action of Jamestown, when Captain Montgomery, who was wounded, returned to Pennsylvania. Had a very pleasant passage of seven days to Philadelphia, where we landed on the 15th. Mrs. Green, wife of the General, came passenger with us. Quartered in the Philadelphia barracks, along with about one hundred and fifty new raised men. Our companies of the southward appear to great advantage. The near approach of the disbandment of the army, and a tardiness in Congress to make provision for a settlement, produced dissatisfaction among the officers in Pennsylvania, as well as among those at head-quarters. To us who were strangers in our own State, this business was unknown. About eighty men from the recruiting rendezvous at Lancaster, turned out and marched to Philadelphia without an officer; were joined by the recruits in the barracks; marched to the State House where Congress were, frightened that body, and broke up their sitting. This proceeding took place about noon, when the officers belonging to the two companies from Charleston were at Governor Dickinson's on an invitation to dinner. The alarm reached us—hastened to the barracks—long roll beat; our two companies fell in to a man; marched to the Governor's house in Market street; several troops of militia horse paraded; great uproar in the city. Although the insurgents had posted sentinels round the State House, the members of Congress made out to escape, after passing a resolution to assemble at Trenton. The officers who were concerned in this business, and who had privately directed the movements, now thought of themselves; they fled and escaped in a light boat down the river; men soon dispersed. A few days brought General Howe from headquarters with a brigade of light troops, for purpose of suppressing the insurrection. Most of the officers who were here previous to our arrival were arrested, and a few taken in close custody. General court martial ordered for their trial. Government were desirous of getting rid of the army in as quiet a manner as possible; at this particular period it was thought best not to be too rigid. Howe had his cue; officers released. Captain Alexander Parker (my uncle), on furlough from Lancaster, was returning home; obtained leave of absence, and accompanied him to Carlisle. Our regiment from southward not yet arrived.

Dec. 3d.—By proclamation of Congress, the American army was disbanded; a few men, under the command of a captain at Fort Pitt, excepted. A resolution soon followed for raising a regiment for the purpose of garrisoning the western posts—this regiment to consist of ten companies, portioned as follows: Pennsylvania—4 companies and Lieut.-Col. Commt. Jersey—1 company. New York—3 companies and a Major. Connecticut—2 companies and a Major.

1784.—The States made the appointments in the first instance, which were confirmed by Congress. The officers were all from those who had been in service. Colonel Harmar was in France; had been sent with the ratification of the treaty. The command of the new regiment was reserved for him, and indeed the Pennsylvania appointments not made until his return. Governor Mifflin at this time was President of Congress, and very popular in Pennsylvania, and Harmar's great friend; but the Colonel's character as a military man stood high; the regiment he brought from the southward eclipsed every thing. I was nominated by Harmar one of his ensigns; the appointment reached me at Carlisle. As soon as they had a knowledge of my acceptance, recruiting instructions were sent me. Marched about a dozen men down to Philadelphia; joined the camp on west side of Schuylkill. The four companies nearly full. Some time spent in equipping and exercising the recruits.

September.—Marched through Lancaster by Carlisle, &c., to Pittsburgh. Waited for the arrival of commissioners appointed to hold a treaty with the Indians. Treaty expected to be holden at Cuyahoga. Commissioners late getting out, season advanced, plan changed, and Indians invited to attend at Fort M'Intosh, about thirty miles below Fort Pitt, on bank of Ohio; to which place we repaired, and found exceeding good quarters.

January, 1785.—About four hundred of the Senecas, Delawares and Wyandots come in. After considerable difficulty, a treaty is agreed to, but with much reluctance on the part of the savages. Amongst the Indians are a number of women and children. The whole a very motley crew—an ugly set of devils all—very few handsome men or women. Colonel Harmar did not join us until we reached Fort Pitt, at which place I was appointed to do the duty of adjutant; this had always been favorite duty of mine.

Fort M'Intosh, 1785.—Winter passed away—no orders for marching; did expect, as soon as the season would permit, to march for Detroit. April and May delightful season—frequent excursions into the country—fishing and hunting. Officers visit Fort Pitt, where we left a lieutenant and thirty men. Fort Pitt and Fort M'Intosh both handsome places. Fort Pitt erected by the British long before the late war—an elegant work, regular pentagon; vast labor and money expended here. Ditch and parapet with pickets and fencing, and every thing in the most complete order. Very considerable quantity of military stores at this place. Indians come in to trade, will get drunk—a white man killed by a drunken Indian at Pittsburgh—people rise and attempt to put the Indian to death. Express sent to Colonel Harmar at M'Intosh. I was ordered to Pitt with certain instructions to Lieutenant Ashton, who commanded there. The Indian guarded to county jail. Pittsburgh in Westmoreland county. Hannahstown, about thirty miles east, the seat of justice. Cornplanter, chief of the Senecas, arrived at Pitt. He had signed the treaty of M'Intosh; was dissatisfied — his people reflected on him; came to revoke. Colonel Harmar was informed of this, and invited up to Pitt—I accompanied him. Meeting appointed in the King's Orchard. Speeches on both sides taken down. Cornplanter dismissed with assurances, &c., but no revoking.

Summer nearly gone. Men have been enlisted but for one year; orders to re-enlist for three. Of the four companies, we re-engaged seventy effective men — rest all discharged. Officers went on the recruiting service. Anxious to know how I was to be disposed of. Proper complement of officers kept for the new company. Did count upon returning over the mountains, but would have preferred remaining at Pittsburgh. Dislike the recruiting service. The new company ordered to prepare to embark for the Great Miami, where another treaty is intended to be held. Generals Butler and Parsons, two of the commissioners, arrive. The party all ready to descend the river, when the Colonel instructed me to prepare and accompany them; this to me was very unexpected. The company has its complement of officers; I was extra. Must move.

29*th.*—I agreed with Mr. Duncan, about the wintering of my mare; he promising to keep her safe in his meadow, while the grass continued, and charge nothing—but the remainder of the winter she should be well fed and kept on good hay, for thirty shillings per month. Having arranged affairs as well as the shortness of my time would afford, I set off for M'Intosh, in company with Mr. O'Hara, but did not arrive until the next morning; the water being exceedingly low, and Mr. O'Hara so unfortunate as to run aground in the night. At ten o'clock set out on horseback for Fort Pitt to make some arrangements; stayed one day. Found the party had sailed. A corporal and six men with small boat left for me. After receiving from the Colonel particular orders relative to myself, I embarked again with Mr. O'Hara. and in a few hours, with brisk rowing, overtook the commissioners, who had halted at Little Beaver creek, where Captain Hutchens and several surveyors were encamped. Here we stayed some minutes. About ten o'clock at night we got to where the troops were encamped, near the mouth of Yellow Creek, 30th September, 1785. A very pretty looking company, commanded by Captain Doughty, of New York, arrived at M'Intosh the same day the other left.

Oct. 3d. — Reached Wheeling. Joined by several of the contractor's boats loaded with provisions. Our fleet now consists of twelve small keels and batteaux, besides two large flats called Kentucky boats. The flats carry cattle, horses, &c.; the others, the troops and goods for the Indians. Ohio river remarkably low — two pilots employed to keep ahead and point out the channel; notwithstanding, some of the boats frequently ground.

8th. — Encamped opposite mouth of Little Kanahwa. My uncle, Captain Parker, owns the ground above Kanahwa; crossed over in light boat; his improvements made just before the war scarcely visible; place grown up; pretty tract of land. Settlement and pre-emption entitle him to fourteen hundred acres. Will be valuable property not long hence.

11*th.*— Passage very tedious; water low and frequent interruptions; made not more than ten and fifteen miles a day. Fine opportunity of hunting and fishing along the shore. Game plenty, particularly turkeys. Some elegant bottoms on both sides of the river; but generally opposite the most prominent parts of the bottoms, the hill makes in and forms what is called narrows. Colonel Monroe, a member of Congress from Virginia, on a visit to Kentucky, took passage with the commissioners. Obliged to meet Congress early in October, and anxious to get on; a light boat got ready; a sergeant, myself, a corporal and six privates, embark with the Colonel— leave the fleet, and after rowing about fifteen miles arrive at Great Kanahwa.

12*th.*—Spent this morning with Colonel Lewis, who is proprietor of the place. Several families reside with him on the point—it is a very pretty situation. Set out about eleven o'clock; kept half our crew at the oars all night.

13*th.* — In the evening passed the Three Islands; narrow channel here; Indian crossing place. Frequent attacks on boats at this place; saw nothing; arrived safe at Limestone, late.

14*th.* — Colonel Monroe having procured horses to carry him to Lexington, left me at ten o'clock. Nothing remarkable here; place only settled this spring; indifferent kind of folks. This is said to be the best and nearest landing place to Lexington — if so, it will in a short time become of some importance.

18th.—Fleet arrive—make a short halt and pass on. I follow in my light boat; encamp early in the evening; men cook provisions for next day.

22d.—Arrive at the Great Miami. Best ground for our station about a mile above the mouth, where the boats were brought and every thing unloaded. All hands set to work chopping, clearing, &c., and preparing timber for block-houses and pickets; and on the 8th instant had ourselves inclosed. Hoisted the United States flag, and christened the place Fort Finney, in compliment to Captain Finney, the commanding officer. Our work is a square stockade fort; substantial block-houses, two stories, twenty-four by eighteen feet in each angle; curtains one hundred feet of stout pickets, four feet in the ground, and nine feet above; situate one hundred and fifty yards from the river, on a rising second bank. A building, eighteen by twenty feet, within the east and west curtains, for the accommodation and reception of contractors' stores and Indian goods; and one small, but strong building, centre of north curtain, for magazine. A council house, twenty by sixty, detached, but within gun shot. Commissioners and their followers pitch their tents within the fort, and erect wooden chimneys. Season very favorable, but growing cool. Men employed finishing the block-houses, and clearing off the timber and brush to some distance outside.

Nov. 13th.—Corporal Thompson arrived with his boat, in company with General Parsons, one of the commissioners.

24th.—Messengers who set out from Pittsburgh to the

Indian towns, to invite the Indians to a treaty at this place, arrive with six chiefs of the Shawanees, Wyandot and Delaware nations, to wit: Captain Johnny, or Red Pole, Half-King, Crane, Pipe, Wingeman and White-Eyes — all very glad to see us *brothers.* Some grog and smoke produced.

25th.—Wrote to Colonel Harmar at Philadelphia, an account of our passage, &c., and of the arrival of the Indians, state of the troops, &c.

27th.—Caught two large Kentucky boats floating down empty — had been unloaded at Limestone, and carried away by a sudden rise of water. Boards served us for floors, sentry boxes and other useful purposes. About one hundred Indians assemble and encamp a couple of miles from us; the greatest part Wyandots, a few Delawares.

Dec. 5th. — Generals Clark, Butler and Parsons leave us on a visit to the Falls of Ohio, about one hundred and fifty miles below. Captain Finney and myself, with a party of soldiers in boat, go to Big Bone Lick, thirty miles down; dig up and collect some astonishing large bones.

Dec. 6th. — Spent this day in the Indian camp by invitation; treated with attention. It was a high day among them, a frolic and feast; several games played—exceedingly active at the game our boys call shinny or common. About forty young men were paraded for this game, equally divided; the ground had been cleared for the purpose. At the centre was a painted post, decorated with pieces of cloth suitable for leggings and breech clouts; the winning side got these. Their ball the size of a man's head, made of deer's hair, covered with skin; their sticks four or five feet long, resembling a racket. The ball was thrown in the air—all endeavored to catch it upon his racket; a fellow would take it in this way and keep in until another more smart overtook him or knocked it abroad, when another scramble took place. They insisted on my joining in one of these games. Several other games were played; some with beans and dishes or bowls, in imitation of backgammon. Our dinner was served upon skins spread on the ground. Had walked to the camp, but must ride back; girl and horse got for me.[1]

---

[1] Elsewhere in a note he says: "I left the garrison in company with Mr. Zane (a man who has been brought up during his youth amongst the Wyandots), to share in the amusements of a frolic that was to take place this day. Accordingly, when we arrived at their encampment we were taken very friendly by the hand, and desired to fall in with them at a game of common. The first thing did was to divide the whole into two parties; this ceremony was performed by two old sachems; and then took post on each side of an elegant decorated post of sugar tree, on the top of which was as much new scarlet cloth as would make a pair of leggings; around the middle was bound a pair of scarlet garters. These were the prizes. When all was ready, one of the old men gave a halloo as a signal to make ready, which was answered by another from each of the company; at that instant the ball was thrown up in the air, then at it we went, and contended for half an hour. At length it was sent past the stage, and the person who struck it declared it aloud, which ended that game—he being presented with the leggings. And in the same manner was the. garter played for; he who hit the ball the last got the prize.

"After dinner another play was introduced, which was called *mamondys*. Having all sat down in a circle, they placed some blankets in the centre, and two of them began the play, with a wooden dish and six plum stones in it, marked on each side something like dice. They shook the dishes about, and from certain marks one would soon exceed the other. With

7th.—The Indian women assembled in our council house and desired the attendance of the chief captain (Captain Finney). We all turned out, heard an oration from one of their elderly ones, the conclusion of which was a request for something to warm their hearts.

12th.—Accompany Isaac Zane, a white man, and two Indians, on a hunting party. We took a light boat, went up the river seven miles, and pitched a camp; had an Indian woman along to keep camp. First day, too anxious in pursuit of buffalo, lost my course; intended to have kept near to Zean; he was led off. I was alone and followed by wolves, yowling occasionally. Zean heard the report of my rifle and came up; was very glad to see him. Concluded to return to camp; he conducted me some distance. Before we parted he killed a doe; opened the udder with his knife—milk collected, of which I drank. Got to camp and stayed there. Party returned home the fourth day, and brought with us the meat of three buffaloes, two bears and parts of a number of deer.

15th.—The same day we returned from our hunt, it rained excessively hard. We were joined by our commissioners from the Rapids, just at the landing; they having received a plentiful quantity of wet that occasioned a near resemblance to drowned rats.

18th.—Three Shawanee Indians arrived with a speech

these and other affairs we diverted ourselves until it grew late, when taking our leave, one who had expressed a great deal of friendship for me, remarked that the road was dirty, that we had three miles to go, and that I would be much the better of a horse—if I would accept of one he would soon have him procured; I assented; accordingly a squaw was dispatched, and soon after we were both mounted and conducted home by two *females*."

from their nation, informing us of their being on their way to this place. This was very agreeable news to our commissioners.

19*th.*—Major Montgomery and Mr. Elliot were sent in a boat, with a sergeant and four privates, up to Limestone, in search of several horses that were stolen from the Indians here, and were heard of at that place.

20*th.*—Commissioners returned a few days since from the Falls; disappointed at not finding more Indians come in. Those with us, about one hundred, are principally Wyandots and Delawares, with whom the treaty at M'Intosh was held. The Shawanees are the fellows the present treaty was intended for; they seem to hang back. Indians treated very kindly—dancing parties in our council house almost every afternoon; the men jump, stamp and exert themselves much, but all keep good time; females glide round, and have a gait or step peculiar to themselves. An old fellow has a keg, with skin drawn over each head—sort of drum on which he beats time—considerable regularity—dance in a circle round the fire—can't dance without something to make their hearts warm, and generally break up pretty merry. Very few went home sober, but those who did were sure to get drunk at night. They would come next day and peremptorily demand a quantity of rum; on being refused they set homeward very much offended, declaring that the next day should move them off, never to be seen as friends again. This day our clothing came.

Dec. 20*th.*—The commissioners are of opinion that a post will be continued here; they think it an eligible position until we are in possession of Detroit, &c. It is convenient to the principal body of the savages who inhabit the head waters of the Miami, and we are about seventy-five miles north of Lexington, to which place a road is now marked out; the Falls of Louisville, below, and Limestone settlement above.

21st.—Sent a return to Colonel Harmar by Mr. Hulings, inclosed in a letter, the copy of which is as follows:

COLONEL—Since my last, the commissioners after sending back the Shawanee chiefs, to bring in their nation and others on the Wabash, &c., have taken a trip to the Rapids, where they left General Clark. Whether he will return or not, is a doubt with us; but General Butler and General Parsons say he will be up in a few days. Our reason for thinking he will scarcely return, is, that while here he had received almost daily complaints from the people on the frontiers of Kentucky, against the Indians, and reflecting on him for trifling, as they think, with some of the savages, while others are plundering *them.* The people are very ripe for a campaign into the towns.

A runner arrived two days since with a speech from the Shawanees, informing us of the whole nation being on their way to this place. But after they do arrive, there are several more nations to be coaxed, so that from every appearance, next spring will bring up the rear of the treaty Much more indulgence is allowed the Indians here than was at M'Intosh. Dancing, playing common, &c. (for which they are well supplied with materials to make their hearts merry), are frequent amusements here. Major Finney is determined they shan't act *Pontiac* with him, for every precaution is taken at that time.

The commissioners are of opinion that this place is the most advantageous spot to keep troops at, until we have possession of others farther northerly, as it is convenient to the principal body of the savages, and nearly an equal distance from the Rapids, the interior part of Kentucky, and Limestone, which is the upper part of the settlement. There has been a road marked out from this place to Lexington, their capital town, from which we can have any supplies we might stand in need of. The distance is about seventy-five miles.

The companies' clothing came to hand yesterday, all in good order. The commissioners made a compliment to Major Finney of as much white half-thicks as made each man a pair of over-alls; they have been worn for some time past, so that their sufferings are not so great as you might imagine. Opportunities are so seldom up the river that I can't possibly send you returns as regular as I could wish, but none shall be neglected.

I have the honor to remain, your very humble servant,

E. D.

23*d.*—General Clark arrived from the Rapids, which was a very agreeable surprise, as few of us expected him.

25*th.*—A very dull Christmas (Sunday).

28*th.*—The chiefs of the Delaware nation (particularly Captain Pipe) made proposals to our commissioners to send once more to their towns, to know why a certain tribe of their's did not come in agreeably to a promise, and likewise, if the commissioners would send a messenger, he should be accompanied by their runners into the Shawanee towns, and to the more western towns, to bring a final answer from them. All was agreed to; and at the request of the commissioners, Mr. Doyle prepared to accompany Mr. Ranken.

29*th.*—New deputation sent to bring the Shawanees, if possible, to treat—Lieutenant Doyle went along—all mounted. The caravan took up the line of march, and was expected would move on in state. Mr. Doyle, with his friend, Mr. Ranken, and a young man, an assistant, with two Indian men and several women, formed the line. They had not been long on the road until a very heavy cold rain came on, from which they must have suffered

5

much; but as the party consisted of old warriors, it was expected they would not be discouraged at any difficulties of that kind, but proceed as men employed on such business ought to.

31*st.*—I set out in company with two Shawanees to provide a few turkeys for the first of the year, and at the request of General Parsons, agreed to meet him, General Butler and Major Finney, at a large pond about six miles up the river; they to go in a boat. After we had rode the distance of four or five miles (for our party was all on horse-back; I was mounted on one of the Indians' wife's horse and saddle), we got amongst the turkeys; and the first thing done was to *charge* upon them, so as to cause them to fly up on the trees, and all the howlings and frightful screeches I ever heard, were given to effect this purpose. As soon as the turkeys rose we alighted and commenced firing. In this manner we sported with two flocks, until we had as many as we could conveniently carry home; then steering our course toward the boat, met a horse belonging to the Indians, and the only one that was left behind; he missing his old companions, got on their track, and having a bell on, alarmed the boat, just as it was putting into the place appointed for our meeting, and occasioned them to make to the other side of the river; so we were obliged to return home without the refreshment which we expected from them.

Jan. 1*st*, 1786.—Agreeably to an invitation, the commissioners and their gentlemen dined with Major Finney, Mr. M'Dowell and myself, in our hut, where we spent a few sociable hours in memory of the late year, and drinking success to the ensuing one. Just as tattoo was striking off, a gun was fired on the river and a light shone that did not a little alarm us, but upon examination was discovered to be a boat passing; we made her come to shore. One of her hands was an old man, who had been lately made a prisoner by the Shawanees. His story is as follows: About two weeks since, himself and his two sons were hunting on the head waters of Yellow Creek; at a time when the sons were after their horses, two Indians came on him, and after inquiring of his company (for they could talk English) moved off very rapidly, taking him along as a prisoner; he says they treated him tolerably, only that his hands were bound; but when they arrived at the Indian town, an old man took the direction and loosed his arms, returning to him his blanket, which had been taken, along with a rifle and some ammunition. He was kept about two hours, when the same old man, who could talk very good English, conducted him from the town, placed him on a path that led to where two of the old man's sons were hunting; he at the same time gave the prisoner a horse, three pints of parched corn and a shell to deliver to these boys, and then sent him off. The prisoner found the boys and delivered the shell; they knowing the horse, and understanding the token, conducted the prisoner down to the Three Islands, about eleven miles above Limestone; and just as they approached the river they discovered a boat on its way down. The Indians being apprehensive of some danger from the boat, did not wait for its coming ashore, but after bidding farewell with the white man, took their horse, which he rode, and moved off. The white man hailed the boat, got on board, and so arrived at this place.

2d.—Major Montgomery and Mr. Elliot arrived with two of the horses that they went in search of; the third one they were not able to get, but expect that Colonel Boon, a very worthy gentleman at Limestone, will recover him.

8th.—Lieutenant Doyle arrived, and informed us that after a disagreeable march of sixty miles, they were met by a party of one hundred and fifty Shawanees, on Sunday, the first of the year. After consulting, it was agreed that he and Mr. Rankin should return, and Wengeanem, the Indian chief, go forward as far as was first intended; indeed, the chief thought, that as Lieutenant Doyle and Mr. Rankin were under his protection, that he ought to have the right of ordering them, and did order them back with the Shawanees. Lieutenant Doyle says that the few nights he was with them their march was conducted with great regularity; that the whole appeared to be formed in certain squads, equal in number, and when any of their young men or hunters would kill meat, it was brought, laid down by the chiefs, one of whom cut it into as many shares as there were squads or fires (for every squad had their own fire) and sent it off by men, who appeared to serve as fatigue men for the day; so there was no one lived better than another, but all fared alike. Every evening after they halted and fixed themselves properly, Captain Johnny, a young Indian who lived with the chiefs, and seemed to act as an *aid*, would take a drum made out of a keg, with skins tied over each end, and beat some kind of a signal; on hearing which, the whole would assemble and spend the greatest part of the night in dancing and feasting. Lieutenant Doyle continued with them until the whole got within twenty miles of the Fort, when hearing that they intended resting at that place, while another party of the same number would join them, he took leave of Mr. Ranken and came with his suite to the garrison.

9th.—George White-Eyes and Pipe's son, set out with dispatches for Muskingum, the purport of which was to have stores and liquors sent down.

14th.—We received information of the Shawanees intending to come into the council house, and that on their approach they would salute us with three rounds per man. Our commissioners knowing them to be a very proud nation, thought it best to pay them the same honors, and ordered preparations in a style rather degrading to the United States, which was, that a party of soldiers should cook and serve out provisions to them in the council house. Now with them, the most decrepit old women are made choice of for that business; and nothing could have occasioned greater laughter than the appearance of soldiers carrying kettles of provisions to them. When the Indians saw them, they cried out, "There come the old women with warriors' coats on," &c. And who knows but they conceived us all old women clad in uniform. In order to return their salute, twelve men were ordered to parade, with three rounds of cartridges, and myself to command them. We waited their approach, which was very solemn. As they came up they gave us Indian music, beat on a keg drum by one of the chiefs, the whole singing at the same time. Their line was formed in rank of file, the women bringing up the rear, all in very regular order. When their firing was over I commenced, and in the intervals gave them a tune on the drum and fife.

After all were seated, their chief warrior, Wiendoohalies, from Wapotomaky, rose and wiped our eyes, opened our hearts, &c. After which our commissioners delivered a speech, informing them of their commission and Congress' desire to treat with all nations between the Mississippi and the St. Lawrence, north of the Ohio, and bidding the Shawanees welcome to the thirteen great fires; that at their next meeting the business would be entered into more fully. The Shawanees then desired to shake hands with the warriors; accordingly the officers paraded in the centre and received them all by the hand. A smoke from their pipes of peace took place next; and about dark a signal was given to march, and off they went.

19*th.*—It snowed until the ground was nearly six inches covered; but immediately after came warm weather which melted the whole, and caused the river to rise.

21*st.*—Bohengeehalus,[1] with about twenty Delawares, arrived. They were saluted in the same manner that the others were. Bohengeehalus is esteemed one of the greatest warriors now among all the Indians. After he

[1] Bohengeehalus, a very large stout man, brother of the "Grenadier Squaw."

had seated himself he discovered General Clark, and knowing him to be a great warrior, rose and saluted him very significantly—instead of taking hold of each other's hands, they gripped nearly at the shoulder, and shook the left hand underneath the right arms.

This evening we were entertained with the Shawanees dancing much in the same manner as was performed by the Wyandots, but the assembly was vastly larger. After they had gone through several of their common dances they prepared for a war dance. The Shawanees have a variety of dances; but the most pleasant one is their social dance, as it is interpreted. As many young men as please, form a ring round the fire, move, dance and sing love songs; the girls looking on for some time—at length they rise one after the other, as the spirit moves them, and seize a partner. The couple stick to each other, dancing and performing every possible gesture, but still keep in the ring, singing and beating time to their music. Now, while busily engaged, the parties exchange some articles of dress, or other things, as a token of their regard. The girls were very fond of getting a few of us engaged in this dance. But the war dance exceeds all—it was performed at the request of the officers. Eight or ten of the most active men stripped themselves quite naked, except the breech clout, painted their bodies and faces, so as to have a horrid appearance; armed with tomahawk and scalping knife, they formed a circle, danced moderately to a mournful kind of tune for ten or fifteen minutes, gave the war-whoop, and sat down together on seats placed for the purpose. They now hung their heads—a dead silence for a short time; one gets up, dances and capers to the music — repeats his exploits, the injuries they had sustained, urging the others to be strong, and rise and revenge themselves upon their enemies. At length they are roused, one after the other, until all get up, when they commence the most tremendous yelling, jumping and figuring about in imitation of shooting, scalping and tomahawking, exerting themselves exceedingly, until a signal is given for silence. A short speech concludes.

24th.—The treaty concluded at M'Intosh was explained to Bohengeehalus and his tribe, to their satisfaction.

25th.—One of the Shawanee chiefs died.

26th.—Shawanees occupied our long house in dancing every day, for ten days past. Officers and young gentlemen attending the commissioners very frequently join them. Business opened this day by an excellent speech from our commissioners to all the Indians — about four hundred present. The boundary lines, designating the lands allotted the several nations, were particularly described and pointed out on the map. They were told that as they had joined the English and taken up the hatchet against the United States, and the war having terminated in favor of the latter, and that the English, also, to obtain peace, had ceded the whole of the country on this side of the lakes to the Americans; that they, the Indians, must now look up to the Americans, and ought to be thankful if allowed to occupy any part of the country, which by the war they had forfeited; nevertheless, more perhaps than they expected would be done for them, but they must leave hostages for their good behavior, &c.

27th. — Shawanees met in council house. Their head warrior, Kickwaypalathey, replied to the speech of yesterday; denied the power and right which the United States assumed; asked if the Great Spirit had given it to them to cut and portion the country in the manner proposed. The Ohio river they would agree to, nothing short; and offered a mixed belt, indicating peace or war. None touched the belt — it was laid on the table; General Clark, with his cane, pushed it off and set his foot on it. Indians very sullen. Commissioners told them it was well, that the United States did not wish war, that two days yet would be allowed to consider of the terms proposed, and six days more with provisions to return home; but after that to take care, for they would certainly feel the force of the United States. Council broke up hastily. Some commotion among the Shawanees. Returned same afternoon and begged another meeting, when their old king, Moluntha, rose and made a short speech, presented a white string, doing away all that their chief warrior had said, prayed that we would have pity on women and children, &c.

Feb. 1st. — Treaty concluded and signed; presents delivered, and provisions furnished each tribe for six days. Five Shawanees left as hostages.

8th.—The commissioners, messengers and attendants, left us; returned in three boats. Wrote to Colonel Harmar at Philadelphia. Our commissioners were heartily sick of continuing so long at this place; their fare was so indifferent for a month past, having nothing but whiskey with beef and bread. Fortunately a boat arrived two days before they determined to start, which supplied them with some liquors for their trip, and a small quantity of sugar, an article they have been out of since the rum was done. After they had prepared and determined to start up in boats, took leave of us in the afternoon, and hoisted sail. We fired a few rounds by way of a salute. They having a fine wind, and their boats, three in number, being well rigged with a sail each, soon got out of sight.

By Lieutenant Doyle, who accompanied the commissioners, I sent two returns to Colonel Harmar, one dated the 1st of January, the other the present date; they were both *inclosed in a letter* a copy of which is as follows, viz:

COLONEL — We were agreeably surprised a few days after I wrote you last, with the arrival of General Clark in a small canoe. I think I mentioned his going to the Rapids with the other commissioners, and not returning with them. I likewise mentioned that the Shawanees were on their way to the treaty; it was true, but their movements were very slow, for they did not arrive until the 14th of January. Lieutenant Doyle and Mr. Rankin (one of the messengers) had set off to go to their towns, but meeting them about sixty miles distant, returned. Lieutenant Doyle's description of their march, and the mode of conduct since they arrived, confirms the character which we had of them, which is a proud, ambitious, smart nation. The young men seem to be under strict subordination to two or three old sachems. They have a white flag, which they marched in with, a drum and several other instruments of music. The pipe of peace is the most elegant I have ever seen. They have a greater command of their appetites than some other nations; as a proof, they absolutely refused receiving any liquor for some days after their arrival.

Twenty-first of January a tribe of Delawares came in. The leader's name is Bohengeehalus. It is said he is the principal warrior amongst the Wyandots and Delawares. Nothing more than an explanation of the treaty at M'Intosh was done with him.

Twenty-sixth, our commissioners delivered a speech to the Shawanees, setting forth their business, &c., and acquainting them of the country which would be allowed them. Next day a reply was made, in which they burlesqued the dividing of lands, and asked if the Great Spirit directed the Americans to cut and divide the land as was proposed; no, they did not understand that part. The Ohio, they thought, was the fittest line, and if we were satisfied, they would agree to let it remain the boundary. At hearing this we began to entertain different notions of matters, but the affair was soon cleared up. The commissioners did not attempt to touch the string which was given, and without rising, determined on an answer, which was, that if they did not agree with the terms proposed, in two days, they should then be furnished with six days provisions to carry them home, and no harm should be done them during that time; but after that take care, for they would certainly feel the force of the United States. Council was not broke up more than fifteen minutes when a messenger came for the commissioners. After they had assembled, the chief took a white string and destroyed the whole of his former speech.

On the 1st instant the treaty was concluded with the Shawanees, and articles similar to those at M'Intosh were signed.

The Half-King of the Wyandots has acted meanly in the business of this treaty: he endeavored to prevent the Shawanees agreeing to our proposal, with a view, we suppose, of expecting a larger quantity of goods that he thought would be a drug on our hands; but when he found they desired peace, and were determined to agree, he then declared that he had not given an answer to the treaty at M'Intosh, nor would he give one here; but when the warm weather would come, he would then go to Congress and hear from them what was to be done with these lands. No reply was made to this. A few days after he desired a council for himself and the Delawares. When they convened, he rose and very strenuously insisted on the commissioners enlarging the country allowed his people and the Delawares. The commissioners told him that matter was settled, and they would not make the smallest alteration. Captain Pipe, of the Delawares (who was sitting listening), rose and said, "Brothers, the Delawares are perfectly contented, they have land enough; and as a proof of our satisfaction, myself and another chief, with several young men (good hunters), will go as soon as we hear of the surveyors being out, and assist them to mark the lines, and (turning to the Half-King) you'll go too. The Half-King was so much confused he said nothing.

The Lord knows when we'll get rid of these creatures.

Major Finney does not expect to leave this place until further orders from you. He has lately received orders from Major Wyllys, dated at M'Intosh, to send him returns of the troops, and that only four rations (extra) were allowed to a complete company. The commissioners think it probable another treaty will be held next summer, somewhere to the northward of this place. They regret the misfortune of not holding this one somewhere near Detroit; however, they all clear themselves of that matter.

Our men have been kept in health with plenty of exercise; but in spring we may expect fever and ague, as the country about here is very low, and frequently covered with water.

Three privates of Captain Doughty's company and two of Captain Hart's, that were here, have returned with the commissioners.

With respect, &c.

E. D.

9*th.*—Captain Dunn had arrived the day before from Lexington, on his way to the Shawanee towns, where he intended spending winter. He took leave and set off with several of the Shawanee chiefs. General Clark left us this day for the Falls.

10*th.*—A canoe came down from Limestone, and informed us that this morning our commissioners were not more than seven miles up the river, but they had got under way early in the morning.

12*th.*—I wrote to Mr. James Parker at Lexington,

relinquishing all claims to our former connection, provided he would clear me of the obligation given Captain Parker for warrants. The bearer was Mr. West.

13*th.*—Mr. Sims passed for Fort Pitt, with whom I sent the following letter to Colonel Harmar:

COLONEL:—I forgot to mention that upon the arrival of the Wyandots, Shawanees and Delawares from White river, we were saluted by them, and having received notice of their approach and intention of firing, we, agreeably to the commissioners' request, returned the salute with three rounds of twelve men each time; and previous to the commissioners leaving the garrison to embark, Major Finney directed me to parade the company, march them down to the bank, which is about one hundred yards from our fort, and there to form, so as to present arms to the commissioners as they passed to the boats; this was done, and when they had taken leave and hoisted sail, I gave them a platoon by way of an acknowledgment.

General Clark left us for the Rapids on the 10th. He did not trouble us with much parade, neither did he take away any of our men. This last was a matter Major Finney endeavored to prevent as much as possible. There would not have gone half the number of soldiers from us up the river, only for the petty messengers who took up as much room as the commissioners, and occasioned a third boat. There were B——, M——, E——, and Mr. K——, all in constant pay at twenty shillings, three dollars, and twenty-five shillings per day, in proportion as they ranked. These men went out together to the towns, returned together, and were waiting here, when we arrived. The Lord knows what service some of them were of, for we can't imagine.

We are now clear of commissioners, messengers, Indians, and every kind of animal except five hostages. Such a sudden change makes me rather melancholy. I feel as if I ought to have gone with them; though my desire is to stay. I would be glad enough to be up, but the season is so cold, that I think the trip would be very disagreeable. I will be very thankful if you will put it in my power to go up in the beginning of

April, or as soon as convenient, and leave for a few weeks, that I might settle some affairs at Carlisle; for if we should go any farther off I shall despair.

E. D.

26*th*.—Captain O'Hara (the contractor) arrived with a large cargo of Indian goods and stores for the commissioners. He came in consequence of the dispatches sent by George White-Eyes on the 9th of January. This was a time when they expected all the western Indians. He likewise brought with him the settlements for last year's service, and two months' cash for the present, with six months' subsistence for the officers.

Captain O'Hara informs us that he lay with the commissioners the night of the 23d instant, about twenty-five miles below the Great Kanahwa; that Captain Beatty, our pay-master, was coming to this place to pay the troops the above mentioned money, but being very unwell, and having orders to return with the commissioners, he put the cash into his hands and went back.

March 1*st*.—Major Finney commenced the payment, and Captain O'Hara opened a cheap assortment of goods, which he disposed of to the soldiers as quick as they received their money.

3*d*, 4*th and* 5*th*.—After they had laid out the greatest part of their settlements for dry goods, reserving only a small share for liquor, they got permission to purchase the same, and toleration to get drunk, so that it would not interfere with their duty; but this charge had no effect; for three days there was scarcely one sober man in the garrison, and God knows how long they would have continued so, if the issues had not been stopped. So between the wet and dry affairs, Captain O'Hara will take nearly the same sum of money back that he brought, except what the officers received.

12*th.* — Two boats called from Fort Pitt, on their way to "O-post," loaded with liquors and flour.

17*th.* — A majority of the men in garrison are Irish. The soldiers requested to have the privilege of celebrating this day, as was customary. Accordingly the bung was opened and every man had permission to purchase and drink what quantity of liquor he pleased; and a pretty good portion did some of them take, for toward the evening we had not six men in the garrison fit for duty, not even the guard excepted.

18*th.* — G. Palfrey died from the effects of too much liquor—and was buried the next day.

20*th.* — Since our establishment at this place a few families had erected a station six miles below us, on the Kentucky side. This morning an express from them informed us that Indians had attacked two of their people, a short distance out, killed one and wounded the other. The wounded person escaped in. I took a light boat, with sergeant and twelve, hastened to the station; found the dead man scalped and cut in several places; buried him, assisted in securing the stockade, &c., and returned.

21*st.* — Mr. Bradshaw arrived about ten o'clock at night, with a boat loaded with provisions; likewise Mr. Devoire and Mr. Le Bere arrived on their way into the Indian country. Mr. Le Bere intends spending a few weeks in the Indian towns and then return by way of Sandusky, to join his company at Muskingum.

24*th.*—This night the five Shawanee hostages deserted from their lodging, and pushed with great expedition toward the towns. They likewise took with them Mr. Sufferins' family, who were encamped about a mile distant—Mr. Sufferins being absent on a hunting party.

25*th.* — Our interpreter, Mr. Sufferins, came in ; very much surprised at finding his people had gone off, and still more when hearing how the hostages had left us. This day we completed a block-house on the bank, to guard the boats.

26*th.* — Mr. Sufferins set off on purpose to overtake his family and the hostages, if possible, and to know the reason of elopement. But after riding twenty miles, only arrived at the place where they lay the night before. The distance he thought they might be in front of him, at the rate they had gone, discouraged him from pursuing any farther, and he turned back with the intention of preparing to go to their towns.

27*th.*—We were surprised by the arrival of Mr. Abner Dunn, an old officer, who had been to the Shawanee towns. He arrived with five Indians (Shawanees) and six white prisoners. Mr. Dunn informed us that their chief, with the six prisoners, had halted about five miles off, being doubtful of the manner in which they would be received, having the night before sent two runners with some tobacco for us to smoke until their arrival, and to get leave for their friends, the hostages, to go and meet them; but when the runners came and could see no hostages they retired undiscovered, and informed their people, which alarmed them; however, Mr. Dunn prevailed on five of them to go in with him and the others to remain until he would send for them. The Indians soon found us to be friends, and sent for the remaining party. After they had all arrived, the White-Horn, their chief, seemed much astonished at the conduct of the hostages. Two speeches were delivered by Johnny Harris from Moluntha, their king; one of them consisted of professions of friendship, &c., the other was information respecting some parties of Cherokees that were out.

30*th*.—Major Finney delivered a speech to the Indians and sent a message to their king, thanking him for his information respecting the Cherokees, after which they marched off. The night preceding, a girl and boy of the prisoners that were delivered up yesterday, eloped.

31*st*.—This night Corporal Thompson and John Geary deserted, and took off one of our best boats.

April 1*st*.—Sergeant Wilcox pursued the deserters.

2*d*.—Captain O'Hara and Mr. Smith left us for Fort Pitt.

4*th*.—Mr. Dunn took leave for the Falls.

Copy of a Letter to Colonel Harmar, dated 31*st March*, 1786.

Sir—The Shawanees have been very slow in executing their business respecting the delivery of the prisoners. They overstayed the time agreed on better than a month; their delay, and an account from the station a few miles below (since evacuated), of five Indians attacking two men of the place, killing one and wounding the other, we suppose frightened off the hostages; for on the night of the 24th of March the whole of them eloped, and we have not heard from them since. But fortunately, two days after there came in two chiefs with six prisoners, whom they delivered up, with a speech from their king apologizing for the delay, &c. We don't apprehend any danger from the Shawanees immediately, but there is now a number of others in the woods for war, that makes our situation rather unsafe. They have killed at Limestone and near the Falls — the last which I have mentioned above, was about four miles distant.

Captain O'Hara arrived here on the 26th of February with the arrearages of pay and clothing for the men who were in service last year; in six months notes and two months for the present in cash, and the same with six months subsistence for the officers. He brought with him a pretty assortment of goods suitable for the soldiers, which he let them have at reasonable prices. I believe he will take back all the notes and cash (which are the same to him), except what the officers received. I mentioned in a letter some months ago that the commissioners had made a compliment to Major Finney of cloth for over-alls for the men. Since, there has some alteration happened or otherwise it was a mistake in me, for as they went up the river they met Captain O'Hara near the Great Kanahwa, and turned the account over to him. He has charged each man that had them with his price.

There was a letter received from Mr. Armstrong, (to which he put his title, Lieut. 1st A. R.) for the purpose of acquainting us of his promotion.

Colonel—as I stand next on the list, am induced to beg your interest to fix me clear of the censure of a number of my friends. For certain it is that I have in some measure lessened, having once served as an officer a grade higher, and that at a more honorable time than at present. But the attachment I have to a military life, and the expectation of rising, persuades me to this duty, hoping that my friends, yourself in particular, will assist me in procuring a lieutenancy — what I once had the honor to hold under you.

I shall ever endeavor to render satisfaction for your assistance in this very material affair, as well as for many past,

While I have the honor to subscribe myself, &c.

E. D.

N. B. Sent a return of the troops with the above.

23*d.* — Captain Blue-Jacket, a chief of the Shawanee nation, came in. He informed us of the good intentions of his people, and that a number of them would hunt this summer near this place, and would bring in the skins; begged that we would receive the Shawanees friendly. As a proof of his friendship, and that we might be assured the nation wished for peace, he left his son, a boy about eighteen years of age, to continue with us until some opportunity would offer for sending him home.

24th.—He took leave, and as he went off said he would go by a hunting camp where there were a number of Indians, and inform them how desirous we were to see them come in to trade.

25th.—In the evening there arrived two young warriors of the Shawanees, with a white boy, a prisoner, whom they delivered up to us; and after receiving a few presents, and being asked if they did not think the boy would run back again, they candidly told us, that he certainly would, if not bound or confined some way. This was enough. Though the boy seemed fond of having it in his power to go to his father's, but yet it was all affected; for in a few hours after a boat came along, bound for the Falls, in which he was put, and in a manner by force; for when he found there was no way of escaping he cried, and appeared to leave the Indian with more regret than he could have done if they had been bearing him away a prisoner from his mother.

26th.—Our friends, the warriors, left us, and took with them Blue-Jacket's son.

May 14th.—We have Shawanees with us every day.

The most of their hunting men are now in the woods around us, at the distance of twenty miles. They intend bringing their peltry to barter at this place. Several of the boys, and even one young woman of the prisoners, made their escape and returned to the Indians. The chiefs who have been in, particularly the White-Horn, say they never mean to break the chain of friendship that now subsists between the Americans and them, and threaten vengeance upon the first who infringes upon the articles of the treaty.

18*th.*—From a letter sent by Major Finney to the commanding officer at Fort M'Intosh, requesting a reinforcement of men at this post, and from several late reports of troops being on their way to us, we prepared a small boat and set out up the river, intending to sail two or three hours for amusement, at the same time thought it probable we might meet them. We had got about four miles, and halted at a spring, when we were very agreeably surprised hy the arrival of Captain Ziegler's company of seventy men—Lieutenant E. Beatty, Doctor Allison, and the Major from Connecticut, Wyllys, commanding.

22*d.*—I received orders to prepare to go on command to the Falls of Ohio.

23*d.*—Set out with sergeant, corporal and twelve men in a barge, for Louisville. River very full. Landed next morning at the place—distance said to be one hundred and fifty miles—run it in twenty-four hours. Four Kentucky boats, which passed Fort Finney the day before I left it, were attacked at the mouth of Kentucky river by the Indians on both sides of the Ohio, supposed to be in number two hundred — fortunately no other damage than a few horses killed. Very alarming accounts of the depredations of Indians in neighborhood of Vincennes — a settlement on the Wabash. Every day fresh accounts of mischief done in the upper counties and on Cumberland. People of Kentucky talk of an expedition against the Indians on the Wabash. Four days I remained at the Falls, and every day there were accounts of men being scalped between that and the upper counties. General Clark informed me that he had frequent intelligence from the different posts on the Mississippi and Wabash, which he took from the British last war, and that if something was not done immediately respecting that country, there will be much more difficulty in subjecting them than there ever was.

After many altercations between General Clark, myself and the two gentlemen who had the artillery in charge, they agreed I should have a piece, with a few shot, which I immediately had put on board.

28*th*.—Having procured a brass three-pounder, with a few boxes of suitable shot, left the Falls; embarked again for our Fort. River very high, and obliged to work up close along shore, giving the savages every possible advantage. This evening, about seventeen miles up, we discovered two bark canoes lying on the bank, and a number of trees barked, which we supposed had not been done longer than two days. We passed on as silent as possible. This night our cable and anchor served to keep us in the middle of the river; but the river rose so high it was of no more use afterward.

30*th*.—About a mile below Kentuck we discovered some appearance of an Indian camp, and saw a black horse with a belt on. We passed the mouth of Kentuck in the night, and lay near a mile above.

31*st*.—We met with such strong water below and above the Big Bone, that we were obliged to drop the oars (though we worked fourteen,) and pull up by the bushes; lay this night five or six miles above Big Bone. We arrived safe at the Fort, near the Miami, in the afternoon, and were received with gladness.

June 1*st*.—Several Delawares came in, who seemed surprised at the field-piece which I lately brought from the Falls, and at our additions to the Fort.

11*th*.—Captain Pipe's brother, with three other Delawares, arrived with a speech from Pipe, the purport of which was, that he hoped we still held the chain of friendship fast, that was made between them and us, at this place, and informing us, that for his part, nothing should be wanting which was in his power to keep the Delawares and the Americans upon the most friendly footing, and begging we would treat his young men (a number of whom were hunting near us) as we have hitherto done.

13*th*.—Mr. Sovereign came in with the Shawanees with a speech from Molunthy, informing us that he was very glad to hear we treated his young men so friendly, and apologizing for the delay in delivering up the prisoners. He says the nation is divided; that the people of Chillicothe will not hear reason; they will not give the prisoners up. In fact, the plain English of which is, that a party of them are as much inclined for war as anything else, from the d——d lies imposed on them by British emissaries. They are fully of the opinion that their king and sachems have sold both land and warriors, and are determined not to agree to what has been done. Molunthy gives us information of four men being killed by the Mingoes, on the waters of the Muskingum. He says that he has advised the Mingoes and Cherokees to be quiet, but they would not hear him. He desires us to have patience. He is striving all he can to fulfill the promises made to our chiefs at the council fire.

14*th*.—Mr. Sovereign returned homeward with a speech to Molunthy, informing him that we still kept the road open, and hoped he would soon send in the prisoners; thanking him for the intelligence he sent, and begging he would endeavor to persuade his contentious people to listen to reason, otherwise the consequence would be fatal; we would wait with patience for a time, until he would fulfill the promises made to our chief at the great council fire, &c.

15*th*.—Major Wyllys left us in a small boat bound up the river, with whom I sent the following letter to Colonel Harmar, with an inspection return:

Sir — After the arrival of Major Wyllys and Captain Ziegler, I was ordered to the Falls to procure and bring up a field-piece, with ammunition, &c. I got a brass three-pounder, with about thirty rounds only of ball and grape-shot. And if it had not been for General Clark, who has always been our friend here, I should have returned as I went, owing to a contentious set of men in civil office there, all of whom are candidates for something, and were afraid would be censured by the public for giving any of the military stores away, at a time when their country is suffering by savage depredations. True it is, that everywhere below us, the Americans have as much reason to be engaged in an Indian war as they ever had. They are daily losing men in the lower part of Kentuck settlement; all which aggravation could not unite the people in a sufficient body to carry on any kind of an expedition—such is the division amongst them.

I brought from the Falls, and delivered to Major Wyllys, all the intelligence I could collect, amongst which are the particulars of two skirmishes which the Americans at St. Vincent had with the Piankeshaw Indians in that neighborhood.

Some Shawanees and Delawares went with us as usual, professing much friendship. The arrival of Captain Ziegler's company has added much to the appearance of this place, and something to the other company. For since, a better spirit of emulation has subsisted, which has been of service. Captain Ziegler tells me the regimental book for last year was left at M'Intosh, and not used very well by the officers last winter; I am sorry for it, but hope you will get it. My coming away from that place in such haste occasioned several neglects; I even forgot my Bible with you.

We long to see you. With respects, &c.

E. D.

26th.—Captain Doyle arrived from M'Intosh; he informed us of the arrival of Colonel Harmar and lady at M'Intosh.

July 4th.—This day was celebrated with three rounds of small arms and three with the field-piece, after which the gentlemen all dined together. When dinner was over thirteen toasts were drunk, each accompanied with a round from the three-pounder, attended in the intervals by two drums, two fifes and a couple of excellent violins. The evening was spent as well as circumstances would allow of.

5th.—Captain Beatty and Mr. M'Dowell left us, having been ordered, by Colonel Harmar, to go up immediately after the arrival of Mr. Doyle. With Mr. M'Dowell I sent a letter to Doctor M'Dowell, desiring him to ask Colonel Harmar for permission for me to go up, &c.

13*th.*—Major Finney received a letter from General Clark, informing him that on the 1st of August he intended marching into the Indian country, with fifteen hundred men, and requested that the field-piece which I brought up might be sent down against that time.

17*th.*—Corporal Thompson, Gairy, and two other deserters, were brought in by three men from Lexington, by whom Major Finney received an account from Colonel Patterson of orders being arrived from the State of Virginia to the County-Lieutenant of Kentucky country, directing them to plan and put into execution an expedition through the Indian country immediately. It is thought General Clark would command.

Captain Armstrong arrived with the boat and men which Major Wyllys took away. He brought a letter from Colonel Harmar to Major Finney, in which there was an order to send up Ensign Denny, for the purpose of acting as adjutant—to repair to a new fort at the mouth of Muskingum, called Fort Harmar, where the Colonel, with Mrs. Harmar, had arrived.

23*d.*—Embarked about noon, in a swift boat, with corporal and six choice men; rowed six oars. River in good order. Anxious to make a quick passage. Had provisions for several days cooked, and boat fitted for anchoring in the stream, &c. Reached few miles above Little Miami.

24*th.*—Met the water rising.

25*th.*—Reached Limestone about same time of the day we left the Fort; this is coming at rate of forty miles a day. Stayed and cooked.

26*th.*—Work along. River risen five feet.

27*th.*—In the evening pass the Scioto river.

28*th.*—Within a few miles of Sandy. Water falling.

29*th.*—Pass Sandy and Guyandot.

30*th.*—Helped forward by a violent storm of wind and rain, directly up the river; reached Great Kanahwa.

31*st.*—Lay by drying our things and cooking.

August 1*st.*—Got within a few miles of Letart's Falls. Water rising rapidly. Met Mr. Le Bere in the evening.

2*d.*—Passed the Falls and anchored ten miles below Flin's Station.

3*d.*—Passed the Scotch Settlement and Flin's, and lay in sight of Little Kanahwa.

4*th.*—In the morning arrived at Muskingum, Fort Harmar, where I met with Colonel Harmar and a number of acquaintances. Here I was received as a brother officer might expect. Though I was ordered up in haste, yet I had some hopes of getting a furlough to go to Philadelphia, as I had not been absent during our service. Having hinted in a letter to Colonel Harmar, before I left the Miami, that a short furlough would be very acceptable and knowing, that if he could with any kind of propriety grant it, he would, I deferred asking. Next day after my arrival he proposed a furlough; I thanked him and accepted it. But as I had no non-commissioned officer from the Miami, he thought it best to send my boat back under the care of Major North and Captain Beatty, just arrived and on their way to the Miami, and to take a passage to Fort Pitt with Mr. Bradford, who was to start on the 10th instant. Fort Harmar is unfinished. Doughty's company from New York, Heart's and Strong's from Connecticut, are here and at work.

9*th*.—Major North and E. Beatty got under way.

10*th*.—Received a furlough for two months; took passage with Lieutenant Bradford, who was ordered to Pitt for artillery, stores, &c.

16*th*.—Arrived at the mouth of Little Beaver; found Mr. Hutchens and the old surveyors encamped there. Hamtramck's company, from New York; Mercer's, from New Jersey, and M'Curdy's, of Pennsylvania, escorting the surveyors.

17*th*.—Reached M'Intosh. Captain Ferguson's company here. Here Mr. Bradford had business, which would detain him a day. Major Finney and myself having no time to lose, agreed to walk to Fort Pitt, thirty miles distant, knowing that when the boat did move, it would take her two days, as the water was very rapid.

18*th*.—We breakfasted with my old friend, Captain M'Curdy, and set off for Fort Pitt. I tripped along after Major Finney exceedingly well, for near two-thirds of the way; but having been confined so long to my boat, and not accustomed to walking, I got much fatigued; however, we reached Fort Pitt about two o'clock, P. M., where we refreshed ourselves upon a tolerable dinner and a glass of claret.

August 22d.—I received my mare, left in care of Mr. Duncan, in miserable order.

23d.—Left Fort Pitt in company with Mr. James Sample. The weather being favorable, we traveled very agreeably together as far as Shippensburg, where we arrived on the 28th.

29th.—I got to Carlisle. Time short—staid a few days. Left Carlisle for Philadelphia, at which place I arrived on the 8th September.

Sept. 12th.—Having completed my business, I parted with my friends, James Campbell and several other acquaintances, and left Philadelphia, with once more my face turned toward the western country.

13th.—Got to Carlisle.

20th.—Left my friends at Carlisle.

25th.—Arrived at my uncle, John M'Clure's, on the Monongahela, seven miles above Pittsburgh, where I left my mare, saddle and bridle, for further use.

26th.—Went in canoe to Pittsburgh, where I met Major North and Captain Beatty, just arrived from the Falls of Ohio, where they left Major Finney and Captain Ziegler with their companies.

30th.—Left Fort Pitt in the boat in which North and Beatty came, and proceeded to Muskingum, at which place I arrived the 3d of October, in the morning.

Fort Harmar, *Oct. 3d.*—John Pratt, formerly Lieutenant and Quarter-master in the 4th Pennsylvania regiment, had originally been of Connecticut, came out now as one of the officers of that State, and appointed Quarter-master, myself announced as adjutant. Strong, Pratt and Kingsbury belonged to one company and formed a mess; I was invited to join them. Very pleasantly fixed.

10*th.*—Captain Doughty and Captain Strong left us with leave of absence until spring.

15*th.*—Captain Tunas, a Delaware Indian, arrived with information that the different nations of Indians from the Wabash, who had collected at the Shawanees towns with a determination to visit this country, had returned home; that one hundred and twenty Shawanees, Mingoes and Cherokees had left Wapotomeky with intention to strike the people on the Ohio; that but few of the Shawanees continued; the greater part of them were in the Kentucky country, scalping and stealing horses. He says Captain Brant, a civilized Indian, had been at Sandusky this summer, but his business was not known. Mr. Johnston, the British agent, had asked all the red people to Niagara; that the Shawanees and a number of other nations had gone, but not any of the Delawares; that Johnston told them they would be no people in a short time, if they did not unite. They should all be one people, and what they did, either to make peace or war, would then be strong.

Nov. 13*th.*—Three men arrived from Limestone, who had been with Colonel Logan against the Shawanee towns. They informed us that Logan left Limestone the 6th of October, marched with eight hundred men in six days, to the Shawanee towns, where he found some men and a number of women. The warriors had all set out to meet General Clark, who was marching with fifteen hundred men toward the Wabash, and only a few sachems remained at home with the squaws. Colonel Logan destroyed all their towns, killed and scalped eleven Indians, amongst whom was the king Moluṇthy, and carried twenty-eight Indian women and children prisoners to Danville, where they were kept in confinement. The old king was tomahawked after he had delivered himself up. Logan found none but old men, women and children in the towns; they made no resistance; the men were literally murdered.

15*th.*—Left Fort Harmar in a light boat, a sergeant and twelve men; arrived at Fort Pitt the 22d.

24*th.*—Rode to Hannahstown, accompanied by Mr. Brison. Viewed several farms and tracts of land in Westmoreland county, belonging to Colonel Harmar, property which he got with Mrs. H.

Dec. 5*th.*—Was ready to return, but the heavy snows and frost had filled the river with ice.

9*th.*—Ohio frozen over in many places. Monongahela and Allegheny both passable on the ice.

13*th.*—Had several days of soft rainy weather. Rivers broke up. The rise of water was sudden. Several boats loaded with goods, &c., carried down with the ice passed Pittsburgh. An attempt made to save them, but fruitless. We had great difficulty to preserve our boat.

16*th.*—Ohio pretty clear of ice. Loaded our boat and sailed for Fort Harmar, where we arrived on the 19th, in the morning. In my absence, Lieutenant Pratt, the

Quarter-master, attended to the ordinary duties of adjutant, but much left undone. Regimental book opened, monthly returns of the regiment, &c., to be made out and transmitted to the War Office.

Fort Harmar, *Mouth of Muskingum River*, *Jan.*, 1787. —No change of movement of any consequence. Officers and men in close quarters. Officers pass and repass up and down to the several posts. Ferguson's company of artillery at M'Intosh. Hamtramck, M'Curdy and Mercer had put up quarters, after the surveying was over, at a place which they called Fort Steuben, about thirty miles below M'Intosh. Doughty, Strong and Heart with their companies at Fort Harmar. Finney and Ziegler's companies had evacuated Fort Finney and erected a small work opposite Louisville. One other company, commanded by Captain Burbeck, of New York, stationed at West Point.

Receiving and digesting the monthly returns of the troops at all these different posts, was a business of some trouble. Those from the post commanded by Hamtramck less difficulty with. Colonel Harmar thinks him one of his best captains.

Feb. 4th.—Mr. M'Dowell arrived on his way to the Rapids of the Ohio. Fortunately there came with him a supply of provisions for the troops at Fort Harmar. For upward of thirty days past they had been on half allowance of flour, with whiskey only one-half their time.

8th.—Major Wyllys and Mr. M'Dowell left us for the Rapids.

19th. — Captain Heart and Lieutenant Beatty arrived from Fort Pitt. The latter brought with him near two months pay and three months subsistence, chiefly in paper money, and likewise part of the annual allowance of clothing for the troops. The money being a particular currency of one State only, the officers at this post (Fort Harmar) objected to receiving it; for though it might answer their present purposes, being in the neighborhood of the State, yet it might be setting a precedent for others, which would be very injurious. Several days spent in deliberating upon the receiving this paper money. Sometimes it was in contemplation to send it back; again they would conceive it more to their advantage to keep it. However, as the Colonel had some business up the river, he postponed the payment until (we suppose) he would consult the officers up the river. Accordingly he, Beatty, Pratt and Mr. Spear set off the forenoon of the 25th.

25th.—This afternoon we were agreeably surprised by the arrival of Major Finney from the Rapids, after a passage of seventeen days to this post. The Major being on the way to visit friends down the country, he only tarried until next morning and set off up the river in hopes to overtake Colonel Harmar.

March 6th.—Mr. Lakesang called, being on his way to the Rapids of the Ohio. He continued over night. By Mr. Lakesang I forwarded to Major Wyllys three hundred hard dollars, and a receipt for thirteen hundred dollars, left with me by Beatty to be sent by the first conveyance (Captain Heart witness). By the same boat, and under Mr. Lakesang's care, I sent the proportion of clothing for the troops at the Rapids, and likewise a new rifle, complete, for Lieutenant Doyle, with a number of letters, &c.

26*th.*— Our commandant, with his suite, arrived from Fort Pitt, about seven o'clock at night, and disappointed the garrison of a little parade that was intended in receiving him.

27*th.* — Major Hamtramck arrived, having been directed by the commandant to muster the troops.

29*th.* — Muster and inspection took place, after which a few manœuvres, &c.

April 1*st.*—The Major left us, bound for Fort Steuben.

10*th.*—Captain Heart ordered to proceed with his company to a place called Venango, on the Allegheny river, about one hundred and fifty miles above Pittsburgh; there to erect a suitable work. This place had formerly been occupied by French and English troops, but burnt down.

15*th.*—Colonel Harmar, Lieutenant Beatty and Pratt, left us, bound for the Rapids. Soon after their departure, Major Hamtramck arrived, having been ordered down to command at Muskingum, owing to the Colonel's absence.

May 10*th.* — At night our Colonel arrived from the Rapids of the Ohio, to no little satisfaction of all the officers at Fort Harmar.

15*th.* — Major Hamtramck set off, accompanied by Captain Beatty, for Fort Steuben. Captain Beatty goes on to New York to obtain a settlement for the regiment up to the first of the present year.

17*th.*—We were surprised with the arrival of Captain Strong, from Connecticut, with dispatches of very considerable importance to Colonel Harmar, from the War Office.

25*th.* — In consequence of the dispatches brought by Captain Strong, Fort Steuben has been ordered to be evacuated; accordingly Lieutenant Kersey, with sixty men, arrived here from that place. Major Hamtramck, with the remainder of the troops, are expected daily. Hamtramck promoted to Major, in room of Fish of New York, who resigned. Lieutenant Smith, captain in place of Hamtramck.

27*th.* — Captain Strong, with his company, embarked on board keel boats for the Rapids of the Ohio.

June 1*st.* — Major Hamtramck, with the whole of the troops under his command, arrived safe.

2*d.* — Captain Mercer, with part of his company, and Lieutenant Kersey, set off for the Rapids, on board two family boats that were passing down. Ensign Spear, with fifty-four men, left us this day for the surveying business.

5*th.* — Captain Smith, with his company, Ensign Sedam, with part of Mercer's company, Lieutenant Peters, Doctor Elliot and myself, left Fort Harmar to join the troops at the Rapids.

10*th.* — In the morning we joined our friends at the Falls.

11*th.*—Our commandant, with Major Hamtramck and

Mr. Pratt, the Quarter-master, &c., arrived in the barge. They bring accounts that Colonel Todd had returned from the Cherokee town on Paint creek, with three or four scalps and six or seven prisoners.

18*th.*—Water favorable. We began to send our boats and stores over the Rapids, for fear of low water. Subaltern's command at landing below the Rapids as guard. Troops wait for a supply of provisions. Some clashing between contractors. Turnbull and Marmie superseded by O'Hara and Duncan. When Bradshaw the agent is at a loss, commanding officer directs the purchase of provisions.

July 2*d.* — Strong's, Mercer's and Smith's companies cross the Ohio from their encampment opposite Louisville, march down and encamp at the landing below the Falls.

3*d.* — Finney's and Ziegler's companies crossed and encamped with the others. This evening Ferguson, with his company of artillery, from M'Intosh, and Daniel Britt, with a cargo of provisions on account of late contractors, arrived.

6*th.* — Captain Ziegler, with a command of a lieutenant, one sergeant, one corporal and sixty-two privates, embarked with all the cattle and horses and a quantity of flour, on board eight Kentucky boats and two keel boats, with orders to proceed down to Pigeon creek, eight miles above Green river, and there wait for the arrival of the troops.

8*th.*—Troops embarked for Pigeon creek, one hundred and eighty miles below the Rapids.

10*th.*—Arrived in the evening at Pigeon creek, where

we found Captain Ziegler, who had arrived the evening before.

11*th.*—The cattle, horses and necessary baggage, with fifteen days flour, taken out of the boats, and the boats, with artillery, stores and heavy baggage, under command of Major Hamtramck, proceeded down the Ohio to mouth of Wabash, with orders to ascend that river and meet the troops as soon as possible at Vincennes. Troops took up the following order of march, (*see Plan,*) and proceeded by the most direct route for Vincennes, agreeably to the advice of a pilot. Columns regulated in their march by signals from the drum. Weather exceedingly warm and woods close. With heavy packs and not lately used to marching, the troops were hard put to. We encamped on a branch of Pigeon creek.

12*th.*—Marched at daylight. Woods not so thick. Crossed Pigeon creek twice, and encamped on its bank.

13*th.*—The troops march with more ease—pass through a level open country. Buffalo numerous in these woods. Several seen standing and gazing at the men, appearing to hearken to the drums. Encamped on the head waters of Pigeon creek.

14*th.*—Marched at the usual time. Fine open country until about twelve o'clock, intercepted by a thicket of plum and rose bushes, which our pilot said reached to a great distance on the right and left. Opened our way through. Some delay and disorder. Columns unable to keep their proper distances. Cattle scattered. Halted until the cattle were collected. Moved on and encamped on bank of Patoka.

15th.—Heavy rain over night. Waited till twelve o'clock. Got on tolerably well considering our tents being very heavy with the rain. Encamped on high ground near a branch of Patoka.

16th.—Marched at daylight. Passed through a very fine rich open country, and arrived at White river about twelve: forded, breast high upon the men. Proceeded to the river De Shay, and encamped.

17th.—Took up the order of march, not until nine o'clock; moved on near to Vincennes. Met by some of the inhabitants. Halted and formed battalion, marched into the village with colors, &c., and encamped close to the American fort, Clark's block-house.

18th.—Moved our encampment about a quarter of a mile up the Wabash, for the sake of good water. Here we found a number of Cherokee Indians, who had fled to the French for refuge. The people on Cumberland, joined by the Chickasaws, had lately made an expedition to their towns and totally defeated them. The Cherokees were very shy of us, but being told by the French that we intended no hostilities, they rejoiced; were thankful and claimed protection.

21st.—The French inhabitants prepared and treated the officers to a very pretty entertainment.

25th.—This day Major Hamtramck, with the boats and baggage, arrived safe, excepting some few articles which could not be brought on, owing to the water being so shoal, and were left at the mouth of Wabash, guarded by Ensign Sedam and a small party of troops. This was a pleasant sight to us, as on leaving the boats we had divested ourselves of everything not indispensably necessary. The six companies having now all assembled, they made a handsome parade. Men well clothed and well disciplined. The order and regularity observed gave the people of Vincennes a very favorable opinion of us. Our little camp, formed agreeably, in every respect, to the regulations, with the company of artillery divided on the right and left; tents new, &c., made no indifferent show. The inhabitants of Vincennes all French, except a few Americans, who found their way here since the war; but few speak English. Had on several occasions been visited by militia from Kentucky, who rather served to alienate and estrange them. They viewed us as belonging to another nation; called us the *real Americans.*

26th. — Lieutenant Armstrong and forty-five privates were detached with craft, to join Ensign Sedam, and assist in bringing up the whole of the stores from the mouth of the Wabash.

27th. — Several persons came in who had been with a party that were defeated coming up the Wabash. They informed us that the day before, just at the Grand Rapids, a party of Indians, about fifteen in number, attacked three perogues, killed three men and took four prisoners, two of whom were French, who were liberated immediately. Among the killed was a soldier of Captain Ziegler's company. One of those who made their escape, informed us that Daniel Britt, with whom we had left six soldiers at the Falls (to help him on, expecting he would overtake our fleet before it would get to the

Wabash), had passed the Wabash unknowingly, and was as low down as Cherokee river; that two of the soldiers had come up from the boat in a canoe, and being satisfied of the mistake, returned. Craft has been sent for Britt's cargo, and is supposed will proceed until they find him.

28*th.*—Two large canoes bearing white flags, appeared coming down the Wabash; they proved to be Piankeshaws, who inhabit the upper waters. Had been invited by Colonel Le Gras to come and see their friends the *true Americans.* Mr. Le Gras appears to be the chief magistrate here; sort of little governor among the French; is looked up to, and has great influence among the neighboring Indians. The Piankeshaws were timorous, having considered the Americans as their enemies. Indeed it was but last year that a formidable expedition went from Kentucky against their towns (but the principal officers, jealous of Clark, who had the command, excited a dissatisfaction among the corps, and when within a day or two's march of the Indians, broke up their camp and returned home). Some pains taken to conciliate and dispel their fear. They seemed to rejoice at their reception, expressed great satisfaction; said we were different Americans from any they had seen. They presented Colonel Harmar with an elegant calumet, and departed, intending to return and bring with them all the chiefs of the Wabash nation.

Aug. 4*th.*—A Mr. Vigo, a gentleman of Post Vincennes, gave the officers of our corps an entertainment. In the evening three Indian men came in, who had been down the Wabash with Lieutenant Armstrong. They brought information that forty Piankeshaws were lying in wait, at the Grand Rapids, for Lieutenant Armstrong's fleet; in consequence of which information, Major Hamtramck, with a captain, one subaltern and fifty-eight men, set out in three keel boats to meet the fleet.

5th.—The whole of our boat stores arrived.

VINCENNES, *9th.* — Colonel Harmar had informed us of his intention to visit Kaskaskia and the settlements on the Mississippi, and had directed me to detail a subaltern and twenty-eight men to accompany him. I felt a desire to see the Mississippi, and offered myself for the command. This the first time I solicited any service; others might do it, but this soliciting service was a business I disapproved. Was living with the Colonel at the time. However, he chose that I should not go. Ensign M'Dowell was ordered in his turn for this pleasant tour. They set out early this morning, accompanied by a very accomplished Frenchman, a Mr. Tardiveau. Major Wyllys, the senior officer, left to command. A Mr. Mason, with a small party, left us this day for the Falls. By him sent several letters, under cover, to Mr. Kingsbury, at the head of the Rapids, addressed to my friends in Pennsylvania. One for P. F., Philadelphia; another for Mr. Lyon, Carlisle, and one for Doctor M'Dowell, at Muskingum, all respecting my rank, &c. I likewise sent per Mr. Bradford, a letter to my friend Parker, at Lexington.

20th. — A gentleman from Kaskaskia arrived, but did

not meet the Colonel's party. Must have been upon different traces. Tells of two hundred Shawanees and Delawares having left their villages on the Miami and settled across the Mississippi, under protection of the Spaniards. That more were expected, as the Spaniards had given them pressing invitations.

21st.—An express arrived from the Rapids, with dispatches for Colonel Harmar from the War Office. By this opportunity I received a letter from Mr. Kingsbury, telling me that he had forwarded my letter for P. F. and the one to Carlisle, per Mr. Abner Dunn, through the wildnerness.

Sept. 2d. — A runner from the Piankeshaws informed Major Wyllys that the chiefs of the tribes invited down had agreed to come, and that he might expect them daily.

3d. — The Colonel and his party returned from the Illinois.

5th.— One hundred of the Piankeshaws and Wyohtomas appeared in great style; all in canoes, but twelve horsemen who guarded the shore. The chiefs' canoes carried white flags. On their approach they gave us three fires. We were prepared for this, and had in readiness twenty men, who returned the salute with three rounds. They all came ashore—expressed much gladness at seeing us as friends. Taking a little milk for nourishment, they set out for town to see their French brothers, giving another fire as they went off.

7th.—Colonel Harmar made a speech to the Indians, the purport of which was, informing them of the peaceable disposition of the United States; that he was directed by the principal chief to take by the hand every tribe of Indians desirous of peace, and authorized to destroy those otherwise inclined. He told them that everything should be done to make them glad; that the road should be kept clear and smooth between them and us, that traders might pass freely and with safety, &c. As a pledge of remembrance of the thirteen great fires (the thirteen United States), he presented each tribe with thirteen strings of white wampum.

8*th.* — Five of the Indian chiefs each made a reply to the Colonel's speech, expressing their gladness at being taken by the hand by their fathers the Bostonians. Professed great friendship; said that they had been misled, were now sensible of their error; hoped their fathers would let all the blood which has been spilt be washed down with the river, never to be seen or thought of more. That they would stand upon fresh ground, keep the road and the stumps between them and their fathers quite smooth; and as a proof and remembrance, each presented the Colonel with a calumet and a string of wampum.

10*th.* — The old chiefs attended, expecting, as was customary, some presents. The Colonel told them that we were warriors, that we did not come to purchase their friendship with trinkets, but barely to take them by the hand if they chose to give it; if they did not, it was a matter of indifference. But, however, since things had been so well settled, he told them his warriors had a few articles, which they would give to the old men only.

The sachems returned thanks. Pleased to take what they could get. The greatest beggars I have seen yet among all the savages.

11*th.*—Two men out of fifteen who had set out on the 9th for the Rapids, returned, having been fired on near the forks of White river, by a party of Indians. From their report it is likely the greater number of their company fell a sacrifice. This story circulating through the town had like to have frightened off all the Indians who had been invited.

13*th.*—The Indians took their departure.

15*th.*—Lieutenant Armstrong, with a party of soldiers and militia, set out to meet a drove of cattle which Mr. Bradshaw, with some hands, was bringing on. Fortunately the two parties met about seven miles off, and came in the same evening. This day Captain Mercer and Mr. Britt arrived from Kaskaskia.

Vincennes, or Post Vincennes, as it is called, is said to be the most capital village in the western country. There are about five hundred souls, French, and about half as many Americans. It is handsomely situated on the left bank of the Wabash, out of danger of the floods. The village is built in the centre of a large prairie, the greater part of which is at present cultivated, but under no inclosure. A sufficiency only is inclosed for their cattle, and is in common. Their houses are chiefly frame work, and many of them covered with bark Five or six families live on the opposite side and have little farms. The land is excellent and the country generally fine for growing. It was first settled by a Monsieur Vincennes, near seventy years ago, from whom it takes its name It is allowed to be one hundred and seventy miles from Post Vincennes to Kaskaskia. The prairies between these two places are remarkable. One, in particular, I am told, is thirty miles in width, and near one hundred miles in length. They run north and south. They are grown up with long grass, free from brush and underwood; here and there a small copse of handsome young trees. The country abounds in buffalo, deer, elk and bear.

Kaskaskia, though more ancient than the Post, is not so extensive a village. Opposite is a settlement called Misére, where a lieutenant and five or six regular soldiers are stationed. About sixty miles above Kaskaskia is Cahokia, and opposite it, on the Spanish side, is St. Louis, where the commandant (a lieutenant-colonel) resides, with about twenty soldiers. Between Kaskaskia and Cahokia there are several small villages, some of them inhabited by Americans only, who have emigrated to that country chiefly since the late war.

Post Vincennes, 30*th*.—Orders issued for Ziegler's and Strong's companies to march next day, with the commandant, for the Rapids of the Ohio. Finney's and Mercer's companies to embark on the 3d October, under command of Major Wyllys, for the same place. Major Hamtramck, with Ferguson's and Smith's companies, to continue at the Post.

Oct. 1*st*.—Set out with the commandant and the two companies; marched to a branch of the river De Shay, supposed to be nine miles.

2d.—Crossed the west fork of White river and encamped on a branch, - - - - - -	20
3d.—Crossed and encamped on north fork of White river, - - - - - -	24
4th.—Reached the Great Lick, - - -	18
5th.—Branch of Patoka, - - - -	16
6th.—Branch of Blue river, - - -	25
7th.—Rapids, - - - - - -	18
	130

In this route we pursued General Clark's trace, made a twelvemonth ago, on his way against the Wabash Indians. First and second day passed through tolerable land; third day very indifferent, owing to the path keeping about three and four miles distant, for thirty miles up the north fork of White river, which led us through neither rich nor level land, but just across the heads of gullies leading into White river. Fourth day's march, passed over a great deal of good land, particularly near the Great Lick, which is not far distant from the road. When within a few miles of the Lick, our hunters had leave to go ahead. Presently heard the report of both their guns, and in a few minutes five buffaloes made their appearance, bearing furiously toward the head of the column. When within fifty paces, the men in front were permitted to fire; this turned the heads of the animals; they passed along and received the fire of the whole line. Three only were shot down, near the rear, where they approached within twenty paces. Fifth day's march, through pretty good land. Sixth, barren. Seventh, broken with knobs and small mountains, until we got within seven or eight miles of the Rapids, when the land became level and of the first quality.

9th. — Mr. Wells set out for Fort Pitt, with two light boats, by whom I sent several letters; one to Esquire Lyon, and inclosed a duplicate of a letter sent from the Post to G. F., and likewise two small letters inclosed to my friends in Carlisle.

21st. — Major Wyllys, with our fleet, consisting of eleven boats, arrived at the foot of the Rapids.

22d. — Baggage brought round the Falls in wagons. The troops marched up to the fort and took quarters with us.

23d and 24th. — The men employed in dragging the boats up through the Falls.

FORT FINNEY, *Rapids of Ohio*, *28th.*—Colonel Harmar received brevet commission, with pay and emoluments of Brigadier-General. He sets out for Fort Harmar. Quarter-master Pratt and myself accompany in a barge, with sergeant and fourteen men. Orders left for Captains Ziegler and Strong with their companies to follow on to-morrow. Major Wyllys, with Finney's and Mercer's companies, to continue at Fort Finney at the head of the Rapids. Got to the eighteen mile Island.

29th, to Kentucky river.

30th, Big Bone creek.

31st, Great Miami.

Nov. 1st, to the Little Miami.

2d, about half way between Little Miami and Limestone.

3*d*, to Limestone.

4*th*, lay still.

5*th*, twenty-two miles up.

6*th*, just below Scioto.

7*th*, thirty miles up.

8*th*, just below Guyandot.

9*th*, within eighteen miles of the Great Kanahwa.

10*th*, six miles above the Great Kanahwa.

11*th*, got five miles above the Little Falls.

12*th*, to the Scioto settlement.

13*th*, arrived at Muskingum, Fort Harmar, after a passage of sixteen days—one other day we spent at Limestone.

20*th*.—Lieutenant Beatty arrived from New York, with some pay for the regiment.

21*st*.—Ziegler's and Strong's companies arrive and take quarters for the winter. Doughty's company we had left here. M'Curdy's, which had been employed through the summer escorting the United States surveyors, was here also.

24*th*.—Alexander Parker and Mr. Dunn arrived on their way to Kentucky, by whom I received several letters from my friends at Carlisle and a box of linen. Parker and Dunn left us the same day, not wishing to lose good weather and high water.

Dec. 6*th*.—Captain Ashton, who had come to this place with Parker and Dunn, set out for the Falls.

10*th*.—Lieutenant Beatty set out again for New York for more cash.

12*th*.—Mr. Jacob Melcher, a candidate for the vacant

ensigncy in the Pennsylvania quota arrived; with whom came John Siddon, a man enlisted for one year to serve as a ranger, and who had been taken prisoner on the Wabash the 26th July last. At the time he was taken, he received a slight wound on the hip. The Indians carried him to their farthermost town on the Wabash and adopted him in a family, where he continued to live peaceably. When an opportunity offered for his escape, he left them and passed through several Delaware towns without any interruption, and arrived safe at Pittsburgh.

25*th.*—The river Ohio bound fast with ice.

Jan. 1*st*, 1788.—The weather continues exceedingly cold.

5*th.*—The thermometer sixteen degrees below zero. Horses, &c., crossed the river on the ice.

20*th.*—The river broke up—much ice floating.

Feb. 4*th.*—The weather intensely cold; the mercury down to fourteen degrees below zero. A messenger arrived from Captain Pipe, with a friendly talk, requesting that the roads might be kept smooth and clear for the Delawares to pass and repass.

24*th.*—The navigation had been shut or interrupted by ice since 20th December last. To-day we had the first arrival. Colonel Blaine, his son James, and Mr. C. Wilkins, all old acquaintances of the officers, came just from Fort Pitt. Very glad to see them. Mr. Wilkins continues here, with a store of goods suitable for the troops.

March 7*th.*—Colonel Blain and his son left us and set out with Mr. Spear, who was ordered to the Rapids to bring up the commissioners' goods, to be in readiness for the intended grand treaty.

8*th.*—Captain Pipe and his tribe came in.

9*th.*—Although the time, for which the men now in service were enlisted, does not expire until midsummer, yet, to provide recruits and to have them out in season, it was thought advisable that a few officers should go to their respective States for that purpose. Accordingly Captains Ziegler and Bradford (the latter in place of Doughty, promoted,) and Lieutenant Pratt, the Quartermaster, all volunteering this service, set out.

17*th.*—Mr. Schuyler pursued the recruiting officer with some dispatches which had been forgotten.

April 6*th.*—Left Fort Harmar, in company with the General and Daniel Britt, the contractor, on board a barge with twelve oars.

7*th.*—Rained all day. Got to the fourth island on the reach.

8*th.*—Fine day, with wind. Lay just below Fish creek.

9*th.*—The river still continues to rise. Had the water remarkably hard. Got to Grave creek.

10*th.*—The water began to lower. Arrived at Wheeling about eleven o'clock, when Mr. Britt took horse to go by land to Pitt.

11*th.*—The river falling fast. Got to Edgington's.

12*th.*—A fine wind. Lay half mile above Beckar's Fort.

13*th.*—Got to M'Intosh early in the evening, where we tarried all night.

14*th.*—With extreme hard work we got to Fort Pitt.

15*th.*—A rainy morning; the water began to rise.

16*th.*—A fine day. 17th, the same. 18th, cold rain.

19th.—Blustering rainy weather.

20th.—A considerable quantity of snow fell. The rivers up to a considerable height; the weather exceedingly cold.

21st.—The weather moderate and the water falls.

22d.—Some rain, and windy. 23d, fine day. Water falls slowly.

24th.—Rained in the morning. Cloudy.

25th.—Wet and disagreeable day. 26th, rain all day.

Sunday, 27th.—It was the General's intention to spend a day or two here, and proceed up the Allegheny river to Fort Franklin (formerly Venango), but a continuation of heavy rains and consequent high water, induced him to delay for a more favorable time; but unwilling to be absent too long, we set out with high water, and rising. This day we passed seven islands, and gained fifteen miles.

28th.—Had severe thunder, with rain. Passed eight islands and several lodges of Indians near Kiskiminitis. Lay five miles above the mouth of that river.

29th.—Clear and cold. River still rising. Passed seven islands, and encamped a mile above Mahoning.

30th.—Last night the contractor's boat, from Venango, passed down on its way back to Pitt; had a passage of fifteen days up. Very hard water to-day. Passed two islands; gained twenty miles.

May 1st.—Current this day very rapid. Passed Stump creek and six islands; made about twenty miles.

2d.—Passed a creek on the east side about nine o'clock. Eleven o'clock passed another, and about half after three another of considerable size, on the west side, supposed to be Sandy. Five islands this day, and rain from morning till night.

3d. — About eight o'clock this morning, after passing one island, we entered the mouth of French creek. The fort stands half a mile up. Several miles below we were discovered by some Indians, who cut across and gave notice to Captain Heart of our approach. The arrival of General Harmar was announced with seven rounds of a six-pounder from the fort. Very kindly received by the Captain and Lieutenant Frothingham, at the head of their command. The company reviewed and dismissed. Spent the day in examining Captain Heart's work, viewing the adjacent country and the old fortifications of the French and British. There is a fine flat of good land here, altogether on the lower side of French creek, sufficient for several farms. The only flat land from Mahoning or Mohelboteetam, up. The hills come in close on the opposite sides, both of French creek and the Allegheny river, and I am informed that the country for at least five miles in all directions, is very much broken with hills and rocks. Captain Heart's Fort, or Fort Franklin, as it is called, is built precisely after the one which had been erected by the British, called Venango. It is a square redoubt, with a block-house three stories high, in the centre; stands better than half a mile up French creek, upon very good ground; but the situation, in my opinion, by no means so eligible as that of old Venango built by the English. This last work stood upon commanding ground pretty close to the bank of the Allegheny, half a mile below French creek, and a mile from Fort Franklin. The cellar wall and huge stack of chimneys of the block-house, are of stone, and yet quite entire. The parapet and some other parts remain perfect, and the whole work might have been rebuilt with half the labor and expense of that built by Heart. The only reason the captain could offer for taking new ground, was the convenience of timber. The French, who made the first establishment here, chose the ground several hundred yards below where the British built. They had a small stockade fort; some remains of it are yet to be seen. But around the British work there is everything to be seen which was not consumed by the fire — ditches and parapets, stone walls, &c. Several handsomely disposed gardens, walks, &c., very visible, and a few fruit trees remaining still; some garden roots, &c., particularly the parsnip, in considerable abundance.

We see a number of the Senecas here. The Senecas, who inhabit the banks of the Allegheny, some three or four day's journey above this, are frequently here. They bring their peltry and exchange it with the traders for such articles as suit them. We saw several families of them; all appeared indolent, dirty, inanimate creatures; most so of any Indians I had seen.

4th. — Left Fort Franklin at five o'clock. Allegheny river flowing brim full; current not less perhaps than six miles an hour. We worked twelve oars steadily. Had two extra hands that afforded some relief; and except about an hour, which was taken up in whole in eating, and a little time spent on an island, we lost no time. Arrived and landed at the fort on the Monongahela side precisely at eight o'clock—fifteen hours passage. After leaving the mouth of French creek, there appeared little else than hills and rocks and rugged looking ridges until as low as Mahoning, or what was originally called Mohelboteetam; from thence the bottoms increased on one side or the other until we reached Pitt. Some very beautiful situations and tracts of land, indeed; old Kittanning a delightful one.

7th.—Accompanied General Harmar on horseback on a visit to his lands in Westmoreland county. Made nearly the same tour I had done last winter was a year. Returned to Pitt on Sunday, the 11th.

13th.—Visited my uncle John M'Clure's family, nine miles above Pitt, on the Monongahela; spent a very pleasant day. Two or three gentle acquaintances were along; they were formerly from Carlisle. A very respectable portion of the society of Pittsburgh are from that place, and this circumstance, no doubt, tends to attract and to create the social intercourse and very great harmony which prevails among them.

15th.—A Mr. White, member of Congress, and some gentlemen of Pittsburgh, accompanied the General in the barge, on a visit up the Monongahela to Braddock's Field. We viewed the battle ground. Saw several small heaps of bones which had been collected, with a little brushwood thrown over them. The bones of the poor soldiers are still lying scattered through the woods, but the ground where the heaviest of the action was is now under cultivation.

17*th.* — Lieutenant Beatty, our pay-master, arrived from New York with cash for the troops.

20*th.* — He set out for Venango by land, escorted by five soldiers. After paying that post, he will return to Pitt to proceed with us in the barge to Fort Harmar.

23*d.*—General Arthur St. Clair, lately appointed Governor of the Western Territory, arrived at Pitt. He has been expected for some time. Had dispatched messengers to the Indian towns to invite them to another treaty. Accompanied by the Governor we took another road to Braddock's Field, and visited the remains of poor Braddock's soldiers. On our return I saw my uncle's family.

27*th.* — The messengers returned from the Indian towns, inform us that no assemblage of them can be had for two or three months. The Governor returns to Ligonier, where his family reside.

28*th.* — General Harmar, Mr. White and myself embarked for Fort Harmar, at which place we arrived about twelve o'clock on the night of the 29th. Here we found Spear and Melcher, two subalterns of the regiment, and Mr. Ephraim Blaine. They had landed a few hours before us. Spear and Melcher, on their way from Vincennes, below the Falls, were fired upon by a party of savages in ambush on the bank, close up which the others were rowing. Two men only were killed. It is a matter of astonishment, that when the Indians do attack our boats in this dastardly way, from the very great advantage they have, that the men in the boats are not all destroyed. There have been too many instances this spring of our people being fired on, but the loss inconsiderable to what it might have been. Preparations are making for another grand treaty. Government have directed it. Our commandant thinks it all idle business. One-half will come in, sign articles and receive presents, while the others are killing, scalping and doing us every possible damage they can.

An association of persons in the New England States, having made a purchase from the United States of a tract of country extending along the Ohio about one hundred and fifty miles, and back perhaps thirty, had formed themselves into a company known by the name of the Ohio Company. A number of the proprietors and directors elected had come on and fixed upon the ground at the confluence of the Muskingum and Ohio rivers, as a central situation from which they could extend their operations, and at the same time be protected by the garrison of Fort Harmar, which was situate on the other side of the Muskingum. These men from New England, many of whom were of the first respectability, old Revolutionary officers, had erected and were now living in huts immediately opposite us. A considerable number of industrious farmers had purchased shares in the company, and more or less arrive every week. A spacious city is laid out here, called Marietta, in honor of the Queen of France. About half a mile up the Muskingum, upon very commanding ground, the site of a very ancient and very extraordinary fortification, was erected a place of arms and security,. called Campus Martius. Building put up of hewn timber, two stories high, forming an oblong square, with strong block-houses in each angle, leaving a considerable area; here their stores, &c., were lodged, and some families perhaps more timid than others, reside, but generally both men and women appear enterprising. Generals Parsons and Varum, two of the company's directors, were also territorial judges. Mr. Symmes, the other judge, was the principal agent in the purchase of another tract of country, including the Miamis.

8*th.*—Jane Beatty arrived from Fort Pitt.

9*th.*—Armstrong embarked for Fort Pitt.

13*th.*—Ensign M'Dowell, with a party of soldiers, set out to escort Mr. Duncan, the provisions and stores intended for a treaty, to the Falls of Muskingum.

June 15*th.*—Major Doughty embarked in the barge for Fort Pitt. His design is to accompany Governor St. Clair to this post.

July 4*th.*—The officers of Fort Harmar were entertained on the point (Marietta side) by the Ohio Company. Heard a very suitable oration delivered by Judge Varum.

8*th.*—Captain Bradford and Lieutenant Ernest arrived from New York, where they had been sent to recruit. Their Legislature not having taken up the requisition of Congress for raising the regiment, these gentlemen were obliged to return without effecting their object.

9*th.*—The arrival of the Governor of the Western Territory (General St. Clair) was announced by the discharge of thirteen rounds from a six-pounder. The garrison turned out, and troops received him with presented arms.

13*th.* — About a month since, Ensign M'Dowell, with a command of thirty men, escorted boats with provisions, &c., to the Falls of Muskingum, about seventy-five miles up, where the intended treaty was to be held. We are informed by express that his party were attacked in their camp yesterday by a party of Tawas; that his picket guard was routed; two soldiers only were killed and one missing. A black servant of Mr. Duncan was killed. The Indians were repulsed with the loss of one killed and left behind.

14*th.* — This evening a party with a craft was sent up the Muskingum to bring off Ensign M'Dowell, command, &c. The treaty, if any, determined to be held at Fort Harmar.

15*th.* — Winthrop Sargent, Secretary of the Territory, and one of the directors of the Ohio Company, had reached this with the ordinance of Congress respecting the government, and with the commissions for the several officers. The people convened on the point; military officers invited over. When assembled, the Secretary read the law and the appointments. Those people appear the most happy folks in the world; greatly satisfied with their new purchase. But they certainly are the best informed, most courteous and civil to strangers of any people I have yet met with. The order and regularity observed by all, their sober deportment and perfect submission to the constituted authorities, &c., must tend much to promote their settlements.

16*th.*—Lieutenant Ford, who had been stationed at Fort M'Intosh, arrived with his party. He is to proceed to Post Vincennes to join his company.

17*th.*—Lieutenant Beatty embarked with part of Ford's command for the Rapids.

20*th.*—Ensign M'Dowell returned. By his address before he left his camp, had managed to get hold of six of the fellows who had made the attack upon him. They were brought down bound, and confined under the garrison guard. They called themselves Tawas and Chippewas.

28*th.*—Two of our Indian prisoners made their escape from the guard. Four of the soldiers had been conducting them, as was usual, to the necessary which stands outside the fort. Those within are used only after night. A corn patch adjoining the necessary. The Indians had previously found that the irons on their hands and fect could be slipped off; when close to the corn, and at a moment when the attention of the guard was taken off, they slipped their shackles, leaped into the corn field, which sheltered them from the view of the sentries, and were soon out of reach.

Aug. 7*th.*—Ensign Thompson sent express to Fort Pitt with orders for Captain Ziegler, who we hear has arrived there with his company.

8*th.*—Lieutenant Ford set out for the Rapids of the Ohio; from thence he is to proceed with the pay-master to Post Vincennes.

17*th.*—Captain Heart arrived from Venango, and Captain Strong set off for Connecticut, by whom I wrote to my friend J. C.

27th. — Judge Symmes, with several boats and families, arrived on their way to his new purchase at the Miami. Has a daughter (Polly) along. They lodge with the General and Mrs. Harmar. Stay three days and depart. If not greatly mistaken, Miss Symmes will make a fine woman. An amiable disposition and highly cultivated mind, about to be buried in the wilderness.

31st. — Captain Smith arrived from New York on his way to the Post to join his company. With him came Ensign Thompson, Mr. Melcher and Mr. Brown, a member of Congress from Kentucky.

Sept. 1st.—Mr. Brown proceeded down the river.

2d. — Captain Heart and Major Doughty set out for Venango. The latter to muster the troops at that post.

9th. — General Richard Butler, commissioner on the part of Pennsylvania, and Captain James O'Hara, the contractor, with Cornplanter and about fifty Senecas, arrive. They were escorted from Pitt by Captain Ziegler's company of recruits. They were received with a salute of three rounds of cannon and the music. Ziegler is a German, had been in Saxon service previous to our late war with England. Takes pride in having the handsomest company in the regiment; and to do him justice, his company has been always considered the first in point of discipline and appearance. Four-fifths of his company have been Germans. Majority of the present are men who served in Germany.

FORT HARMAR, *11th.*—Mitchell arrived express from

the Falls, by whom we learn that Lieutenant Peters with a command of thirty men, had been defeated near the mouth of the Wabash. Eight of his men were killed and ten wounded. That one boat loaded with provisions fell into the hands of the enemy. That Mr. Peters retreated down the Ohio, and was making for Kaskaskia. By the same express are told that Captain Hardin, from Kentucky, had conducted thirty active woodsmen (militia) into the Indian country about the mouth of the Wabash, and it was supposed had fallen in with the Indians who defeated Peters; that he had returned to the Falls with thirty horses taken and ten scalps. Messengers arrive from the Indian towns. Say the nations in grand council had agreed to attend the treaty. Saw the young men return daily with scalps.

12*th.*—A singular occurrence took place to-day in sight of the fort, between two of the Seneca Indians. Both among the best looking men, and duly sober, met, drew their knives and fought until both sank under their wounds. It seems that they had formerly lived together as brothers. One of them, a married man, was obliged to go on a mission to some distant nations, and unable to take along his wife, left her in charge of his friend, who was to provide for and protect her. When the husband returned he found that his poor frail wife had been left in care of a savage. She was seduced and carried out of the nation. He bore this with manly fortitude, but resolved if they ever met, one of them must die. It seems that they had a knowledge of each other coming here, and were prepared for the meeting and for what took place. The fellow who had eloped with the woman came last from the Shawanee towns, where it is said he lately killed a girl for refusing to comply with his wishes.

14*th.*—A messenger arrived from the Indian towns with speeches, &c. They report that all the nations will attend the grand treaty as soon as possible for them to arrive. That they had been counciling at the Miami town, where they had agreed on the above; at the same time scalps were daily brought in by the young men.

15*th.*—Mr. Ernest and Mr. Wilkins set out for Fort Pitt, the former with orders to relieve Lieutenant Schuyler, who is stationed there. By the latter I sent a letter to my sister Nancy, and inclosed a bank note of twenty dollars.

21*st.*—Lieutenant Armstrong arrived on his way to the Falls.

22*d.*—Lieutenant Kersey, with forty-eight Jersey recruits, and Ensign Hartshorn, with twenty-nine from Connecticut, arrived.

29*th.*—Major Doughty arrived from Venango, where he had been sent to muster Captain Heart's command. With him came Major Alexander and several other gentlemen.

Oct. 4*th.*—Captain M'Curdy, with Ensign Hartshorn and cadet Morgan, and about forty men, were detached to escort the geographer to the Scioto river.

13*th.*—Doctor Knight joined the regiment in character of a substitute for Doctor Sumner, who had occasion to remain at home longer than his furlough specified.

One of the two savages mentioned on the 12th September as having fought respecting a woman, is found drowned in the Muskingum. It is said the tribe generally wished for his exit, and that some of them must have been the instruments of his death. Every possible attention was paid by the Senecas, as well as by the surgeon of the garrison, to the husband. His life was despaired of. The other totally neglected, an outcast, left to shift for himself, to dress himself; a small portion of victuals sent daily from the fort, and left in his reach where he lay near the bank. Notwithstanding, and contrary to the expectation and wishes, was recovering and able to crawl about, when now, a month after the fight, and all hopes of his death having ceased, he is found drowned in the Muskingum. Some one or two of his nation had in the night dragged him down the bank and put him in the river. From the appearance of the ground being torn up where he lay and along to the water's edge, he must have made considerable resistance.

19*th.*—General Gibson, a commissioner on the part of the State of Pennsylvania, arrived from Fort Pitt. He and General Butler are appointed by the State to treat with the Indians, particularly the Senecas, and to make them compensation for a tract of country lying on Lake Erie, and including Presqu' Isle, which the State has purchased of Congress.

20*th.*—Notwithstanding the treaty was solicited by the savages, it is doubtful whether the chiefs will come in or not. A late message from them says, that they have been informed by good authority, that we have poisoned the whiskey which we intend for them; and infection for the small pox has been put in the blankets to be presented them. This message, with the daily accounts of mischief doing in some quarter or other, seem to indicate as if they had no mind to treat. Three canoes arrived last night from Limestone, brought accounts that Lieutenant Armstrong's boat was fired on near the Scioto; that one of his men was shot through the cheek. The Indians have lately killed a soldier in the vicinity of the fort at the Rapids, and not content with scalping him, cut him in four quarters and hung them up on the bushes.

28*th.* — G. W., a trusty Indian messenger who had been sent to the towns, arrived with an account that the chiefs were preparing to attend the treaty, and might be expected in twelve or fifteen days.

Nov. 1*st.* — Captain M'Curdy, with his command, and the geographer, arrived.

7*th.*—Messengers Wilson and Rankin return from the Indian towns. With them came Captain Davie, of the Six Nations, and several others. These last are from Grand river, on the British side of Lake Erie. Brant is expected in a few days.

Dec. 13*th.* — About two hundred Indians arrive—consist of Delawares, Wyandots, Senecas, Tawas, Pottowattamies, Chippewas and Socks. No Shawanees.

14*th.*—Meeting in council house to welcome each other, &c.

15*th.*—Met in council. Treaty opened. This evening Captains Ferguson and Beatty set out, and Ensign M'-Dowell arrived, who had been escorting Mr. Marten surveying up the Scioto.

20th.—The weather extremely cold. The river driving with ice. The Governor and Indians have had frequent meetings in the council house, but nothing conclusive yet.

29th.—A grand council was held. The old Wyandot chief, Shandotto, addressed the Governor in behalf of all the nations present. He began by telling their origin and how the thirteen fires had gotten possession of their country; how we nad in two instances cheated them. The first, he said, was in a bargain made with them for just as much ground as an ox's hide would cover, merely to build one fire upon. The Americans cut the hide into strings and claimed all the ground they could encompass therewith. The second case was a bargain for such an extent of country, in a certain direction, as a white man would travel to and back in one day. A surprising walker was found, who went as far and back again the same day as any of their swiftest men could do in two. These, said he, were submitted to, as you were strangers in our country, and professed to be our friends, but you have gone on from one step to another, so that we don't know when you will stop. At a treaty concluded to the northward, before the late war, he said, they had given up all the country south of the Ohio river. That boundary was a very plain one. It was such as could not be altered or mistaken; there could be no dispute about it. Concluded by saying that all the nations present had determined to grant no more of the country, but were willing to abide by the treaty which established the river Ohio as the boundary line. He presented a large belt of wampum with a black stripe running through the middle of it, representing the Ohio river dividing, &c. The Governor replied, and told them that he could not possibly make the least deviation from the treaties which had been concluded at Fort Stanwix, at Fort M'Intosh and at the Miami river. That at these treaties the several boundaries had been fixed, and were unalterable. Council adjourned. Several days pass over. Indians pow-wowing. The Ohio rising and driving with ice.

Jan. 6th, 1789.—All hands assemble again. The Governor made a speech to the Indians. Explained to them by a simile how they had forfeited their country. He supposed the Wyandots and some distant nation at war with each other. The Shawanees living between, were desired by the Wyandots to lie still, which was agreed to, but the Shawanees being of a restless disposition, and easy persuaded, took up the hatchet against their neighbors the Wyandots; notwithstanding, the Wyandots conquered their enemies, and obliged them to sue for peace, and the Shawanees' lands were given as a price for the same. Now, whether had not the Wyandots a good claim to the lands? They all agreed it was but just; then, said he, this is exactly your case, you took up the hatchet against the United States, and joined the English in the late war. The English, to obtain peace, ceded to the United States all the country south of the great lakes. He told them that they had been all summer endeavoring to meet, but it seemed to be to no purpose. The United States, he said, were much inclined to be at peace with all the Indians, but if the Indians wanted war they should have war. He told them that if they would renew the articles which had been agreed to and signed at M'Intosh and at the other treaties, he would add another article, and allow them the privilege of hunting any where in the United States' territory, and would deliver over to them a certain quantity of goods, such as might be agreed on. Adjourned.

8*th.* — Lieutenant Pratt joined us, from Connecticut, with about seventy recruits.

9*th.* —In council once more. The old Wyandot chief, Shandotto, who spoke for all the nations present, said he was sorry the Governor talked of war. It was not long since both had felt the effects of it. For their part, they wished for no more. He said they all had a great regard for the thirteen fires, and would do everything in their power to accommodate them for the sake of peace, only hoped the line would be removed a little way.

11*th.*—This was the last act of the farce. The articles were signed.

13*th.* — The goods were given out to the different nations of Indians. The death of General Vernum, one of the judges of the territory, who was buried this afternoon, is generally lamented. The officers of the fort attended his funeral.

22*d.*—The Indians mostly dispersed. Mr. Thompson, Luce and Schuyler, embarked for the Rapids.

28*th.* — The Governor, Pennsylvania commissioners, and sundry other gentlemen attending the grand treaty, left us for Fort Pitt.

Feb. 15*th.* — Captain Bradford, with his company, embarked for the Rapids. Dr. Carmichael proceeded with him as far as the Great Miami, there to join Lieutenant Kersey.

22*d.*—Married this evening, Captain David Ziegler, of the first regiment, to Miss Sheffield, only single daughter of Mrs. Sheffield, of Campus Martius, city of Marietta. On this occasion I played the captain's aid, and at his request, the memorandums made. I exhibited a character not more awkward than strange, at the celebration of Captain Ziegler's nuptials, the first of the kind I had been a witness to.

March 18*th.*—Lieutenant Kingsbury was sent to conduct a number of M'Curdy's discharged men to Fort Pitt.

April 19*th.*—Ensign Hartshorn detached with a party for Wheeling, where he expected to meet Mr. Ludlow, with whom he was to proceed to run the northern boundary of the Ohio Company purchase.

May 1*st.*—The Indians attack and kill a Mr. King, a proprietor in the Ohio Company, just below the Little Kanahwa, where a settlement is forming. The directors apply to General Harmar for a few soldiers for the protection of the place. A sergeant, corporal and fifteen men, detached to protect the settlement below, called Belpre, and a corporal and eight sent up the Muskingum to Wolf creek, where the people are making another settlement.

5*th.*—The commission of first Lieutenant, which ought to have been sent me last year, was received but to-day. It is dated 28th of March last; the detention occasioned by a claim of Mr. Spear for the same appointment.

Spear had filled a vacant ensigncy twelve months after our appointments, but having been an older subaltern in the Revolutionary war, thought he was still entitled to the right. Our State, where the appointments originate, decided against him. This evening Lieutenant Ford, with Captain Mercer's company, arrived from Vincennes. Captain Mercer and Lieutenant Peters came also, on their way home

28th. — Two parties of a corporal and nine men each were detached to escort the surveyors of the Ohio Company in running out certain ranges upon the river, and to the extension of the purchase westward. They took two men and provisions.

June 4th. — Lieutenant Kingsbury, Mr. Tupper and myself set out in a small boat with four men, to visit the settlements made by the New England people on donation lands, called Belpre settlement. We got down about one o'clock — found everything appeared as well as industry could make.

5th. — We embarked and returned up within seven miles of the garrison. Landed and struck off on a west line, and at the distance of one mile, got upon Mr. Kingsbury's one hundred and sixty acre lot, and mine, which adjoins his. We found mine to be tolerably good land, having a branch of the Little Hockhocking running directly through it. A great deal of poplar, walnut, locust, cherry, shellbark hickory and black oak. Returned to the boat and got home about dark.

9th. — Ensign Hartshorn and his party returned from escorting Mr. Ludlow, the surveyor, who was running the northern boundary of the Ohio Company purchase. They completed the business without the least molestation.

9*th.*—Major Wyllys, Ensign Sedam and Dr. Allison, arrived from the Rapids on their way to New York.

28*th.*—A young Delaware came in with information that George Washington was wounded by some person in ambush, on the Tuscarawas branch of the Muskingum. They are willing to lay it to Brant's people, but at the same time think the mischief done by militia from Wheeling.

July 7*th.*—Major Doughty joined us from New York.

14*th.*—Captain M'Curdy and Ensign M'Dowell came with forty-four recruits—good looking fellows.

Aug. 9*th.*—Captain Strong, with his two subalterns, Lieutenant Kingsbury and Ensign Hartshorn, and a complete company of seventy men, embark for the Miami.

11*th.*—Captain Ferguson joined us with his recruits. Major Doughty follows Captain Strong for the purpose of choosing ground and laying out a new work intended for the protection of persons who have settled within the limits of Judge Symme's purchase.

21*st.*—A corporal and six men escorting surveyors of the Ohio Company, attacked by the Indians. The corporal only escaped.

Sept. 4*th.*—Ferguson with his company ordered to join Strong in erecting a fort near the Miami. Lieutenant Pratt, the quarter-master, ordered to the same place.

14*th.*—At a meeting of the agents of the Ohio Land Company, a tract of land lying at or near the mouth of

Tyger's or Kyger's creek, on the Ohio, about four or five miles above the Great Kanahwa, was granted to an association of thirty-five proprietors, formed for settling the same; each to have one hundred acres at least. The 1st September, 1790, is the time allowed for commencing the settlement. Captain Beatty and myself are of the association.

22*d.*—Captain Heart, with his company from Fort Franklin, arrive here.

Nov. 10*th.*—The General intends removing to headquarters very shortly, to the new fort building by Major Doughty, opposite the mouth of Licking creek. Had hinted that a short furlough would be very desirable before I went lower down, and if I could be excused from the regiment, would proceed to Philadelphia, and complete some business of his and of the officers of the Pennsylvania quota. I had, in the absence of quartermaster, performed both duties of adjutant and quartermaster. Mr. Pratt I always found ready and willing. On this occasion he volunteered, and I obtained a furlough until 1st May. Embarked in a twelve oar boat with Doctor Scott.

11*th.*—Lay near the upper end of the Long Reach.

12*th.*—Met a rise of water, and got one mile above Sunfish.

13*th.*—Rainy weather. Lay all night at Mr. Mahan's, seven miles below Wheeling.

14*th.*—Deposited with Esquire Zeens sundry articles found with Rogers (drowned), to be sent to his wife at Marietta. Got to Carpenter's at Short creek.

15*th.*—High water. Lay one mile above Holliday's Cove.

16*th.*—The river continued to rise. With hard work we made Dawson's, opposite the mouth of Little Beaver, about eight o'clock at night.

17*th.*—As we turned up Beaver creek, to go to the block-house two miles up, where an officer and party is stationed, we met General Parson's canoe, with some property, floating down. Found the old gentleman, in attempting to pass the Falls, about five miles up, was cast out and drowned, with one man who accompanied him. Judge Parsons was esteemed a useful, enterprising citizen. He had an interest in Salt Spring tract, on the Mahoning, and anxious to prove the navigation of the Falls practicable, the experiment cost him his life. It is said that his life was insured in New York.

18*th.*—Set out after breakfast and got as high as the lower end of Montour's Island.

19*th.*—Arrived at Pittsburgh about two o'clock, P. M., when to our great satisfaction we found Major Wyllys, Captain Mercer, Captain Beatty, Lieutenant Peters, Ensign Sedam and Doctor Allison, all on their way to join the regiment.

PITTSBURGH, *Dec.* 4*th.*—With Beatty, the pay-master, I had business which detained me here longer than was intended. My boat and crew were taken back by these officers. Got upon the road this afternoon.

12*th.*—Reached Carlisle.

Jan. 9*th*, 1790.—Left Carlisle in company with Mr.

Nesbit. That evening reached the Susquehanna on my way to Philadelphia.

13*th.*—Arrived in the city after a cold and tedious ride.

26*th.*—Having settled all my business fully, took leave of the pleasing amusements of the city and got back to my friends at Carlisle on the 29th. Had been here but a few days, when a strange indisposition came on me, altogether unaccountable. Few persons have been favored with better health than I have enjoyed all my life; once only, in South Carolina was I laid up for a while. Temperance and an active life may have contributed to exempt when few escaped, but never was without a grateful sense of the favor of Divine Providence. In the present case endeavored for several days to keep up, when it was discovered that I had taken the measles, a disease very prevalent here at this time, and which it was supposed I had had. This sickness could not have taken me at a more convenient or happy time — was in the house with my mother and sisters. In the space of a couple of weeks was again about, and as soon as it was prudent to be exposed to the roads and weather, left my kind and affectionate relations, and arrived at Pittsburgh on the 22d. March.

April 11*th.* — No place appears to me more inviting than this; could willingly remain here awhile, but my furlough draws to a close, nor would I go over it one day, for a week of pleasure anywhere. Besides, I know that nothing short of unavoidable delay would do in my case. The only conveyance for one down the river is a Kentucky boat loaded with flour for head-quarters. The boat and hands are put under my charge, and with three soldiers, making seven of us, we set sail.

12*th.*—Buffalo creek.

14*th.*—Land at Fort Harmar, mouth of Muskingum, a place where I had spent most part of the last two years with much satisfaction. It was now in a manner deserted. Head-quarters had been removed to Fort Washington, opposite the mouth of Licking. Spent one day with some old friends of the Ohio Company. Accounts from below that Indians are in force on the river near Scioto.

17*th.*—Reached the Great Kanahwa, where were several boats waiting to increase their force. An express had arrived from Limestone to Colonel Lewis, with accounts that the savages had attacked and taken several boats at the mouth of Scioto.

18*th.*—While waiting to enlarge our fleet, Mr. Kingsbury arrived from the Miami, by whom I received a letter from the General, but too late for me to execute his business.

19*th.*—Having examined the several boats and the people on board, the arms, &c., and made such disposition of the whole as was thought most judicious, sailed at the head of sixteen Kentuck boats and two keels. The Kentucky boats were lashed three together and kept in one line. Women, children and stock all put into the middle boats. Outside boats only manned and worked. The men belonging to each block of boats had their own commanding officer, and the whole could repair to either side as necessity might require. The keels kept on each flank. The river is in good navigable order, and weather pleasant. The boats were enabled to keep their stations. Passed the Scioto about daylight.

20th.—About eight o'clock in the morning a storm of wind and rain met us. Such a one I had never before seen on the river. The boats had to be cut loose, and even when single were in danger of filling every instant. At this time were supposed to be about five miles below Scioto and close upon the Indian shore. Any apprehension from the Indians by me was forgotten; I was clear for making the nearest land, headed my boat for shore, and made the signal for the others to follow. One only obeyed the signal and landed along side of me. The rest passed and made for the Kentucky side, at the hazard of their lives. They, however, got safe, with no other damage than shipping large quantities of water. In this situation we were obliged to remain the whole day. As the sun went down the storm ceased. I fired a gun and put off—the boats all followed, and next morning reached Limestone.

LIMESTONE, *21st.*—Upon landing here was informed that an officer of the regiment, with soldiers, was on the opposite shore. Procured a light boat and crossed the river, where I found Lieutenant Pratt with a small party of men. He informed me that General Harmar, with about three hundred regulars and volunteers, had marched the morning before for Paint creek, which empties into the Scioto about sixty miles up, at which place it was expected the Indians who had been on the Ohio, would be found with their plunder. Here I found that the General had calculated my time, for expecting that Mr. Pratt would see me, he had left instructions for me to proceed to Fort Washington. Parted with Pratt in the evening.

22d.—Arrived at Fort Washington about twelve o'clock.

FORT WASHINGTON, *May 2d.*—The troops returned from Paint creek, under command of Captain Ferguson. General Harmar parted with them at mouth of Scioto, and proceeded in his barge for Muskingum.

July 11th.—Governor St. Clair arrived at Fort Washington from the Illinois, where he had spent part of the winter and spring in organizing the several counties in that quarter of the territory, and establishing a system of government. General Harmar had returned to headquarters some weeks since. The Governor remained with us but three days. In the mean time it was agreed and determined that General Harmar should conduct an expedition against the Maumee towns, the residence of all the renegade Indians, from whence issued all the parties who infest our frontiers. One thousand militia were ordered from Kentucky, and the Governor on his way to New York, the seat of the general government, was to order five hundred from the back counties of Pennsylvania. 15th September was the time appointed for the militia to assemble at Fort Washington.

15th.—The General commenced his preparations; calculations of provisions, horses, stores, &c., were immediately made out and ordered accordingly. Every day employed in the most industrious manner. Captain Ferguson, with his company, engaged in getting in complete order the artillery and military stores. Indeed every officer was busily employed in something or other necessary for the expedition, but particularly the quartermaster, Pratt. No time was lost.

Sept. 18*th.*—The Kentucky militia began to come in, but not such as we had been accustomed to see on the frontiers. They appear to be raw and unused to the gun or the woods; indeed many are without guns, and many of those they have want repairing. Our artificers employed in putting to right the militia arms. General much disheartened at the kind of people from Kentucky. One-half certainly serve no other purpose than to swell their number. If the leading *patriots* of Kentucky don't turn out rascals, then some men that I know are greatly mistaken.

19*th.*—A battalion of Pennsylvania militia arrived.

22*d.*—Governor St. Clair returned from New York.

25*th.*—Major Doughty, with two companies of the first regiment, brought from Fort Harmar, joined, and also the residue of the Pennsylvania militia. These last are similar to the Kentuckians; too many substitutes. Much difficulty in regulating and organizing the militia. Colonels dispute about the command. The General, after much trouble, effects a compromise and reconciliation. Kentuckians compose three battalions under Majors Hall, M'Millen and Ray, and Lieutenant-Colonel commandant Trotter. Pennsylvania militia into one battalion, under Lieutenant-Colonel Truby and Major Paul. The whole to be commanded by Colonel John Hardin from Kentucky, subject to the orders of General Harmar

26th. — The whole of the militia took the field under the direction of Colonel Hardin, an old continental officer, amounting to one thousand one hundred and thirty-three. They marched on the direct route to the Indian towns.

29th. — General Harmar moved out with the federal troops and joined the militia.

30th. — The General having got forward the supplies, moved on with the federal troops, formed into two small battalions under the immediate command of Majors Wyllys and Doughty, together with Captain Ferguson's company of artillery, who took along three light brass pieces.

Oct. 2d. — Their number three hundred and twenty. Total, one thousand four hundred and fifty-three.

3d. — Joined the advance troops early in the morning. Spent this day in forming the line of march, encampment and battle, and explaining the same to the militia officers. Major James Fontaine appointed volunteer aid-de-camp to the General. Mr. Stephen Ormsby brigade-major to the militia, and Mr. John Bellie quarrer-master. Doctor Slater surgeon to Colonel Trotter's tegiment. Encamped on waters of Little Miami, thirty-one miles from Fort Washington.

4th.—The army took up the line of march and gained eleven miles. Encamped on branch of the Little Miami, forty-two miles from Fort Washington.

5th. — Joined by a small reinforcement of horsemen and mounted infantry. The horse formed into two troops, and with the company of mounted infantry, put under

the command of Major Fontaine. The army now consists of

3	battalions	Kentucky militia,	1,133
1	do.	Pennsylvania militia,	
1	do.	light troops mounted,	
2	do.	of regular troops, -	320
		Total, - -	1,453

Much trouble in keeping the officers, with their commands, in their proper order, and the pack horses, &c., compact. Encamped this evening on Glade creek, a branch of Little Miami, about fifty-two miles from Fort Washington.

6th.—Passed through a beautiful open country. Encamped three miles north of old Chillicothe, sixty-two from Fort Washington.

7th.—Open country. Encamped on Mad river on Pickaway fork of Great Miami, seventy-one miles from Fort Washington.

8th.—Gained about nine miles. Encamped on waters of Great Miami, about eighty miles advance.

9th.—Marched at usual hour and gained ten miles. Encamped on waters of Great Miami, about ninety miles from Fort Washington.

10th.—Same waters. Encamp about one hundred miles from Fort Washington.

11th.—Encamp five miles north-west of a place called the French Store, about one hundred and twelve miles from Fort Washington.

12th.—Encamp about seven miles north-west of new

Chillicothe, on Grave creek, a branch of the Miami or Omee, which empties into Lake Erie, and about one hundred and twenty-five miles from Fort Washington. Half pound powder and one pound lead served out to each rifleman, and twenty-four rounds cartridges to the musquetry. Commanding officers of battalions to see that their men's arms are in good order and loaded.

13*th.* — Early this morning a patrol of horsemen captured a Shawanee Indian. Marched through a thick brushy country. Encamped on great branch of the Miami or Omee river, near the ruins of La Source's old house, about one hundred and thirty-five miles from Fort Washington.

14*th.* — Colonel Hardin detached early this morning with six hundred light troops, to push for the Miami village. This detachment sent forward in consequence of intelligence gained of the prisoner, which was that the Indians were clearing out as fast as possible, and that the towns would be evacuated before our arrival. As it was impossible for the army to hasten their march much, the General thought proper to send on Colonel Hardin in hope of doing something before they would all be able to clear out. Marched this day about ten miles. Beech and white oak land generally, and no running water. Country very flat, and appears as if at particular seasons it was altogether under water. Encamped about one hundred and forty-five miles from Fort Washington. This night the horses were ordered to be tied up, that the army might start by daylight, with a view of keeping as near to Colonel Hardin as possible. The distance to the Indian towns this morning, when the detachment went ahead, supposed to be about thirty-five miles.

15*th*.—Every exertion made to get forward the main body. Difficult march this day over beech roots and brush. Encamped on the waters of the Omee about one hundred and fifty-three miles from Fort Washington. Horses were again tied, grass cut and brought to them that the army might not be detained next morning, as had frequently been the case; for although repeated orders were given to the horse-masters to hopple well their horses, and directions to the officers and men not to suffer them to pass through the lines, many of them, owing to the scarcity of food, broke loose and passed the chain of sentries and were lost. Patrols of horsemen are ordered out every morning at daylight to scour the neighboring woods and bring in any horses that might have passed the lines; and the pickets turned out small parties for the same purpose. The cattle, also, every pains taken to secure them. At evening, when the army halts, the cattle guard, which is composed of an officer and thirty men, build a yard always within the chain of sentries, sometimes in the square of the encampment, and place themselves round the inclosure, which secures them.

16*th*.—March through beech and swamp oak land. Met an express from Colonel Hardin, who informed us that the enemy had abandoned every place. Encamped within seven miles of the Miami village, and about one hundred and sixty-three from Fort Washington. Horses tied up again and grass brought them.

17*th.* — About noon the army arrived at the Miami village, or Maumee towns, on the Omee river, distant from Fort Washington about one hundred and seventy miles. Two very considerable branches meet here, the St. Joseph from the north-west, and the St. Mary from the south-west, which form the Miami or Omee, emptying into Lake Erie. Several little towns on both branches, but the principal one is below the confluence on the north side. Several tolerable good log houses, said to have been occupied by British traders; a few pretty good gardens with some fruit trees, and vast fields of corn in almost every direction. The militia picked up as much plunder as loaded some of them home. A great deal is found hidden and buried about, and many things left as if the enemy went off in a hurry.

18*th.* — Colonel Trotter was ordered out with three hundred men, militia and regulars, to reconnoitre the country and to make some discovery of the enemy. He marched a few miles, when his advance horsemen overtook and killed two of the savages — one of the militia slightly wounded. The Colonel proceeded no farther, marched back to camp the same evening. Colonel Hardin, commanding officer of the militia, showed displeasure at Trotter's return without executing the orders he had received, and desired the General to give him the command of the detachment. The men were furnished with two days provisions, and Hardin marched on the morning of the 19th. I saw that the men moved off with great reluctance, and am satisfied that when three miles from camp he had not more than two-thirds of his command; they dropped out of the ranks and returned to camp. Hardin proceeded, and about ten miles from camp, not expecting to be near the enemy, he suddenly came upon a party supposed to be about one hundred only, and owing to the bad order of his men, and their dastardly conduct, was entirely defeated. The Indians made the first discovery, and commenced a fire at the distance of one hundred and fifty yards, and advanced. The greatest number of the militia fled without firing a shot; some few, with thirty regulars that were of the detachment, stood and were cut to pieces. Of the militia forty are missing, but it is well known that very few of these were forward in the fight. The conjecture is, that most of them ran back from the rear and have pushed for the Ohio. Twenty-five of the regulars are missing. The army moved from the Miami village this morning; encamped at Chillicothe (a Shawanee town), two miles east, for the convenience of burning and destroying the houses and corn. Last night, a Captain M'Clure and M'Quircy of the militia, took a notion to trap some of the Indians, who we suspected lurked about after night and carried off straggling horses. A short distance outside the sentries they close hoppled a horse with a bell on, and took their station in a hazel thicket but a few yards off. It was not long until an Indian stalked up and seized the horse. The captains rushed upon him, cut off his head and brought it into camp, and claimed at least the price of a wolf's scalp. Detachments employed collecting and burning corn, &c.

20*th.*—The army all engaged burning and destroying

everything that could be of use: corn, beans, pumpkins, stacks of hay, fencing and cabins, &c. Twelve or fifteen of the savages made their appearance this day near to one of our burning parties. Some of Major Fontaine's corps got on their flank undiscovered. A few shots were exchanged, and two of the Indians were killed, without any loss on our side.

21*st.*—The army having burned five villages, besides the capital town, and consumed and destroyed twenty thousand bushels of corn in ears, took up their line of march back to Fort Washington, and encamped eight miles from the ruins.

Nine o'clock at night.—The General ordered out four hundred choice men, militia and regulars, to be under the command of Major Wyllys, to return to the towns, intending to surprise any parties that might be assembled there, expecting the Indians would collect to see how things were left. The Major marched about midnight in three divisions, at the distance of a few hundred yards apart, intending to cross the Omee as day broke, and come upon the principal ruins all at the same instant, but at different quarters. The wings commanded by Majors Hall and M'Millen came upon a few Indians immediately after crossing the Omee, put them to flight, and contrary to orders, pursued up the St. Joseph for several miles. The centre division, composed chiefly of the regular troops, were left unsupported. It would seem as if the enemy designed to draw the principal part of the force after a few of their people, while their main body attacked Major Wyllys. The centre division sustained a very unequal fight for some time; they were obliged at length to give way. The few that escaped fled in the direction to where the militia had gone, and met them returning from the pursuit of the scattering Indians. The enemy followed and were met by the militia several miles up the St. Joseph; this narrow creek was between the parties; a smart fire commenced and was kept up. The Indians attempted to force their way across but were repulsed, and at length withdrew. Our parties collected their wounded, and returned slowly to camp. One of Major Fontaine's corps, who was attached to the centre division, immediately after the defeat of Wyllys, escaped to camp, and gives a very imperfect account of the business. He got in about eleven o'clock, A. M. Major Ray with his battalion was immediately dispatched to support the parties, but met Colonel Hardin returning to camp with his wounded. Hardin had been an officer in the Revolutionary war; on this expedition under Wyllys, he had volunteered his services, with a view of retrieving his affair of the 19th, and had assumed the command of the militia. He declares, as well as other officers, whose veracity cannot be doubted, that the enemy must have lost one hundred killed, besides a number who were seen carried off wounded. The federals lost forty-eight men and two officers (Major Wyllys and Lieutenant Frothingham,) in the business of this day; the militia not so many. The whole of the killed and missing of the army amounts to one hundred and eighty-three, but it is verily believed that a number of the militia who are missing have deserted, and are on their way to Kentucky. Major Fontaine, who commanded the cavalry and was with the centre division, charged the enemy, but was not supported—his men faltered; himself far in front, was singled out and fell. The design of sending back Major Wyllys with his command, was evident to all the army, and would have answered the fullest expectations, provided due obedience had been observed on the part of the militia, but owing to their ungovernable disposition, an excellent laid plan has in some measure been defeated, and our loss is equal if not greater than the savages'. The General advised with his principal officers about returning to the towns. It was agreed not to return.

22*d.*—Continued in our encampment, fixing up biers for the wounded and making repairs, &c. The frost had destroyed the food early on our march out, and the horses of the army were now very much reduced, so much so that it was utterly impossible for the main body to perform anything rapidly, and to get back upon the road which we had so lately passed was attended with difficulty.

23*d.*—The army took up the line of march; proceeded slowly. Every attention paid to keep the men compact. Vigilance was the order of the day.

Nov. 3*d.*—Got back to Fort Washington.

4*th.*—At Fort Washington. The militia mustered this afternoon in their camp on the south side of the Ohio, and discharged by a general order; those from Kentucky to receive pay and rations up to the 10th instant.

5*th and* 6*th.*—The militia began to move off in small

parties for their homes. It was an arduous task to keep the militia in order or within reasonable bounds, at any time, but when we had gotten so far on our way home as to consider ourselves in some measure out of the enemy's country, they broke out and became altogether ungovernable. The General was under the necessity of punishing one of them for discharging his piece in presence of several officers, contrary to a special order. This fellow, it seems, is the son of a Baptist preacher in Kentucky. His officers and many of his men would have opposed the punishment, and although there was much forbearance on the part of the General through the whole campaign, I have no doubt but a hue and cry will be raised against him in Kentucky as soon as those fellows get home. If he is blamable, it is only for being too indulgent to the militia. I feel conscious of having acted my part. As the adjutant of the General, I had not only my regimental duties to attend to, but the duty of adjutant to the army, brigade-major, &c., and in most instances, when militia field officers were upon duty, had, at the request of the General, to station the guards and go the rounds. The general detail of all guards and detachments kept and made out by myself; their examination on the grand parade daily, was also my duty; regulating the march, keeping the columns in their proper places, assisting the quarter-master in keeping up the baggage, looking after and correcting accidents and delays, was no trifling employment; and every morning half an hour before daylight, agreeably to orders, it was my particular duty to see the army all under arms. However, I feel amply rewarded. I know that I have the approbation of my commanding officer, and that is enough; but hope never to be employed in a similar situation with such *materials.*

7th. — Left head-quarters for the seat of government; passed through Lexington, the crab orchard and wilderness, and after a most inclement ride, arrived at Philadelphia the 12th December. High water and very bad roads.

PHILADELPHIA, *April 1st,* 1791. — It was expected when I left head-quarters that I would return across the mountains in time to descend the Ohio with the first spring flood. I frequently pressed for my departure, but was delayed. Congress having added a second regiment to the establishment, and at the close of the session passed a law for raising two thousand levies, or six months men, for another expedition against the Indians. Governor St. Clair appointed major-general, and to conduct the campaign himself. Captain Beatty, our late pay-master, had spent the winter in the city settling up his accounts. He and myself the only officers of the regiment at this time in Philadelphia. Beatty ordered to New Brunswick on the recruiting service. He was desirous that I should accompany him, and prevailed on the Secretary of War, who rather requested that I would assist in raising the company, after which I am at liberty to return to the regiment in any manner I please. Took the stage at three o'clock; lay by awhile at Princeton, and reached Brunswick early next day. Remained here a few days with Beatty and proceeded to New York.

Made arrangements and commenced recruiting. An excellent sergeant and corporal did the business for me. We were very successful. Recruits sent to New Brunswick weekly by the packet. Beatty ordered to march. I repair to New Brunswick; accompany him to Newton, in Bucks county, file off myself to Philadelphia; detained there three days; from thence to Carlisle, where I met Beatty, who had been joined by a new raised company from Lancaster, commanded by Captain Doyle.

July 4th.—Spent the 4th of July together.

5th.—The two companies took up their march for Fort Pitt. Stayed with my friends till the 10th.

10th.—I set out and arrived in Fort Pitt on the 15th; companies arrived a few days after. Found two battalions of the levies here; two other battalions from Virginia had sailed. Several companies of the second regiment had also gone on.

PITTSBURGH, *August 7th.*—Beatty's and Doyle's companies embark; took passage with them, but owing to the very low state of the river, did not reach Fort Washington until the last of the month. Camp formed at Mill creek, three miles out; the artillery only doing duty in the fort. Business obliged me to remain here with General Harmar, who had his family in the fort.

FORT WASHINGTON, *Sept. 1st.*—General St. Clair appears exceedingly impatient at the delay or detention of some of the corps. The quarter-master general, Hodgden, not yet come on, and General Butler, the second in command, is also back. Preparations for the campaign very backward. General Harmar seems determined to quit the service; has positively refused going on the campaign, and takes no command.

7th.—General Butler, and Hodgden, the quarter-master general, with Captain Newman's company of the second regiment, arrive. General Harmar solicits a court of inquiry to examine into his conduct on the last campaign. The court is ordered — General Richard Butler the president. Several days spent in examining the testimony. The court make a report to the commander-in-chief, highly honorable to General Harmar. It was impossible for me not to be affected by the determination of General Harmar. I knew that he only waited for the march of the army, when he would ascend the river with his family and retire to civil life. My secret wish was to accompany him; he discovered it, and informed me that he would apply for an officer's command to escort and work his boat to Pittsburgh, and had no doubt but that General St. Clair, upon being asked, would order me on that service. I made the request in writing. Was answered that it could not be granted. I stayed with General Harmar and his family until the last moment. He conversed frequently and freely with a few of his friends on the probable result of the campaign—predicted a defeat. He suspected a disposition in me to resign; discouraged the idea. "You must," said he, "go on the campaign; some will escape, and you may be among the number."

26th. — Left Fort Washington and proceeded to join my regiment. Arrived at the army next day. Found a pleasant encampment twenty-three miles from Fort

Washington, on the Great Miami. The principal part of the troops have been at this place since the 15th, building a stockade fort with four bastions. Barracks to accommodate one hundred men.

29th.—Commenced my duty as adjutant, Major Hamtramck the commanding officer of the regiment. We are informed that upward of one hundred horses have been stolen, supposed by the enemy, from the vicinity of Fort Washington, some of them cut from their fastenings under the walls of the fort.

30th.—Appointed aid-de-camp to the commander-in-chief. With much difficulty finished and handed in a set of monthly returns.

Oct. 1st.—Joined the General's family, found to consist of Colonel Sargent, the adjutant-general, Count Malartie, a young Frenchman from Gallipolis, in character of volunteer aid, and the General.

2d.—Accompany commander-in-chief to Fort Washington. Three hundred militia had just reached that place from Kentucky.

3d.—A number of the militia are reported to have deserted already.

4th.—A sergeant and nine of the militia deserted last night.

5th.—An officer from the army arrives in pursuit of deserters. A sergeant and twenty-five deserted on the night of the 3d.

6th.—After some difficulty in getting the militia equipped, they march to join the army. Public dispatches forwarded to seat of government by way of Lexington.

7th.—Set out about nine o'clock; arrive at Fort Hamilton in the afternoon. The army had marched on the 4th.

8th.—We cross the Miami twenty-five miles from Fort Washington, and follow the army; their course north sixteen degrees. Passed four encampments and the militia on their march. Joined in the evening as troops were encamping. Distance from Fort Washington forty-four and one-fourth miles. The army is five days from Fort Hamilton, at the fording of the Miami, to this place (not four miles a day).

9th.—The army marched this morning at ten o'clock, and encamped about three; gained only five miles. The country, thus far from the Miami, level, rich and exceedingly well watered with small branches.

10th.—Army in motion at eight o'clock. Country more flat. Crossed a number of small rivulets running east. Timber chiefly beech. Gained about eight miles and encamped at four o'clock. The horses had been all tied up last night, which enabled an early start this morning.

11th.—Ten o'clock this morning before the troops took up the line of march. Horses missing, which occasioned the delay. About twelve arrived at a pretty little creek running west, supposed to be a branch of White river. Fresh trails of Indians discovered. Two o'clock came directly upon an extensive wet prairie; army obliged to halt and encamp. Marched this day not more than six miles. Country very level, well watered and timbered.

12th.—This morning spent in searching the prairie and examining for a passage across. General Butler with a party set out early toward the east; myself, with a captain and fifty riflemen, to examine westerly. After proceeding about three miles we made out to cross the prairie, but with difficulty got my horse through. From this place we had a view for several miles west; the prairie rather appearing to increase. On the north side came upon a deep beaten Indian path, which we followed about two miles, turned and recrossed the prairie, examined further, could find no place possible for the army to cross without bridging at least three hundred yards. General Butler's report favorable. He found a pretty good way by going three miles round. Twelve o'clock the army marched, altering their course to north-east thirty-five degrees. Passed several small prairies, all of them swampy. Fell in with an Indian path, leading through and avoiding the wet land. March this day five and one-half miles over excellent country, watered with pretty, small runs winding about in every direction.

13*th.*—The General, with a few attendants, reconnoitres the country. Makes choice of ground to erect another fort for purpose of a deposit. The army moved about one o'clock, one mile, near to this ground and encamped.

14*th.*—Two hundred men employed, under direction of Major Ferguson, at the new fort. It is to be a square work, curtains thirty-five yards; regular bastions in each angle. The whole raised with logs laid horizontally; the face of the curtains forming the rear of the barracks.

15*th.*—Cold and wet. Heavy rain last night and continues all the day.

16*th.*—Rain all last night. Express from Fort Washington with information of the mountain leader and twenty Indians of the Chickasaw nation on their way from Fort Washington, and also of sixty horse loads of flour.

17*th.*—The new fort goes on but slowly. Weather very bad; constant rain night and day. A rifleman of the militia, a few miles from camp with leave to hunt, fired upon by a single Indian and wounded through the hip, but made his escape into camp. Men desert; four of the first regiment went off since our arrival here.

18*th.*—A continuation of wet, disagreeable weather. The army would have been without bread after to-day, had not a small supply of forty-eight horse loads arrived.

19*th.*—All the horses of the army, quarter-master's as well as contractors, sent back for a supply of flour. Unpardonable mismanagement in the provision department. Troops put on half allowance of flour. Colonel Oldham, commanding officer of militia, directed to furnish an escort to go back with the horses. His men declare if they are sent on that duty they will not return. Falconer's company of levies escort the horses back.

20*th.*—The time for which the levies were enlisted begins to expire. Ten were discharged this morning; several a few days ago. The levies from Virginia claim their discharge. All of Captain Hanah's company from Alexandria, discharged. An express this day from Fort Washington. Captain Buel's company of the second regiment had arrived there from the eastward.

21*st.*—Very severe frost last night; ice upon the waters near a half inch thick. The food of our horses and cattle had been injured by slight frosts as early as the 4th. A strong guard escort the cattle and horses to the best pasture, and every afternoon one-half the army off duty turn out and bring grass from the prairie to serve them over night.

22d.—For want of sufficiency of flour, the General has been under the necessity of keeping the troops upon half a pound of that article daily, but the ration is made up of beef. This, however, would not satisfy militia; twenty of them deserted last night, and some more this morning. An officer near Lexington, who joined us this day with about sixty men, happened to meet those who went off this morning, and brought them back. He informed us that a number of the militia who had deserted from Fort Washington, and on the march, had been apprehended in Kentucky and were confined in the jails. Two brigades of horses loaded with flour arrived this day, estimated at one thousand eight hundred pounds; also a small drove of cattle. The quarter-master general is ordered to Fort Washington to make some more certain arrangement with regard to supplies of provisions—the contractor not to be depended on.

23d.—Two artillery men attempted to desert to the enemy, were taken, tried and sentenced to suffer death; were hanged along with one of the levies for shooting his comrade. The country for ten miles round has been well explored. Many large wet prairies, especially to the west. Upland thin, covered chiefly with white oak. Fine springs which feed the prairies. Any quantity of meadow ground—natural meadow.

24th.—The army took up their line of march about nine o'clock. Pursued the old Indian path leading north through a fine open woods. The soil and timber of a superior quality. Gained six miles and encamped along the bank of a handsome creek running east; a large prairie on our left.[1] A captain's command left at the new fort, called Fort Jefferson, with all the men unable to march. The commander-in-chief has been unwell for some time past, but to-day scarcely able to accompany the army.

25th.—Rain almost all last night. Troops continued encamped.

26th.—Remain encamped. A party of fifty militia sent to reconnoitre the country north-west, fell in with five of the enemy about fifteen miles from camp, but owing to mismanagement, the Indians made their escape, leaving behind in their camp, blankets, tomahawks, paint, &c., to the value of twenty-two dollars. An express from the quarter-master general, respecting provisions. The commander-in-chief very ill.

27th.—The army wait for a supply of flour to enable them to proceed. The last pound served out this day, and should none arrive, on to-morrow the men will be without bread. Much dissatisfaction among the militia and levies; the latter claim their discharge; say they have served longer than the term for which they have enlisted. The enlistments are indeed somewhat extraordinary; they specify six months after assembling at the rendezvous on the frontier, but there has been no uni-

---

[1] This camp called afterward by Wayne, "Greenville."

formity observed; some corps have inserted Winchester, some Fort Pitt, and others Fort Washington, but the bulk of the men say and declare that they engaged to serve but for six months from the date of their enlistment. These circumstances have been made a cause of complaint to the General, who has had much trouble. Piamingo and nineteen Chickasaws join the camp. The season so far advanced it will be impracticable to continue the campaign. Forage entirely destroyed; horses failing and cannot be kept up; provisions from hand to mouth. A party of men engaged in throwing a bridge over the creek in front of the camp. Some hail and snow to-day.

28*th.* — Seventy-four horses loaded with flour arrive; about twelve thousand pounds. This supply will afford four days' allowance to the army. A few horses came loaded with clothing for the first regiment, the officers of which were directed to fill up their companies, if possible, from the levies. The new clothing has a good effect; near forty have already enlisted. Two privates of Major Butler's battalion were fired upon about three miles from camp, one of them killed, the other wounded, but made his escape to camp. Two of the militia some miles out, were pursued by four Indians; one only got in, it is supposed the other is a prisoner, as the savages endeavored to catch him when they might have shot with certainty. In the general orders of this day the troops directed to be under arms at the first tap of the drum, which is to be given at daylight, and to continue paraded until dismissed.

29*th.*—One of the sentries which form the chain round the encampment, alarmed the troops last night about nine o'clock, and put them all under arms. He imagined that he saw an Indian, and fired three times at some object. The first and second regiment of regulars compose about one-third the army, and although chiefly recruits, are tolerably well disciplined, but the remainder (excepting the few militia,) being levies and raised but for six months, and their times expiring daily, they take great liberties. This morning there was a constant firing kept up round the camp, notwithstanding it is known there is a general order against it; in fact, at present they are more troublesome and far inferior to the militia. A bridge thrown across the creek. One hundred and twenty men, properly officered, were ordered forward to open the road for the army. Two hundred militia go as a covering party. Piamingo and his nineteen warriors, accompanied by Captain Sparks of the levies, with four riflemen, set out on a scout; their object to take a prisoner. The battalion of levies from the territory south-east of the Ohio being so small, it was blended with the one from Virginia. Supernumerary officers went home. Three days flour issued to the troops in order that horses may be had to carry the baggage; most of the baggage horses having been sent with the quarter-master general for provisions.

30*th.*—The army took up the line of march about nine o'clock, crossed the creek upon the bridge, and left a very handsome encampment. The creek which runs along in front of this ground, twenty-five yards wide, is said to

11

be a principal branch of the Miami. Gained seven miles this day; course north-west twenty-five degrees. The soil and timber of a superior quality. The General has been so very ill since we left Fort Jefferson, that it was supposed he would not be able to proceed.

31*st.*—A very unpleasant camp in the woods; soil rich and timber thick and heavy. Last evening had a gust with severe lightning and thunder; directly after night the wind rose and blew violently until daybreak. The trees and limbs falling around and in the midst of us, with the darkness of the night and in an enemy's country, occasioned some concern. About twelve o'clock at night, for the first time, at the request of the General, I visited all the guards.

Army continued encamped, waiting for several brigades of pack horses loaded with flour, which had reached Fort Jefferson last night. The troops are supplied for to-day and to-morrow, and the contractor has enough for one other day; but should we move, the supply behind would be too late or lost; besides it was found yesterday that the horses with the army were not sufficient to carry the baggage, part of which had to be left on the road. The tents and other baggage sent back for and brought up. Militia show great impatience; their officers appear to have little influence. One-third turn out with a determination to go back, a few are prevailed on to stay; between sixty and seventy, however, march off in despite of everything, and swear they will stop the pack horses with provisions. The first regiment dispatched after them, not with an expectation of bringing them back, but with that idea and to prevent future desertions, and principally to protect the convoys. This evening two hundred and twelve horses, loaded with flour, arrived; one hundred and fifty pounds the average weight.

Nov. 1st.—The army remain encamped. A party advanced to open the road. Prepare for marching to-morrow. A deposit made here of heavy articles and such as could be dispensed with, to lighten the horses.

2d.—The army marched at nine o'clock; about twelve o'clock crossed a creek fifteen yards wide, running east. The country very flat and marshy. Joined this afternoon by another Indian path much frequented. Gained eight miles and encamped. Course north twenty-five degrees east this day, and total distance from Fort Washington eighty-nine miles. A scout sent out yesterday fell in with an Indian camp, got some plunder and seven horses branded United States, supposed to have been stolen from Fort Washington. We had a light snow all this day.

3d.—Marched at nine o'clock. The first four miles very flat and wet. About twelve passed over dry ground and descended gradually for three miles to a small creek, supposed to be a branch of the waters emptying into Lake Erie; proceeded two miles farther, and encamped on pleasant dry ground, on bank of a creek about twenty yards wide, said to be the Pickaway fork of the Omee.[1] Distance this day about nine miles; general course northwest thirty degrees. Fresh signs of the savages appeared to-day in several places; parties of riflemen detached

---

[1] Known since to be a branch of the Wabash.

after them, but without success. It was later than usual when the army reached the ground this evening, and the men much fatigued prevented the General from having some works of defense immediately erected. Major Ferguson, commanding officer of artillery, sent for, and a plan agreed on intended to be commenced early on to-morrow. The high dry ground barely sufficient to encamp the army; lines rather contracted. Parallel with the front line runs the creek, about twenty yards wide. On both flanks low wet ground, and along most part of the rear. Militia advanced across the creek about three hundred yards. Had accompanied the quarter-master in the afternoon, on to this ground; it was farther than could have been wished, but no place short of it appeared so suitable. I was much pleased with it; returned and made report; found the army halted and about to encamp on flat land, and with no good water; although it was late, the march was continued till just dark, when we reached the creek.

4th.—Camp on a creek twenty yards wide, supposed to be the Pickaway fork of the Omee, ninety-eight miles from Fort Washington. The frequent firing of the sentinels through the night had disturbed the camp, and excited some concern among the officers. The guards had reported the Indians to lie skulking about in considerable numbers. About ten o'clock at night General Butler, who commanded the right wing, was desired to send out an intelligent officer and party to make discoveries. Captain Slough, with two subalterns and thirty men, I saw parade at General Butler's tent for this purpose, and heard the General give Captain Slough very particular verbal orders how to proceed. Myself and two or three officers staid with the General until late, when I returned to the commander-in-chief, whose tent was at some distance on the left, and who was unable to be up.

The troops paraded this morning at the usual time, and had been dismissed from the lines but a few minutes, the sun not yet up, when the woods in front rung with the yells and fire of the savages. The poor militia, who were but three hundred yards in front, had scarcely time to return a shot—they fled into our camp. The troops were under arms in an instant, and a smart fire from the front line met the enemy. It was but a few minutes, however, until the men were engaged in every quarter. The enemy from the front filed off to the right and left, and completely surrounded the camp, killed and cut off nearly all the guards, and approached close to the lines. They advanced from one tree, log, or stump to another, under cover of the smoke of our fire. The artillery and musketry made a tremendous noise, but did little execution. The Indians seemed to brave everything, and when fairly fixed around us they made no noise other than their fire, which they kept up very constant and which seldom failed to tell, although scarcely heard. Our left flank, probably from the nature of the ground, gave way first; the enemy got possession of that part of the encampment, but it being pretty clear ground, they were too much exposed and were soon repulsed. Was at this time with the General engaged toward the right; he was on foot and led the party himself that drove the enemy and regained our ground on the left. The battalions in the rear charged several times and forced the savages from their shelter, but they always turned with the battalions and fired upon them back; indeed they seemed not to fear anything we could do. They could skip out of reach of the bayonet and return, as they pleased. They were visible only when raised by a charge. The ground was literally covered with the dead. The wounded were taken to the centre, where it was thought most safe, and where a great many who had quit their posts unhurt, had crowded together. The General, with other officers, endeavored to rally these men, and twice they were taken out to the lines. It appeared as if the officers had been singled out; a very great proportion fell, or were wounded and obliged to retire from the lines early in the action. General Butler was among the latter, as well as several other of the most experienced officers. The men being thus left with few officers, became fearful, despaired of success, gave up the fight, and to save themselves for the moment, abandoned entirely their duty and ground, and crowded in toward the centre of the field, and no exertions could put them in any order even for defense; perfectly ungovernable. The enemy at length got possession of the artillery, though not until the officers were all killed but one, and he badly wounded, and the men almost all cut off, and not until the pieces were spiked. As our lines were deserted the Indians contracted theirs until their shot centred from all points, and now meeting with little opposition, took more deliberate aim and did great execution. Exposed to a cross fire, men and officers were seen falling in every direction; the distress too of the wounded made the scene such as can scarcely be conceived; a few minutes longer, and a retreat would have been impracticable. The only hope left was, that perhaps the savages would be so taken up with the camp as not to follow. Delay was death; no preparation could be made; numbers of brave men must be left a sacrifice, there was no alternative. It was past nine o'clock, when repeated orders were given to charge toward the road. The action had continued between two and three hours. Both officers and men seemed confounded, incapable of doing anything; they could not move until it was told that a retreat was intended. A few officers put themselves in front, the men followed, the enemy gave way, and perhaps not being aware of the design, we were for a few minutes left undisturbed. The stoutest and most active now took the lead, and those who were foremost in breaking the enemy's line, were soon left behind. At the moment of the retreat, one of the few horses saved had been procured for the General; he was on foot until then; I kept by him, and he delayed to see the rear. The enemy soon discovered the movement and pursued, though not more than four or five miles, and but few so far; they turned to share the spoil. Soon after the firing ceased, I was directed to endeavor to gain the front, and if possible, to cause a short halt that the rear might get up. I had been on horseback from the first alarm, and well mounted; pushed forward, but met with so many difficulties and interruptions from the people, that I was two hours at least laboring to reach the front. With the assistance of two or three officers I caused a short halt, but the men grew impatient and would move on. I got Lieutenants Sedam and Morgan, with half a dozen stout men, to fill up the road and to move slowly, I halted myself until the General came up. By this time the remains of the army had got somewhat compact, but in the most miserable and defenseless state. The wounded who came off left their arms in the field, and one-half of the others threw theirs away on the retreat. The road for miles was covered with firelocks, cartridge boxes and regimentals. How fortunate that the pursuit was discontinued; a single Indian might have followed with safety upon either flank. Such a panic had seized the men, that I believe it would not have been possible to have brought any of them to engage again. In the afternoon Lieutenant Kersey, with a detachment of the first regiment, met us. This regiment, the only complete and best disciplined portion of the army, had been ordered back upon the road on the 31st of October. They were thirty miles from the battle ground when they heard distinctly the firing of the cannon, were hastening forward and had marched about nine miles when met by some of the militia, who informed Major Hamtramck, the commanding officer, that the army was totally destroyed. The Major judged it best to send on a subaltern to obtain some knowledge of things, and to return himself with the regiment to Fort Jefferson, eight miles back, and to secure at all events that post. He had made some arrangements, and as we arrived in the evening, found him preparing again to meet us. Stragglers continued to come in for hours after we reached the fort.

The remnant of the army, with the first regiment, were now at Fort Jefferson, twenty-nine miles from the field of action, without provisions, and the former without having eaten anything for twenty-four hours. A convoy was known to be upon the road, and within a day's march. The General determined to move with the first regiment and all the levies able to march. Those of the wounded and others unable to go on, were lodged as comfortably as possible within the fort. Accordingly we set out a little after ten and continued our route until within an hour of daylight, then halted and waited for day and until the rear came up. Moved on again about nine o'clock; the morning of the 5th we met the convoy. Stopped a sufficiency to subsist us to Fort Hamilton; sent the remainder on to Jefferson under an additional escort of a captain and sixty men; proceeded, and at the first water halted, partly cooked and eat for the first time since the night preceding the action. At one o'clock moved on, and continued our route until nine at night, when we halted and made fires within fifteen miles of Fort Hamilton. Marched again just before day, the General soon after rode on to the fort. Troops reached in the afternoon.

7th.— Fort Hamilton command was ordered off with a small supply for the wounded, &c. About twelve same day continued our march, and halted before night within fifteen miles of Fort Washington, which place we reached the afternoon of the 8th.

The prediction of General Harmar, before the army set out on the campaign, was founded upon his experience and particular knowledge of things. He saw with what material the bulk of the army was composed; men collected from the streets and prisons of the cities, hurried out into the enemy's country, and with the officers commanding them, totally unacquainted with the business in which they were engaged, it was utterly impossible they could be otherwise. Besides, not any one department was sufficiently prepared; both quarter-master and contractors extremely deficient. It was a matter of astonishment to him that the commanding general, who was acknowledged to be perfectly competent, should think of hazarding, with such people, and under such circumstances, his reputation and life, and the lives of so many others, knowing, too, as both did, the enemy with whom he was going to contend; an enemy brought up from infancy to war, and perhaps superior to an equal number of the best men that could be taken against them. It is a truth, I had hopes that the noise and show which the army made on their march might possibly deter the enemy from attempting a serious and general attack. It was unfortunate that *both* the general officers were, and had been disabled by sickness; in such situation it is possible that some essential matters might be overlooked. The adjutant-general, Colonel Sargent, an old Revolutionary officer, was, however, constantly on the alert; he took upon himself the burden of everything, and a very serious and troublesome task he had. But one most important object was wanting, can't say neglected, but more might have been done toward obtaining it; this was, *a knowledge of the collected force and situation of the enemy; of this we were perfectly ignorant.* Some few scouts out, but to no great distance. The one which left camp on the 29th of October, under direction of Captain Sparks, and composed chiefly of the friendly Indians, had missed the enemy altogether, and on their return to join the army, the morning after the defeat, met an Indian runner who had been in the engagement, of him they got the news which enabled them to escape. When the army advanced from Fort Jefferson, it did not exceed two thousand men; discharges, desertions and the absence of the first regiment, reduced the effective strength on the day of action to about fourteen hundred. The second regiment had but one battalion with the army—it was well appointed, but young in service. The officers and men, however, did their duty; *they*, with the battalion of artillery, were nearly all cut off. The whole loss, as now ascertained by the different returns, is thirty-seven officers and five hundred and ninety-three privates killed and missing; thirty-one officers and two hundred and fifty-two privates wounded.

LIST OF THE KILLED AND WOUNDED.

Officers in the army of the United States, commanded by General Arthur St. Clair, November 4th, 1791.

ARTILLERY.

KILLED.	WOUNDED.
Major Ferguson,	Capt. Ford.
Capt. Bradford,	
Lieut. Spear.	

CAVALRY.

KILLED.	WOUNDED.
	Capt. Trueman,
	Lieut. Debutts,
	Cornet Bhines.

FIRST REGIMENT.

KILLED.	WOUNDED.
	Capt. Doyle.[1]

SECOND REGIMENT

KILLED.	WOUNDED.
Major Heart,	Lieut. Graton.
Capt. Phelon,	
Capt. Newman,	
Capt. Kirkwood,	
Lieut. Warren,	
Ensign Balsh,	
Ensign Cobb.	

FIRST REGIMENT OF LEVIES.

KILLED.	WOUNDED.
Capt. Vanswearingen,	Lieut.-Col. Dark,
Capt. Tibton,	Capt. Dark,
Capt. Price,	Capt. Buchanan,
Lieut. M'Math,	Lieut. Morgan,

[1] Captain Doyle was on guard when the first regiment was ordered back, he had been relieved, but was without any command. Attached himself to the artillery.

KILLED.	WOUNDED.
Lieut. Boyd,	Lieut. Lyle,
Ensign Wilson,	Lieut. Rhea,
Ensign Reaves,	Lieut. Davidson,
Ensign Brooks	Lieut. Price,
Ensign Chase,	Adjt. Whistler.
Ensign Turner,[1]	
Adjt. Burges,	
Dr. Grayson.	

SECOND REGIMENT OF LEVIES.

Capt. Cribbs,	Lieut.-Col. Gibson,[2]
Capt. Piatt,	Major Butler,
Capt. Smith,	Capt. Slough,
Capt. Purdy,	Lieut. Thompson,
Lieut. Kelso,	Lieut. Cummins,
Lieut. Lukins,	Lieut. Read,
Ensign M'Michle,	Ensign Moorhead,
Ensign Beatty,	Adjt. Crawford.
Ensign Purdy,	
Adjt. Anderson,	

KENTUCKY MILITIA.

Lieut.-Col. Oldham,	Capt. Thomas,
Capt. Lemmon,	Capt. Maddison,
Lieut. Briggs,	Lieut. Owens,
Ensign Montgomery.	Lieut. Stagner,
	Ensign Walter,
	Dr. Gano.

---

[1] Ensign Turner commanded one of the guards. He was taken and carried to Detroit — returned by Montreal — saw him in Philadelphia the next April. He either was or affected to be deranged.

[2] Colonel Gibson died of his wounds at Fort Jefferson.

Major General Butler, killed; Colonel Sargent, adjutant general, and Viscount Malartie, acting as aid-de-camp, wounded.

Fort Washington, *Nov.* 18*th.*—The remains of our wretched and miserable army are encamped in front of the fort. Every necessary provision ordered to make the men as comfortable as possible, but the weather has been cold and wet, with snow, and a very considerable number of officers and men are laid up. The General, too, has been much indisposed. On the 9th, the day after we reached this, he made out to forward to government, by way of Kentucky, a short dispatch, but has scarcely had his head off the pillow.

On the 10th a detachment of fresh troops marched for Fort Jefferson, with a small supply for that post, and on the 11th the first regiment followed. Such of the officers in camp who are capable, have been engaged making returns, pay rolls, &c., and preparing for their men's discharge. All the wounded able to be moved from Fort Jefferson, reached here yesterday. The General has at length completed his particular dispatches, and on to-morrow I once again ascend the river for the seat of government. He purposes, as soon as he is able to travel, to set out on horseback for the same place.

19*th.*—In the evening take leave of our friends at Fort Washington and embark on board a fourteen oar barge. The boat's company consists of Captain Edward Butler and twenty-two of his men, who were raised about Pittsburgh, and for the sake of getting home have volunteered this service. Passengers are Captain Buel, of the second regiment, who arrived at Fort Washington some short time after the army marched from thence, and where he chose to remain—he is now returning home; and Adjutant Crawford and Quarter-master Semple, of the Pennsylvania levies. Crawford is an old Revolutionary officer of some merit. He received a shot in the late action, which is lodged somewhere about the chest, but appears not at all disabled. Semple is a fine companionable man, who has seen better times. We promise ourselves as pleasant a passage as circumstances and the lateness of the season will admit.

Dec. 9th.—Arrive at Wheeling, after an extremely hard and tedious passage of twenty days; the same journey have more than once made in fifteen—but the winter seemed to have set in earlier than usual. The river had swollen considerably before we started, and heavy rains and snows almost every day on our way up, kept the water constantly on the rise. The last two nights covered the river with ice, and it was with difficulty the boat was worked to this place.

10*th.*—Hired a boy and horses, took the road through Washington, and reached Pittsburgh on the night of the 11th.

13*th.*—In the morning leave Pittsburgh, and arrive at Philadelphia late on the 19th.

19*th.*—Waited immediately upon the Secretary of War. Since I left Fort Washington, have endeavored to banish from my mind, as much as possible, every idea of the slaughter and defeat of the army; to talk at all on the subject is an unpleasant task to me, but there are certain persons to whom I must make a full communications. My friends at Pittsburgh, and on to this place, seem to view me as escaped from the dead — astonishment takes place of pleasure; and having in some degree got over those feelings myself, am considered as little better than one of the savages — but all this will soon be forgotten.

The morning after my arrival here, General Knox, the Secretary of War, called at my quarters and took me to the President's, where we breakfasted with the family, and afterward had much talk on the subject of the campaign and defeat. With the Secretary, at his office, I have also endeavored to afford every possible satisfaction. It is a pleasing reflection to believe that I have fulfilled all that could be expected of me. The attention and kindness which I receive, is a flattering consolation and assurance of having done my duty. Among the friends I met at this place, I have found none who appeared more sincerely pleased to see me than General Harmar and his family. They left Fort Washington at the time the army marched out, and arrived here safe about three weeks since. The first business the General attended to was the settlement of his public accounts, which was soon done. Indeed there could be no difficulty, for in my opinion, there is not a better accountant than himself; nor is it possible for any man to have been more exact or punctual than he was in all his transactions. He resigns his commission at the end of the present month.

29th.—This day I received the appointment of captain

in the first regiment. Several other regular promotions made. Hamtramck will command the regiment; Ziegler and Strong, majors.

February, 1792.—General St. Clair and several officers of the levies arrive at the city. My friend Captain Pratt, late quarter-master, with whom I lived and messed for five years while adjutant of the regiment, passed on his way home to Connecticut, to recruit a company for himself. A new raised company now at this place, has been assigned to me; but for the present, as it is a question with me whether I will continue in the service, have excused myself from the command. I feel perfectly weary and sick of the noise and bustle of a military life, and long for a change for a domestic situation.

March.—General St. Clair is determined to have an investigation into the causes of the defeat. He resigns the command of the army. As it will be some time before the investigation can commence, and having little now to do, I leave Philadelphia for Pittsburgh, by way of Carlisle, with a view of making arrangements to retire from the army. The little horse that served me so well in the campaign and in the action, was brought round by the General, and carries me on this journey. Our good fortune, I hope, will attend us. See my friends at Carlisle. Proceeded to Pittsburgh, where I make some engagements, and determine upon quitting the service. Return to the city after an absence of four weeks.

April.—General Anthony Wayne appointed commander-in-chief, in place of General St. Clair, who had resigned. The army is to be augmented to four regiments of infantry, besides a corps of cavalry; the whole, with artillery, to consist of five thousand men. The committee of Congress commence their inquiry into the causes of the defeat. Several hours spent every day for a week past, examining officers and others examined on oath. They adjourn, and finally report to the House,

> "That, in their opinion, the failure of the late expedition can in no respect be imputed to the conduct of the commanding general, either at any time before or during the action."

May 1*st.*—Resigned my commission; next day left the city for Pittsburgh.

In the winter of 1793–4 the western frontiers of Pennsylvania lay much exposed to the inroads of the Indians; frequent depredations were committed. General Wayne had removed and taken with him down the Ohio, the whole of the troops of the United States, leaving at Fort Franklin only a subaltern and twenty men. I had occasion to be in Philadelphia about this time, when Governor Mifflin communicated to me a plan which he recommended to the Legislature for the protection of the western frontiers. This plan was adopted, and an act passed authorizing him to appoint and raise in Philadelphia a company of artillery, and in the western counties three companies of riflemen. A very favorite object of the Governor, and which was approved by the Legislature, was the establishment of a post at Presqu' Isle, on Lake Erie. The command intended for this favorite object was to be composed of detachments from each of the four companies, to consist of a captain, four subalterns and one hundred and seven non-commissioned and privates.

March 1*st*, 1794.—I was commissioned captain of the company to be raised in the county of Allegheny, and especially appointed to the command of the Presqu' Isle detachment. It was expected that a post at Presqu' Isle would cut off the intercourse between the Six Nations, who had become wavering and suspicious, and the hostile Indians, and would favor General Wayne, who was preparing to march against the latter. Another important object was to afford protection to commissioners appointed to lay out towns at Le Bœuf and Presqu' Isle, and to force settlements at each of these places, under cover of the troops.

20*th*.—General Wilkins came from Philadelphia with the law for raising four companies of State troops, and the commission of captain for myself, with orders to command the detachment of one hundred and seven men, when raised, destined for Presqu' Isle. Samuel Murphy and James Patterson appointed the subalterns to the Allegheny company.

April 4*th*.—Mr. Patterson's commission did not come on until to-day. I went to his home and delivered it, with money and recruiting instructions. Lieutenant Murphy has been out since the 24th of March in Fayette.

9*th*.—Set out to Westmoreland to recruit and to hurry on the quota of that county. Had written to the inspectors of Washington and Westmoreland, some days previous, requesting that their men might be sent on as soon as possible, as a covering party was wanted to make a deposit somewhere near the head navigation of French creek.

13*th.*—Finding that the detachments would not join us as soon as they were wanted, joined with General Wilkins in requesting a party of volunteers for covering the boats and stores.

19*th.*—The volunteers assembled. Twenty men with Lieutenant Miller arrived from Washington.

21*st.*—Ensign Mahaffy came in with his quota from Westmoreland. They marched along with Miller's men; each with a sergeant, corporal and twenty men. They would join the volunteers next morning. Lieutenant Miller returned to Washington to recruit.

The State troops under Mahaffy, - -	43
Four sent with boats, - - - - - -	4
	47
Volunteers, - - - - - - -	32

May 7th.—The detachment of artillery (thirty-two) under Lieutenant Hazlewood, arrived from Philadelphia.

23*d.*—Received a letter from the Governor entreating that nothing might be omitted to have the law for laying out the town at Presqu' Isle executed, and empowering us to order out militia if necessary. Mr. Ellicott and Mr. Wilkins, who was just from Fort Franklin, joined in requesting a company from the three counties. Accordingly the men were ordered out.

30*th.*—Orders came from the Governor for turning out one thousand militia to assist in making the establishment at Presqu' Isle, but left to the discretion of General Irvine, who was expected to be here.

June 1*st.*—General Irvine came to town. He was of opinion that five hundred of the militia ordered out would answer the purpose, but not less. Two days ago the Indians attacked a canoe upon the Allegheny; there were three men in it. They killed one and wounded the other two, but got nothing. The accident happened five miles above the Kiskiminetas. The Indians, disappointed in that attack, crossed to the Kiskiminetas and unfortunately fell in with a Kentucky boat full of women and children, with but four men, laying to feeding their cattle. The men were ashore, received a fire without much damage, got into the boat, all but one, who fled to a house not far distant. The Indians fired into the boat, killed two men and wounded the third. The boat had been set afloat and drifted down in that helpless condition, twenty-four women and children on board.

2*d.*—Orders from the Governor suspending our expedition to Presqu' Isle, and directing me to remain with my detachment at Le Bœuf. Wrote to the inspectors to forward me the enlistments of the recruits from Westmoreland and Washington counties.

6*th.*—Wrote to the Governor.

7*th.*—Lieutenant Hazlewood, with his detachment of artillery from Philadelphia, thirty-two, having joined us, we crossed the Allegheny with seventy men, the remainder of my command, and took up our march for Le Bœuf. Encamped one mile from Robinson's.

8*th.*—Detained until late in the day waiting for a

drove of cattle which we wished to have along. Twenty-two were brought over. We moved seven miles and halted.

9th.—Found that the cattle had returned in the night back to the river. We were obliged to send after them. It was two o'clock when they were brought up. We marched about fourteen miles, and encamped on a branch of Brush creek.

10*th.*—Marched at seven o'clock; crossed Connekeness; halted one hour; took the route again, and encamped one mile beyond Muddy creek. This day's march twenty-three miles.

11*th.*—Marched at eight o'clock. Passed over a rich level country. Stopped at Slippery Rock, where we saw one of the best natural mill seats and plenty of water. A fine situation for a village. Went on and encamped at a spring—twenty miles.

12*th.*—Marched at seven o'clock through thickets of brush—few trees—but the land good. Rain for two days past. Passed the graves of two men who were killed a few days ago, eighteen miles from Franklin. Halted awhile. Proceeded and got to the fort (mouth of French creek) between four and five o'clock in the afternoon—twenty miles—distance from Pittsburgh seventy miles.

13*th.*—Lay encamped drying, cleaning and putting our arms in order.

14*th.*—Mr. Ellicott made a request in writing for me to remain until the arrival of the Cornplanter—stating that he and General Wilkins had sent for him. Agreed.

15th.—Found Fort Franklin in a wretched state of defense. The men in the fort, about twenty, almost all invalids and unable to make any repairs. The officer and his command under great apprehension of an attack from the Indians, who were in considerable numbers about the place, and very insulting. There was good reason to fear mischief from the Six Nations. Two men were murdered the day before we arrived, eighteen miles on the road to Pittsburgh. They had left the fort, and it was supposed had been followed by some of the rascals who are now here. Sensible of the importance of the post, and the connection which we must necessarily have with it, could not think of advancing and leaving it in such bad condition. The garrison for some time past had suffered every inconvenience of a close siege; gates were kept locked day and night. But both gates and pickets served more to cover the enemy, than for any defense of the people within. Accordingly we set to work. A new set of pickets was brought from the woods, and in four days an entire new work erected round the block-house, which we left in tolerable defensible order. Lieutenant Polhemus, who commands here, is of opinion that General Knox intends the fort shall go to wreck—says he has often represented the condition of the place; but no provision had been made for repairing it. The block-house cannot last more than another year or two, and then it will be easier building upon the old British work (which ought to have been done at first) than to repair the present one.

21st.—Took up our march. Crossed French creek in

canoes; the water high and rapid. Marched twelve miles over a fine country. Forded Big Sugar creek waist deep. Encamped on a fine piece of ground.

22*d.* — Marched at seven. The road and land from Franklin to Cussewago excellent. Got to the settlement about three o'clock, where we found some people "forted," as it is called. This the only place where a settlement has been attempted this side of Pittsburgh.

23*d.*—The cattle strayed. Did not get all until eleven o'clock. Marched twelve miles. The country very level and rich.

24*th.*—Marched at eight through pine swamps and bad roads. Came upon French creek, seven miles below Le Bœuf; the country thence up beautiful, and the road good. Joined our people about four o'clock. The distance from Fort Franklin to Le Bœuf, by way of Cussewago, about fifty-five miles. The first part may be made good, but the other will be very difficult until the country is opened. A direct road north from Franklin to Le Bœuf, it is said, will not exceed forty-five miles; but it is yet uncertain what kind of a road that route will afford. Ensign Mehaffy and his detachment we found fenced in. The quarters of the men who were here before us, and the whole place, in the most abominable filthy condition, and one-third of the men ill with the flux. Boats had all been got up safe and unloaded. Stores of every kind deposited in a temporary warehouse. To our very great mortification, I received orders from the Governor suspending our march to Presqu' Isle, and to proceed for the present no farther. This circumstance he laments. The President of the United States has made a special request of it; apprehensive of giving disgust to the Six Nations and extending the sphere of Indian hostilities. Information communicated to the department of war, by Israel Chapin, Indian Agent, stating the great probability of an immediate rupture with the Six Nations if we proceed to Presqu' Isle, has produced this interposition of the President.

25*th.* — The evening of our arrival I received a letter from Israel Chapin, superintendent for the Six Nations, informing me that he had just landed at Presqu' Isle with William Johnson, a British agent, and sixteen chiefs and warriors—a deputation from the Buffalo council, and that they would be with us by two o'clock next day.

26*th.*—Lay encamped under cover of two block-houses. Chapin with his party came in, and saluted us as they passed. We returned the salute with a discharge of the small arms out of the block-houses, and one six-pounder. The Indians encamped down on the river bank.

27*th.*—Met the Indians to hear their message. It was from the Buffalo council "to the armed people at Presqu' Isle and Le Bœuf," and amounted to nothing more or less than an order to remove back. That if we did, they would consider us as friends, but if not, we would not be considered as such. I disliked the presence of Johnson, and felt a very strong disposition to take him into custody. Abused Chapin for coming upon such business. He excused himself by declaring that he had been in a manner compelled. He is an old man. Johnson, the British and Indian agent, acted (slily) as prompter to their old chief who spoke. They denied having sold their land. Told us that the paper (deed) which they signed at Fort Harmar, was thought by them then to be no more than a treaty of peace, and that the goods which were given them they considered as presents. Money, they say they never received any. They were very inquisitive—wished to know if any surveyors were out, and told us to stop every person from going forward. They were told that we were ordered here by our great council, and could not remove from hence until orders came for that purpose.

28*th.*—Chapin and the deputation of Indians left us and returned to Presqu' Isle, where they had left their boats, and would proceed home to Buffalo by water, the way they came.

29*th.*—Wrote to the Governor; inclosed the Indian message and a return of the troops.

30*th.*—Commenced our fatigue with as many hands as we dare venture abroad, getting pickets and block-house logs.

July 1*st.*—Laid off ground on the old French and British site, and began a work sufficient for my command. Four block-houses forming a square, fifty-four feet apart; lower story of house seventeen feet, upper story twenty feet, connected by stout pickets set two and a half feet in the ground and ten and a half out. The seam inside covered by a smaller picket six feet high. Sides of block-houses covered by an angle in the line of pickets extending from the centre of each curtain. Sides of the angles, eighteen feet. The ground handsomely elevated. Washed on the east by Le Bœuf creek, fifteen and twenty yards wide. An extensive cleared plain all around.

2d.—All hands at work. Erected another curtain.

3d.—Inclosed ourselves so as to secure us from any attempts the Indians could make.

4th.—Block-houses up to the square pickets planted on three sides. Rested this day from labor.

5th.—Mr. Nesbitt, Mr. Tannehill and Mr. Gibson, left us to return home. Wrote to the Governor. Employed in getting in timber, leveling the fort, &c.

6th.—Sunday. Rested from labor.

7th, 8th, 9th and 10th.—Employed in raising two buildings; one for the contractor and one for quarter-master's and military stores.

11th and 12th.—Pulled down some old buildings and got up our fourth line of pickets. Filled up two old French cellars that were within our work, and leveled the parade. An Indian express arrived from Franklin with a packet for Mr. Ellicott.

13th.—No fatigue.

17th.—Sent Lieutenant Murphy, the quarter-master, a sergeant and fifteen men, with a six ox team, to bring up our other twelve-pounder from where it was left, seven miles below on the creek. They returned in the afternoon.

18th.—An express came from Franklin with the proceedings of the Buffalo council, held the 4th instant; sent by General Chapin.

19th.—Ensign Mehaffy, with six men, started for Pittsburgh with dispatches, and with orders to bring us on a supply of provisions.

25th.—Obliged to stop our work for want of provisions.

26th.—Discovered three Indians viewing the fort. Sent out a couple of men with a white flag, but the fellows cleared off. This evening received letters from Pitt and one from the Governor, dated 13th of June.

27th.—Heard the report of two cannon toward Presqu' Isle. Sent two men on there to observe if there were any people at that place.

28th.—The men sent to Presqu' Isle returned after being all over the place. Made no discoveries.

Aug. 1*st.*—Dispatched Sergeant Holladay and two men to Pittsburgh, with letters and returns for the Governor. Sent along a draught of our fort, which is now nearly finished. In the second story of each of the western block-houses is mounted a six-pounder; and aloft on each of the eastern houses is a swivel. In the eastern angle, fronting the creek, constructed of heavy timber laid horizontally, we have a battery of two twelve-pounders. Around the curtains are erected banquettes of hewn timber, for the men to mount on to fire through the ports. Men quarter in the block-houses. Officers have two small buildings, for quarter-master and contractor's stores, besides magazine and guard house.

2*d.*—Served the troops with a half a ration of meat only, and a ration and a half of flour. The weather remarkably warm and dry; no rain since the 20th of July.

3*d.*—Extreme sultry weather. The creek totally useless. In the evening appearance of rain at a distance, all round; only a few drops reached us. The wind has continued south-west during this dry spell.

5th.—Cloudy, with wind, but no rain.

6th.—Received a supply of cattle, thirteen head, but miserably poor.

7th.—Last night one of the sentries fired at an Indian very near the fort, about two o'clock in the morning. The garrison was alarmed and under arms.

9th.—The weather changed. Wind from the south-east.

10th.—A steady rain all last evening and this morning. An appearance of more.

11th.—Dry warm weather. A young Indian came express from Cussewago, with information that a Mr. Dickenson had, the day before, been fired upon within one hundred perches of the town, and was wounded in three places, a fourth shot cut the crown of his hat. One of the balls lodged in his body, but there were hopes of his recovery. David Mead begged for some protection.

12th.—Sent a trusty corporal and twelve men to Cussewago to remain there. A man of that place fired on within one hundred and fifty perches of the block-house, and wounded in three places. Nothing of the kind has yet occurred with us. Our sentries have twice in the night fired at objects which they took for Indians, and had us all at our stations. Have no doubt but they were frequently near us. A few days since three fellows appeared on the edge of the plain; I sent a sergeant with a flag toward them, but they made off.

17th.—Sherman Morrow, of the artillery, missing; supposed to have deserted. Our whiskey run out.

18*th.* — Sent a party in search of Morrow; found no trace of him.

19*th.*—A further search made, but no trace or sign.

20*th.*—Set in to rain very early, and continued all day. The creek rose considerably. Morrow came in about two o'clock. Says he was lost; traveled to Lake Erie, was at Presqu' Isle.

23*d.* — In the evening three canoes made out to bring us some flour from Cussewago. Each canoe had five barrels of flour.

24*th.*—The people returned to Cussewago.

25*th.*—Last night a few of our fellows broke open the commissary store, outside the garrison, where the commissioners had a cask of brandy, and carried off the barrel. The men were paraded early. George Depue, John Depue, Walker and Glenn, who were found drunk, were confined. A canteen of the brandy was found in Walker's berth, and a number of the men appeared to have had a small share. Mitchel, of the artillery, called out, that it was damned wrong these men should be confined. I ordered him to be secured. He snatched up a musket, and swore he would shoot the first man who would attempt to lay hands on him. The guard was backward. I advanced toward him; he snapped the piece at me and called to the men to join him. Elliot, one of the prisoners, jumped up to his assistance, and hallooed, "Now's the time, my boys, let's join." Two of the other prisoners endeavored to escape out of the gate. In the mean time Mitchel was loading his piece, and had got it primed, but before it was charged Lieutenant

Murphy, seconded by Sergeant Smith, jumped upon him and disarmed him with considerable difficulty. Mr. Ellicott, who was at the gate at the time, prevented Glenn and Depue from running off. Elliot was the only one who offered to assist Mitchel, and coming up at the time Lieutenant Murphy was engaged with Mitchel, Mr. Murphy settled his business. The troops about this time were under arms, and as soon as possible we had Mitchel in irons. He, however, was not settled, but damned himself if he would not shoot both Murphy and myself. Knowing him to be a dangerous fellow, and having no authority to punish so capital a crime, and keeping him confined with us would have been attended with some risk, I dispatched him off under a corporal and three men, to Fort Franklin, with a request to Captain Heth to keep him secured. The same party of rascals broke down the oven some time in the night, with a view of putting a stop to any more bread being issued.

Lieutenant Miller is blamed for encouraging the breaking of the oven. He has been heard say that it was wrong not to let the men have flour, and went so far as to tell me the men ought to have flour. I mentioned at the time that if he would be answerable for any charge the contractor would bring against me, that his detachment should have flour; but he would not agree to that. When the men have been talking to him of the hardness of the times, he would reply that "they were hard enough," and being exceedingly familiar with all ranks, eating and sleeping with his, sitting down and entering into social conversation with the meanest of them, and drinking with them upon all occasions, notwithstanding my repeated advice to him, this conduct led the other gentlemen to suspect him of being concerned. However, he was very quiet during our fray. About ten o'clock the barrel was found concealed under a heap of brush, with about half the liquor in it.

Lieutenant Hazlewood informs me, that Lieutenant Miller told him he was not doing right in suffering a man of the artillery detachment to bake bread—that *he*, Miller, would not allow one of *his* detachment to do so, if he had ever so many bakers; and mentioned that the man who baked had the curses of all the garrison. Upon further inquiry, we find there were no less than seven concerned in robbing the store.

27*th.*—Ensign Mehaffy, with his party, arrived with thirteen head of very small cattle, and a few horse loads of flour and whiskey—ten in number.

Sept. 3*d.*—Wrote to the Governor and inclosed returns, dated the 1st. Also wrote to General Harmar.

6*th.*—Received a small supply of flour from Cussewago in two canoes. A few days past considerable rain fell. The waters risen five or six inches.

7*th.*—Last night was very cold.

8*th.*—Still colder.

9*th.*—In the morning the whole country white with frost. The officers of the fort have all expressed a desire to see Presqu' Isle, and they have received some encouragement, provided circumstances would allow it. A few days since a letter was received by Mr. Ellicott from Mr. Adlum, who had returned to Fort Franklin from the

Cornplanter. The letter informs us that a treaty was to be held at Buffalo, on the 15th of this month, by the Six Nations, and commissioners appointed by the United States; recommending it to us, by all means, to have a stock of provisions laid in; that if the treaty did not terminate as the Indians wished, that war was inevitable, and that the Cornplanter desired him to tell us not to carry much provision to Le Bœuf, for fear we would have to run of and leave it before long. Before this information came, I had told Mr. Hazlewood we would endeavor to let him go to Presqu' Isle soon. But since, being obliged to employ more of the men in strengthening the fort, and not thinking it prudent to let him select sixteen men to go just upon the day he pleased, he made a formal tender to me of his commission, telling me it was to see the country that he came out, and if he could not have that liberty, he did not choose to serve any longer; he wished to resign his appointment, he would then go where he pleased. I informed him that it was not in my power to accept it; but the next time that I wrote to the Governor, would mention it, and if he approved of the resignation it would be well; but that it was impossible for him to quit until an answer came from the Governor. He replied, that his time would be out against then, and took back the commission.

Besides the information which has been mentioned as received from John Adlum, he tells us also, that a number of Indians had come across the lake to guard the frontiers of the Six Nations. Now it is more than probable that a party of these Indians are constantly about

Presqu' Isle, that place being the grand point in question. And to suffer an officer and fifteen or twenty men to go there at this time, might precipitate a war, which is dreaded. The night after Lieutenant Hazlewood had shown me a list of sixteen men that he wanted to go to the lake with him, and before he wished to quit the service; I took an opportunity of mentioning to him the impropriety of going at this time. Told him that I was as desirous of going as any person could be, but that I was determined never to do a thing that might disgrace me; that probably there was not much danger, but it was uncertain what would happen. That one or two men might not be discovered, but an officer and such a party as he wanted, would very likely be seen and intercepted. Any accident would injure me. He appeared satisfied with this; but to my astonishment, next day he wanted to resign.

11*th.*—Received a letter from Ensign Vanhorn at Cussewago, complaining much of Mr. Wilkins having ordered the two six-pounders from there to Franklin, and begging for some more men. Wrote by the two men to General Wilkins, and inclosed a letter to an inspector for fifty men to be kept at Cussewago; mentioned the hostile determination of the Six Nations, &c.

The pack horses in the employ of the contractor left us two or three days ago, with orders to load at Cussewago with flour, and return as soon as possible. I sent two men along with them, and ordered the corporal who is stationed there, to add four of his men to the party when they started for this place.

15*th.*—No whiskey for the troops.

18*th.*—The pack horses not returned. Whiskey out. Beef very poor. Men complain. A board of officers inspect it, and judge a pound and a half to be no more than right. Sent a man to Cussewago to know what detains the horses.

20*th.*—The express returned from Cussewago and says that the pack horses had arrived there from Franklin the day before yesterday; that the one-half of them were lost; that but five were coming on. By the same express Mr. Mead informs us that on Sunday last he was at Franklin, where he learned that Governor Simco had marched with a party of British troops from Niagara to dispossess Captain Williamson of a handsome establishment which he had made on Lake Ontario, in the State of New York. Yesterday two spies were discovered viewing our fort. This evening the horses arrived. One lost on the road from Cussewago, and the load (salt) was left behind. Matthew Wilson, the express from Cussewago to Pittsburgh, returned; only eight days gone. By him I received letters from the Governor and General Wilkins.

21*st.*—Sent a boat off for corn to Cussewago, and for some more flour. We have had some rain almost every day for three weeks past, but not to affect the creek until now; nor has there been any chance to employ boats since the 4th of July until the present time.

28*th.*—On the morning of this day the meat was complained of. A court was ordered to inspect it. They reported it poor and unwholesome; consequently not fit to be issued. Mr. Ellicott and myself looked at it, but could not agree with the court. The beef was put into store, the best meat picked out, and delivered without a murmur. Some of the officers who were on the court, particularly Lieutenant Miller, scolded his sergeant, and forbid the men taking it, telling them it was all condemned. This encouraged others, and they thinking that the contractor and quarter-master were imposing upon them meat which had not passed inspection, refused the second time. I desired the court to go and give their opinion of what the contractor had selected. They did; and Lieutenant Hazlewood reported that they were of the same opinion as before, that the meat was unfit for use. I examined it, with some other gentlemen, but excepting a few pieces which had been taken out the first time, the rest was as sweet as any meat could be. I waited upon the court, and told them there was no resource (it was all we had), that there might be a chance piece not so good, but that the commissary should pick it; and as I had understood from the men that the poorness was what they complained of, that a pound was not sufficient for the ration, if they would look at it again and report what additional quantity might be allowed, that I would order it. Lieutenant Miller cursed himself and said he would report no more about it, that if they had done right they would have thrown it into the creek. Lieutenant Hazlewood and Ensign Mehaffy were willing to make the report, while they thought that the others refusing, would prevent them. But upon my telling them that any two would be sufficient, or that Lieutenant

Murphy should be ordered in the room of Lieutenant Miller, Lieutenant Hazlewood replied that he or they could not have anything more to do with it; that any other opinion now would be condemning the first report, and therefore declined. This was plain enough, that all the meat was looked upon by the court to be bad and unfit to be issued.

29th.—Two canoes came with seven barrels of whiskey and six barrels of flour. Cold rains. The creek in fine condition for boating.

30th.—Very cold for the season.

Oct. 1st.—Wrote to the Governor and inclosed a return of the troops. My communications to the Governor have been once a month, and oftener when necessary. Men are all in fine health and exercised every day. Our numbers the same as when we set out; that is, four subalterns, a quarter-master, seven sergeants, six corporals, one drummer and ninety-six privates.

2d.—Cold raw east wind, with rain. The creek falls.

3d.—Cold, and considerable rain.

4th.—A light snow in the morning. The day clear and cold.

5th.—Last night a cold rain; cleared up and changed to snow. The country covered about four inches. The woods around have a beautiful appearance. The creek keeps in good boating order. Received a supply of beef this afternoon in time to save the life of our milch cow.

6th.—Hard frost, clear and cold.

7th.—This morning woods white with frost. Considerable ice. The creek keeps up finely.

8th.—Clear and moderate.

9th.—Cloudy and cold, with some rain. Received two messages lately from the Cornplanter. He pretends to be friendly, but says we must leave the place or we will be driven off. The Senecas, of whom he is chief, are a tribe of the Six Nations; they live high up the Allegheny river, and in case of hostilities are much exposed. John Adlum, a surveyor, who was lately at Cornplanter's town, writes from Franklin, and says that a number of the Indians from the British side were with the Cornplanter, and threaten this post. Our movements into this country no doubt have prevented these people from joining the western Indians, and a continuance of peace with them will depend altogether upon the success of General Wayne.

10th.—Very winter-like weather. A canoe with whiskey, flour and salt arrived this afternoon from Cussewago. About dark an express from Pitt, with letters from Mr. Wilkins and Governor Mifflin; a copy of an act for maintaining my command, which is to be increased to one hundred and thirty men; orders to re-enlist.

11th.—Fine day.

12th.—A canoe with twelve barrels flour. Answered Mr. Wilkins' letter by Matthew Wilson.

13th.—Pleasant weather. The Indian summer here. Frosty nights. The creek begins to fall.

14th, 15th, 16th and 17th.—Remarkable fine days and clear, dry, frosty nights.

18th.—Set out with twelve men, accompanied by Mr. Ellicott, on a visit to Presqu' Isle. Went by what is called the grubbed road. It seems that after the French had opened the Indian path from Presqu' Isle to Le Bœuf, and wagoned considerably upon it, they found that it was some miles about, and that they had commenced the road upon a wrong plan; that it would take more labor to keep it in repair than would open one upon a straight line, notwithstanding, near five miles was cross-way'd, and no road can be had from the lake to French creek with less. However, the direct course was found, and they began with cutting it out forty feet in width, which was pursued from the ford on Mill creek all the way to Le Bœuf. They also erected several large bridges, thirty, forty, fifty feet in length, across hollow ways and deep runs, overlaid with puncheons about eighteen feet long. But there does not appear to have been any cross-way done. Though it will certainly want as much as the old road, yet there has been a vast deal of digging. The course being straight, the way unavoidably led up and down every little precipice that presented, but all these were leveled; every point and sidling ground was made easy, and is still so. But the bridging has decayed and fallen down in the centre. But what appears the most extraordinary is the grubbing. The country through is covered with a vast deal of heavy timber, notwithstanding every tree, from one end to the other, has been taken up by the roots and rolled out. However, it does not appear that ever they made use of this road; for when the trees were taken up the holes were yet so deep as to make it bad for a horse. No doubt the road was intended for a grand way. It is now grown up with small wood, but the largest to be seen does not exceed six inches. It is supposed that eight men could cut out a mile in a day. After that there must be a cross-way for four or five miles, and some of the old bridges repaired, the root holes filled; in places ditching would be very serviceable. The distance is between ten and twelve miles. We left Le Bœuf about eight o'clock and were at Presqu' Isle about two. Spent the afternoon along the lake and looking round the old fort. The situation grand. A perfect seaboard prospect, and one of the most beautiful. The bank along the lake is high and dry, perhaps about forty feet. Six or eight feet of the bottom is a slate rock. For a mile and a half, the country round the fort has been cleared, but is now grown up with young chestnut timber. Even within the fort the brush is so thick that it is difficult passing. There have been very fine gardens here; parsnips, currant bushes and many other things growing wild. The old fort a regular pentagon; about one thousand feet round the parapet, overlooking and commanding the basin or harbor, and affording a boundless view of the lake. It has been a handsome but light work; neither ditch nor parapet are sufficiently large. Five feet is about the base and height. The ditch perhaps three feet, and four in width. There must have been some other defense, pickets or fraising. The walls of the magazine are yet good, and the well wants nothing but cleaning out. The chimneys of the houses, some brick, others stone, are still standing; and the walls of a stone house, down by the old mill, are yet tolerably good.

19*th*.—Left Presqu' Isle about seven o'clock. Returned by the old cart road. Got back to Le Bœuf about two o'clock. The old road appears now to be dryer than the grubbed one. Indeed in many places where the cross-waying is, the ground does not appear to want it. The country upon both roads is wet; will make fine grazing farm. Many excellent plantations might be made. There is a variety of soil and timber. Some places and large bottoms, are as rich as any land that can be found; the timber, walnut, sugar-tree and shell-bark hickory. But the greater part is but middling, except for pasture; the timber, hemlock or spruce pine, and beech. Along the lake, for two or three miles back, the country is high and dry, a light soil, chestnut and oak of a large growth. Although we had severe frosts at Le Bœuf since the middle of last month, and almost constant, we could not discover that there had been any at Presqu' Isle, at least nothing appeared touched, not even the pea vine. This temperature of the weather must be owing to the large body of water which had received in the summer a degree of heat not easily chilled; consequently until that warmth in the lake is overcome, the air around will be influenced and kept temperate. The same cause is operating now upon the air. On the contrary, in the spring, keeps back the season and all vegetation. It is from this cause, I suppose, that apple orchards and some other fruits are so certain upon the lakes. Letters from Pitt inform us that in August General Wayne had given the western Indians a severe drubbing. This will be very apt to quiet the Six Nations, the instigations of the British to the contrary notwithstanding.

20th.—The French creek fallen near three feet since the last rains. Two men from the landing, ten miles down, left their boat and canoes there. They came up for assistance. The creek too low for their boat. The weather changing. Considerable rain fell this afternoon.

21st.—Rain, off and on, all night, with a strong south wind. About daylight shifted to the north-west. Thick squalls of snow all day, with hail.

22d.—Cold and like for snow. The creek rose last night a few inches. The keel boat, after putting part of her load into canoes, made out to reach this place.

23d.—Mr. Ellicott set out in the Mohawk boat for Fort Pitt.

24th.—Set in to snow early in the morning; continued all day, night, and the most part of next day.

25th.—In the afternoon changed to a light rain. Had the ground been frozen and the snow not so wet, we would have had it twelve or fourteen inches deep. It was six inches this morning.

26th.—Sunday. Very foggy, cold and wet.

27th.—The snow all gone; weather moderate; creek rising. Robert M'Near, with a party of men, came on to open the road to Presqu' Isle.

28th.—Cloudy and raw weather. The creek in excellent boating order.

29th.—Moderate rain all day and most part of the night.

30*th*.—Partly clear; no rain to-day.

31*st*.—Rained last night and moderately all day. The creek higher than we have ever seen it before.

Nov. 1*st*.—Cleared off pleasant.

2*d*.—Fine day.

3*d*.—Hard rain all last night, and violent storms of wind and rain all day. The creek over its banks.

4*th*.—A constant rain all day and night.

5*th*.—Cleared away—moderate.

6*th*.—Pleasant, dry day; the creek beginning to fall.

7*th*.—Dry. The creek not yet within its banks.

8*th*.—A light rain off and on all last night; wet drizzling rain all day. The creek fell within its banks.

9*th*.—Sunday. Cloudy and raw.

10*th*.—Some snow and rain. This afternoon received instructions from the Governor to re-enlist the detachment.

11*th*.—Read the Governor's letter to the men.

12*th*.—Find that the men don't incline to enlist for six months. They are naked and dispirited, and no money among us to tempt them. Concluded upon engaging volunteers for a month. Cold and snow.

13*th*.—Snowed hard all day. Find a difficulty in persuading any of the men to stay even for one month.

14*th*.—Constant snow. Engaged as many as nineteen volunteers to stay and help the garrison until a relief comes on, which is promised before the 1st of January.

15*th*.—Moderate, with some snow. The creek falling fast, owing to the frosty nights.

16*th*.—Sunday. Deep snow last night; snowed hard all day. Preparing to start down the river.

17*th.*—Left Ensign Mehaffy, Quarter-master M'Cutcheon, and nineteen men, and embarked with the rest of my command in boats for Pitt. Hard snow all day. The creek tolerably full of water and difficult to navigate, owing to the great number of trees which fill up the channel. Two of our canoes overset and a couple of rifles lost. The day very cold; many of the men wet, being obliged frequently to jump into the water, and some thrown out. Halted six miles short of Cussewago.

18*th.*—Got under way very early, and was at Cussewago for breakfast; remained all day fixing the craft and repairing a keel boat which we found necessary to take along.

19*th.*—Fine day. Took the detachment that was at Cussewago on board the keel boat, with myself and a few men out of the canoes, and left that place about nine o'clock; got to Franklin about three without any difficulty.

20*th.*—Drew provisions at Franklin and cooked breakfast. The day very wet and cold. Got down within twelve or fifteen miles of Stump creek.

21*st.*—Very cold snowy day. The Allegheny high. Lay this night a few miles below Green's.

22*d.*—Reached Pittsburgh.

24*th.*—The Governor had left this but a few days. I found a new arrangement of the detachment intended for my command; that a Mr. Buchanan had been appointed captain, and already recruiting; had raised a number of men for Le Bœuf. Doctor Kennedy appointed surgeon to the detachment, and a flattering letter for me, with the appointment of Major. This was pleasing information, as I had some doubts about getting recruits in time to relieve Ensign Mehaffy. Our leaving Le Bœuf so soon as we did, was that we might have the more time to enlist men, as we found it impossible to persuade any of them to engage there. No money to be had for the men.

25th and 26th.—Discharged the men.

Dec. 13*th.*—Started up Captain Buchanan for Le Bœuf with thirty-five recruits. The party lay four days on the opposite side of the river, waiting for pack horses; four only were provided. Doctor Kennedy was obliged to remain behind for want of a conveyance for his baggage.

Jan. 4*th,* 1795.—Ensign Mehaffy and Ensign M'-Cutcheon, with the men left at Le Bœuf, arrived.

5*th.*—Discharged the remains of our command.

11*th.*—Lieutenant Hazlewood resigned his commission and took abrupt departure for Philadelphia.

Have leave of absence, with liberty, if necessary, to visit Philadelphia.

May 31*st.*—As every difficulty seems to have ceased, and my young family not in a situation to be left, have recommended the Governor to transfer the command and the duty of escorting the commissioners in laying out the towns, the only business now to be done, to Captain Buchanan, who appears well qualified for this service.

APPENDICES.

APPENDIX No. I.

LETTERS.

IN illustration of the foregoing Journal of Major Denny, it was thought that the letters of his friend and commander, written during the same period, on the same topics, might be interesting. With that view, the family of General Harmar kindly intrusted to us his whole military correspondence. Many letters were selected for publication for the reference they make to persons and occurrences there mentioned, and some indeed, for their own merit and their public value.

Lieut.-Col. Josiah Harmar to Thomas Mifflin, President of Congress.

NEW YORK, January 19th, 1784.

SIR—I have the honor to inform your Excellency that I arrived here this day. I left Annapolis the morning of the 15th, in the stage. On my arrival in Baltimore, I hired a sleigh, which conveyed me that night as far as Leggett's. Here I found a stage. On the morning of the 16th I took passage in it, and that night gained the head of Elk. Fortunately I here met his Excellency the Minister of France, who delivered me his dispatches. On the morning of the 17th, before day, I left the head of Elk in the stage, and gained Philadelphia in the evening. I instantly waited upon the honorable Mr. Morris, and produced to him the act of Congress, directing him to supply me with cash to bear my necessary expenses. He gave me one hundred and three pounds fifteen shillings cash, and a credit upon Paris. I then waited upon his Excellency the President of the State, and delivered him his letters. I engaged a sleigh to go on with me the next morning—lodged at your house that night—left the ladies, Mrs. Suckey and Miss Beccy well. Sarago awakened me before day on Sunday morning, the 18th, and the sleigh being at the door, I was conveyed by fresh horses with great celerity that night as far as Newark, eighty-six miles. On the 19th, in the morning, the day being excessively stormy, I left Newark, and with great difficulty in the passage of the North river, arrived in New York that evening. I then instantly went on board the French packet, and was introduced to Monsieur D'Aboville, the captain, the Minister having given me a letter to him. I shall use every exertion at L'Orient to get forward to Paris and deliver the ratification of the treaty in time.

I have the honor to be, with the greatest esteem and affection,

Your Excellency's most obedient servant,

JOS. HARMAR.

His Excellency, THOMAS MIFFLIN, Esq., President of Congress, Annapolis.

Same to same.

PARIS, April 8th, 1784.

SIR—I had the honor of addressing your Excellency on the 21st of February last, the day we left Sandyhook. I now have the pleasure to inform you of my safe arrival at L'Orient on the 25th ult., after a rough and stormy passage of thirty-three days. When we were seventeen days out we were near Cape Finisterre, which gave us every reason to expect our voyage would be completed in twenty days; but on the European coast, the strong eastwardly winds set in, which detained us a fortnight longer. Immediately upon my landing at L'Orient, I hired a voiture and went day and night by post—arrived at Paris on the 29th—delivered the dispatches Congress was pleased to intrust me with to his Excellency, Doctor Franklin, that evening, and took the necessary receipt for the same, agreeably to the private instructions received from your Excellency. In conversation the day before yesterday with Doctor Franklin, I informed him that I should send your Excellency advice of the time of my arrival and delivery of the public dispatches, and begged to know whether he thought any difficulties were likely to arise on account of the treaty not being exchanged agreeably to the stipulated time. The doctor gave me for answer, that he had written some time since to Laurens on the subject, and desired him to inform Mr. Hartley (the British commissioner) that the reason of the treaty not having arrived, must be owing to the inclemency of the season in America; and that if it should be judged necessary by the court of Great Britain, he thought that Mr. Laurens would do well to enter into an agreement for an extension of time. Mr. Hartley was accordingly informed of the above circumstances by Mr. Laurens, and his reply to Mr. Laurens was, that the court were satisfied with the reasons advanced, and that an extension of time was unnecessary. I therefore have the satisfaction to inform your Excellency *all is well.*

The Marquis de la Fayette intends sailing for America about the latter end of next month, and has very politely offered me a passage in the same vessel with him, which I shall embrace with pleasure. I had the honor of delivering your Excellency's letter to him; he desires me to present you his particular compliments.

For British politics, I beg leave to refer your Excellency to the inclosed papers, which the Marquis has been obliging enough to favor me with Mr. Pitt is prime minister, and Mr. Fox has gained the Westminster election. I have the honor to be, &c.,

JOS. HARMAR.

P. S.—No intelligence as yet of the arrival of Lieut. Colonel Franks at London with the triplicate of the treaty.

Same to same.

LONDON, May 5th, 1784.

SIR—Colonel Franks, whom I left in Paris, arrived about twelve days after me, and delivered his dispatches in London. The attention of the British nation seems to be at present principally engaged in the issue of the Westminister election. Your Excellency will be pleased to receive the inclosed papers. Fox and no Fox, is all the cry.

In the letter which I had the honor of writing you from Paris, I informed your Excellency that Mr. Fox had gained his point; but I was then mistaken; however, it is now beyond a doubt that he will succeed. I shall return to France the 12th of this month, and expect the Marquis de la Fayette, whom I shall accompany. Will be ready to sail about the 1st June. I have the honor to be, &c.,

JOS. HARMAR.

Same to John Dickinson, Esq.

FORT M'INTOSH, January 15, 1785.

SIR—A few days since the treaty commenced, and I believe will be satisfactorily concluded against the latter end of this mouth; although the chiefs of the Wyandots, Chippewas, Delawares and Ottawas (which are the nations that are assembled here), in a speech which they delivered at the council-fire yesterday, held out an idea to the continental commissioners, that they still looked upon the lands which the United States held by the treaty with Great Britain, as their own. But the commissioners have answered them in a high tone; the purport of which was, that as they had adhered during the war to the King of Great Britain, they were considered by us as a conquered people, and therefore had nothing to expect from the United States, but must depend altogether upon their lenity and generosity. This spirited answer, it is supposed, will have the desired effect.

The State commissioners will not have the least difficulty in transacting their business, which lays with the Wyandot and Delaware nations.

I have the honor, &c.,

JOS. HARMAR,

Lt.-Col. Com'g. 1st Am. Reg't.

His Excellency JOHN DICKINSON, Esq., President the Honorable the Supreme Executive Council.

Same to John Armstrong, Secretary to Council, Philadelphia.

FORT M'INTOSH, May 24, 1785.

SIR—Inclosed be pleased to find a list of the officers who are willing to continue upon the present establishment.

Names and rank of the officers of the Pennsylvania line, who are at present in the service of the United States, and are willing to remain upon the establishment, agreeably to the Act of Congress of the 7th April, 1785.

NAMES.	RANK.	DATES OF APPOINTMENT.
Josiah Harmar,	Lieut.-Colonel,	12th August, 1784.
Walter Finney,	Captain,	12th August, 1784.
David Ziegler,	Captain,	12th August, 1784.
William M'Curdy,	Captain,	12th August, 1784.
Thomas Douglas,	Captain,	12th August, 1784.
Joseph Aston,	Lieutenant,	12th August, 1784.
Stewart Herbert,	Lieutenant,	12th August, 1784.
Ercureus Beatty,	Lieutenant,	12th August, 1784.
Thomas Doyle,	Lieutenant,	12th August, 1784.
John Armstrong,	Ensign,	12th August, 1784.
Ebenezer Denny,	Ensign,	12th August, 1784.
Nathan M'Dowell,	Ensign,	21st October, 1784.
John M'Dowell,	Surgeon,	12th August, 1784.
Richard Allison,	Mate,	12th August, 1784.

Your most obedient and very humble servant,

JOS. HARMAR.

Same to General Knox.

FORT M'INTOSH, June 1, 1785.

SIR—The Wyandot and Delaware nations have brought in their prisoners (fifteen in number), agreeably to the treaty, and the hostages left in my possession are now dismissed. These nations are friendly. The Shawanees make great professions of peace. The Cherokees are hostile, and have killed and scalped seven people near the mouth of the Scioto, about three hundred and seventy miles from hence.

Speeches have been continually sending by the British, from Detroit to the Indians, since the treaty, and I have good intelligence that several traders have been amongst them, using all means to make them entertain a bad opinion of the Americans. One Simon Girty, I am informed, has been at Sandusky for that purpose.

Your most obedient servant,

JOS. HARMAR.

Same to Colonel Francis Johnston.

FORT M'INTOSH, June 21, 1785.

DEAR JOHNSTON—I am hourly expecting the arrival of the commissioners, as I understand a treaty is to be held at Post St. Vincent.

Between you and me, my dear Johnston, vain and ineffectual will all treaties be, until we take possession of the posts. One treaty held at Detroit would give dignity and consequence to the United States, and answer every purpose.

The British have been sending speeches among the Indians, continually, since the treaty was held at this place, the purport of which, you may be assured, was for no good. The first grand object, therefore (in my humble opinion), would be to dispossess them, and then we shall have the Indians friendly to our interest. The nations down the river have killed and scalped several adventurers who have settled on their lands.

I wish you were here to view the beauties of Fort M'Intosh. What think you of pike of 25 lbs.; perch of 15 to 20 lbs.; cat-fish of 40 lbs.; bass, pickerel, sturgeon, &c., &c.? You would certainly enjoy yourself. It is very fortunate there is such abundance of fish, as the contractor for this place, some time past, has failed in his supplies of beef. This would be a glorious season for Colonel Wood, or any extravagant lover of strawberries; the earth is most luxuriantly covered with them—we have them in such plenty that I am almost surfeited with them; the addition of fine rich cream is not lacking.

JOS. HARMAR.

Same to General Mifflin.

FORT M'INTOSH, June 25, 1785.

DEAR GENERAL—I am honored with your letter of the 7th May last, sent me by Major Prevost, of Pittsburgh. The pitiful reduction of the officers' pay, I am at a loss to account for.

The commissioners are daily expected for the treaty on the Wabash. In confidence, my dear General, I'll assure you, in my opinion, all these treaties will be ineffectual. Possessing the British posts ought to be the first grand object, then a treaty at Detroit would answer all purposes. The United States will never have either dignity or consequence among the Indians, until this is effected.

The official letter, inclosing you Dr. Franklin's receipt for the delivery of the treaty, &c., I hope you have received.

P. S.—The Indians down the river, viz., the Shawanees, Miamis, Cherokees and Kickapoos, have killed and scalped several adventurers—settlers on their lands.

Same to General Knox.

FORT M'INTOSH, July 1, 1785.

SIR—The cockade we wear is the union (black and white.) Perhaps it will be necessary to have a national one; if so, be pleased to send me your directions about the color. And if you should approve of a *national march* (without copying French or British), I should be glad to be instructed.

Same to same.

FORT M'INTOSH, July 16th, 1785.

SIR—On the 11th instant, I was informed that three chiefs (and twenty-five Indians) of the Six Nations had arrived at Fort Pitt, and wished very much to speak with the commanding officer. Agreeably to their desire, I rode up to Pittsburgh and met them in council; when to my great surprise the Cornplanter, the principal chief, had the original articles of the treaty which was concluded with them at Fort Stanwix, along with him, and toward the close of the speech, said they were burthensome, and wished to deliver them up. I have the honor to inclose to you their speech and my answer to it.

It is reported that a Mr. Brant has lately arrived from London, who (with the commanding officer of the British in that quarter) has informed the Six Nations that their lands were never ceded to the Americans by the King of Great Britain. In consequence of which, these chiefs complain of being accused by their nations of treachery, and say they are in danger of their own people.

They have left Fort Pitt highly satisfied to appearance with the answer to their speech; but as long as the British keep possession of the posts, it is very evident that all treaties held by us with the Indians, will have but little weight with them.

Your most obedient servant,

JOS. HARMAR.

The Honorable Major-General KNOX, Secretary at War, New York.

Same to Hon. Arthur Lee.

PHILADELPHIA, December 28, 1785.

DEAR SIR—The bearer, Doctor Wilkins, has some thoughts of contracting to supply the regiment with rations. From the recommendation of General Irvine of Carlisle, who offers to be his security for the performance of his engagements, I am induced to believe that he will use every exertion to please both officers and men. If, therefore, the terms which he may give in should be lower or as low as other applicants, I would beg leave to recommend him to your notice.

Same to General Knox.

PHILADELPHIA, May 7th, 1786.

I have just received the inclosed letters from Captain Finney at the Miami. The intelligence is truly alarming, and notwithstanding the fair reports of the commissioners concerning the peaceable disposition of the Indians, I am well convinced all their treaties are farcical, as long as the British possess the posts. The party of Indians alluded to in this letter as a reconnoitering party from Detroit, were discovered by Captain Strong near the garrison at M'Intosh. Upon a party being sent out, they fled, being about twenty in number. Duncan and Wilson's reports I have not inclosed, as they contain some reflections on General Butler, particularly mentioning his small influence among the different tribes of Indians. If you wish to see them, I shall inclose them per next opportunity.

Same to General Knox.

FORT PITT, July 3, 1786.

SIR—One John Bull (called by the Indians Shebo,) informs me that he left Detroit on the 29th April, in company with one hundred Moravian Indians, men, women and children, and are at present about four miles from Cuyahoga—that they have crossed the lake with the intention to settle near their old towns on the Muskingum, where a party of the Indians were formerly massacred; but as they are too late in the season for planting, their intention is to remain and hunt near Cuyahoga until fall.

He further informs me, that on the 7th ultimo Commodore Grant, with Captain M'Kee, Simon Girty and Matthew Elliott, with forty Indians, among whom were the Half-King, Baubee, Koon and Gusheways, a chief of the Ottawas and Chippewas, sailed from the mouth of Sandusky river for Canada. They gave out that they were going as far as Quebec, with a design to purchase the lands on the north side of the lake from the Indians, but it was generally supposed they were going no farther than Niagara to a treaty which Sir John Johnson (who was there) had invited them and the Six Nations to.

These Moravian Indians (among whom Bull resides), by what I can learn, have ever been friendly to the United States.

Same to Captain Finney, commanding officer of the Miami.

FORT HARMAR, at the mouth of the Muskingum,
July 27, 1786.

SIR—I intend to appoint Mr. Denny Adjutant to the regiment, for which purpose he must repair here as soon as possible.

JOS. HARMAR.

Same to General Knox.

FORT HARMAR, August 10, 1786.

SIR—Since I had the honor of addressing you on the 4th instant, Ensign Denny has arrived from the Miami, and brings intelligence that an expedition is forming under the command of General Clark, and authorized by the State of Virginia, to attack the Indians.

Extract from the Order Book of Lieut.-Col. Comm't. Josiah Harmar.

GARRISON ORDERS.

FORT HARMAR, at the mouth of the Muskingum,
October 3, 1786.

Ensign Denny is appointed Adjutant of the regiment, and is accordingly to be obeyed and respected.

Same to Thomas Mifflin, Speaker of the House of Assembly, Pennsylvania.

FORT PITT, March 17, 1787.

The Muskingum river is about one hundred and eighty miles distant from here, at the mouth of which the fort stands. I have often wished during the hunting season (viz., the months of November and December), for the honor of your company at my post. Venison, bear, turkey, geese, ducks, &c., &c. You should have regaled upon the greatest abundance.

Be pleased to view the inclosed plan of the remains of some ancient works on the Muskingum, taken by a captain of mine, with his explanations.

Various are the conjectures concerning these fortifications. From their regularity I conceive them to be the works of some civilized people. Who they were, I know not. Certain it is, the present race of savages are strangers to any thing of the kind.

Same to Major Hamtramck.

FORT HARMAR, April 7, 1787

SIR—Permit me to congratulate you upon your promotion. I observe that the council of appointment have directed that you take rank from the 21st October, 1786. Lieut. Bradford is captain of artillery; Lieut. Smith, a captain of infantry; Ensign Peters, a lieutenant of infantry; Ensign Schuyler, lieutenant of artillery, and Matthew Ernest, lieutenant of infantry; the latter I conceive to be a new appointment.

Same to General Knox, Secretary at War.

FORT HARMAR, May 14, 1787.

During my short stay at the Falls, I endeavored to make myself acquainted with the politics of the country, and to gain as perfect a knowledge as I possibly could, of what was going forward amongst the inhabitants of Kentucky. The free navigation of the Mississippi is the general subject of discourse amongst them. The inhabitants to the westward of the Allegheny mountains are unanimously opposed to its being closed; if such a measure should take place they will look upon it as the greatest grievance, as the prosperity of the western world depends entirely upon this outlet.

Kentucky at present, by the returns of their county lieutenants, musters five thousand fighting men. You will please to judge what a flourishing country this must be in the course of a few years, from the number of emigrants to it. Curiosity prompted me to order the officer of the day (Lieut. Denny) to take an account of the number of the boats, &c., which passed this garrison from the 10th of October, 1786, until the 12th of May, 1787: one hundred and seventy-seven boats, two thousand six hundred and eighty-nine souls, thirteen hundred and thirty-three horses, seven hundred and sixty-six cattle, and one hundred and two wagons, have passed Muskingum, bound for Limestone and the Rapids. If Congress should be of opinion that it will be expedient to shut the navigation, I think a respectable post at the mouth of the Ohio, or the Wabash, will be necessary; otherwise, from all appearances, the people will become so strong, in the course of a little time, as to force a trade, at all events.

Same to same.

CAMP AT VINCENNES, August 7, 1787.

Post Vincennes is a very considerable village, situate upon the Wabash, about one hundred and twenty miles from its mouth. It contains nearly four hundred houses (log and bark), out-houses, barns, &c. The number of inhabitants about nine hundred (souls) French, and about four hundred (souls) Americans. Monsieur Vincennes, the French officer from whom it derives its name, I am informed, was here and commenced the settlement sixty years ago.

I have the honor to acknowledge the receipt of your letter of 1st June, inclosing the contract of Mr. O'Hara with the Board of Treasury for the supply of the troops, &c.

Same to same.

KASKASKIA, November 24, 1787.

SIR—I marched on the 9th August from the post (Vincennes), with a subaltern, Ensign M'Dowell, and thirty men, through the prairies, and arrived at Kaskaskia on the 16th of the same month. Our march was very fatiguing, as the weather was excessively warm, and water very bad and scarce on the route. The distance is about one hundred and sixty miles; the French call it eighty leagues. I was accompanied by two Indians (Pachan, a Miami chief, and his comrade), who hunted and supplied the party with meat (buffalo and deer), both on the march and upon our return.

The prairies are very extensive, natural meadows, covered with long grass; one in particular, which we crossed, was eight leagues in breadth. They run, in general, from north to south, and like the ocean, as far as the eye can see, the view is terminated by the horizon. Here and there a copse of wood is interspersed. They are free from brush and underwood, and not the least vestige of their ever having been cultivated. The country is excellent for grazing, and abounds in buffalo, deer, bear, &c. It is a matter of speculation to account for the formation of the prairies. The western side of the Wabash is overflown in the spring, for several miles.

On the 17th, I was visited by the magistrate and principal inhabitants of Kaskaskia, welcoming us upon our arrival. Baptiste De Coigne, the chief of the Kaskaskia Indians, paid me a visit in the afternoon, and delivered me a speech expressive of the greatest friendship for the United States; and at the same time presented me with one of the calumets, or pipes of peace, which is now sent on. Some of the Peoria Indians likewise visited me. The Kaskaskias, Peorias, Cahokia and Mitchi tribes compose the Illinois Indians. They are almost extinct at present, not exceeding forty or fifty, total.

Kaskaskia is a handsome little village, situate on a river of the same name, which empties into the Mississippi at two leagues distant from it. It is one hundred and five miles from the mouth of the Ohio; the situation low and unhealthy, and subject to inundation. The inhabitants are French, and much of the same class as those at Post Vincennes; their number is one hundred and ninety-one, old men and young. Having but very little time to spare, I left Lieutenant M'Dowell with the party at Kaskaskia, and on the 18th set out, accompanied by Mr. Tardiveau and the gentlemen of the village, for Cahokia. We gained Prairie du Rocher, a small village five French leagues distant from Kaskaskia, where we halted for the night.

On the 19th we passed through St. Philip, a trifling village three leagues distant from Prairie du Rocher, and dined at La Bellefontaine, six leagues farther. La Bellefontaine is a small stockade, inhabited altogether by Americans, who have seated themselves there without authority. It is a beautiful situation, fine fertile land, no taxation; and the inhabitants have abundance to live upon. They were exceedingly alarmed when I informed them of their precarious state respecting a title to their possessions, and have now sent on a petition to Congress by Mr. Tardiveau. On the same day we passed another small stockade, called Grand Ruisseau, inhabited by the same sort of Americans as those at La Bellefontaine, and arrived at Cahokia that evening. Cahokia is a village nearly of the size as that of Kaskaskia, and inhabited by the same kind of people; their number two hundred and thirty-nine, old men and young. I was received with the greatest hospitalitp by the inhabitants. There was a decent submission and respect in their behavior. Cahokia is distant from Kaskaskia twenty-two French leagues, which is about fifty miles.

On the 21st, in consequence of an invitation from Monsieur Cruzat, the Spanish commandant at St. Louis, we crossed the Mississippi, and were very politely entertained by him. After dinner, we returned to Cahokia.

St. Louis (nicknamed Pancour) is much the handsomest and genteelest village I have seen on the Mississippi. It is about four miles distant from Cahokia, and five leagues above it the river Missouri unites with the Mississippi. The inhabitants are of the same sort as before described, excepting that they are more wealthy. About twenty regular Spanish troops are stationed here.

Exclusive of the intruders already described, there are about thirty more Americans settled on the rich fertile bottoms of the Mississippi, who are likewise petitioning by this conveyance.

On the 23d, I passed by the ruins of Fort Chartres, which is one league above the Prairie du Rocher, and situate on the Mississippi. It was built of stone, and must have been a considerable fortification formerly, but the post next the river has been carried away by the floods, and it is of no consequence at present. I staid about a quarter of an hour, but had not time to view it minutely, as it was all a thicket within. Several iron pieces of cannon are here at present, and also at the different villages. This evening I returned to Kaskaskia.

On the 24th, Monsieur Peruse, the Spanish commandant at St. Genevieve, sent me an invitation to pay him a visit. We crossed the Mississippi accordingly; were politely entertained, and after dinner returned to Kaskaskia.

St. Genevieve (nicknamed Misēre) is a village much inferior in every respect to St. Louis; it is about four miles (including the passage of the Mississippi,) from Kaskaskia. About eight or ten regular Spanish troops are stationed here.

We arrived, on the 7th of October, at the rapids of the Ohio. The distance from Post Vincennes is about one hundred and thirty miles. We saw no Indians nor signs of Indians. We had an action with five buffalo, who would have run through the column had they not been prevented by the men facing and firing a volley at them. They killed three of them.

I am happy to hear of General St. Clair's appointment as Governor of the Western Territory, as it will add to the dignity of Congress.

Same to General St. Clair.

FORT HARMAR, November 25th, 1787.

MY DEAR GENERAL—I am happy, very happy, to hear by Captain Beatty of your appointment to the government of the Western Territory. Permit me sincerely to congratulate you upon it.

Congress have been pleased to honor me with a brevet commission of Brigadier-General. I should be justly accused of ingratitude was I not to thank my old friend for his friendship and influence upon this occasion. I shall ever hold them in most grateful remembrance.

Mrs. Harmar sends her kind compliments to you. Major Duncan left here yesterday for the Falls.

I have the honor to be, my dear General,
Your obliged friend and humble servant,
JOS. HARMAR.

His Excellency ARTHUR ST. CLAIR, Esq., President of Congress.

Same to Major Wyllys, commanding at the Rapids of the Ohio.

FORT HARMAR, December 6, 1787.

DEAR MAJOR—General Knox has written to me, that there are some apprehensions that Brant, with a number of confederated Indians, may be hostile. It will therefore be expedient that each post should be upon its guard. You will please to inform Major Hamtramck of it.

Yours, sincerely,
JOS. HARMAR.

P. S.—You will perceive by the inclosed paper the inflammatory letter written by Captain Sullivan to the Spanish Minister. If he should set his foot on the western territory, I have orders to seize and confine him.

Same to General Knox.

FORT HARMAR, December 9, 1787.

I have continued to order the officer of the day to take an account of the people emigrating down the river. From the 1st of June to this day there passed this garrison, bound for Kentucky, 146 boats, 3,196 souls, 1,371 horses, 165 wagons, 191 cattle, 245 sheep, and 24 hogs.

Same to Captain Heart, commanding officer at Venango.

FORT HARMAR, December 19, 1787.

SIR—Your letters of the 12th and 25th June inform me of the peaceable disposition of the Indians at that period; but my latest letters from the War Office inform me, that there is great reason to suppose that the Indians will confederate under Brant, and that hostilities will commence on their part.

General St. Clair is appointed Governor of the Western Territory, and is to hold a grand treaty with them sometime next spring. In the meantime the utmost precaution is necessary on the part of the officers commanding at the different posts in order to guard against surprises.

You wish a name for your fortress. As it is in the State of Pennsylvani, let it be named *Fort Franklin.*

Same to General Knox.

FORT HARMAR, January 10, 1788.

On the 6th of last month I wrote to Major Wyllys at the Rapids of the Ohio, and inclosed him a copy of the inflammatory letter written by Mr. Sullivan to his Excellency the Spanish Minister, and informed him, that if the said Sullivan should be found in the federal territory, I had orders to seize and confine him.

It is the universal sentiment of the inhabitants westward of the Allegheny mountains, that they ought to enjoy the free navigation of the Mississippi, but I very much question whether the Kentucky, Cumberland people, and those below, will have the audacity to attempt to seize upon the Natchez and New Orleans. Such an enterprise would certainly be a disgrace to the United States. I know of no cannon and the necessary apparatus which they have in their possession to carry on such an expedition. I shall transmit the duplicate of your letter of the 14th November and a copy of Sullivan's * letter to Major Brown and to Major Wyllys (as soon as the weather permits), with strict orders to watch closely and know the designs of those fellows down the river. I shall likewise give him directions to send an officer and two or three confidential persons to Franklin and Kentucky under pretense of exploring the country, in order that we may be made acquainted with their intended manœuvres. It appears to me that this matter will not be so serious as is imagined, but rather an evidence of the mutinous disposition of Sullivan and an insignificant banditti. Sullivan was the principal ringleader in the mutiny of the Pennsylvania line during the late war, and it is high time to put an end to his career. If he can be apprehended in Franklin,

* Captain Sullivan, formerly in Moylan's dragoons.

or out of the federal territory, I should suppose myself justifiable in giving orders for that purpose.

We have had a remarkable spell of hard weather here ever since Christmas. The thermometer has been sixteen degrees below the zero point. The river is now fast bound with ice. As soon as the weather will permit, I shall send Major Wyllys the necessary orders respecting Sullivan and his adherents. If from the intellignce which I have given you respecting the inundation of the lands at the mouth of the Ohio, it should be judged advisable to fix upon some other tract of country to satisfy the claims of the late army, wherever Congress may be pleased to pitch upon said tract, I shall (agreeably to your directions) station an adequate body of troops in the vicinity thereof, in order that the surveyors may be protected in the execution of their business. I beg leave to observe that Fort M'Intosh is by no means tenable. The small party stationed there at present I propose to order to Fort Pitt, to receive stores, clothing, &c., and that the officer commanding there may forward them, also, any dispatches which may arrive from the War Office. It should have been evacuated last spring, but for the orders received from you countermanding the same. I shall direct Major Doughty to proceed there with a party early in the spring, and to dismantle it. The fort is built of hewn timber; it will be easy to raft it to this post, where it will be of service. If a communication should be wanting to Lake Erie, a block-house for the reception of stores can instantly be built near the Big Beaver.

Agreeably to your directions I have sent orders to the officers commanding at the several posts, to put the troops perfectly upon their guard, in order to avoid surprise, as from the intelligence you have transmitted me, there may be a probability of the Indians confederating under Brant, and committing hostilities. I am in hopes the general treaty, which the Governor of the Western Territory means to hold in the spring, will pacify the savages and settle all differences. Respecting the land reserved to satisfy the claims of the late army, to the best of my knowledge, the million of acres which is to be bounded south by the Ohio Company purchase, will be found to be excellent land, especially if it should take the land on the Muskingum and its branches, which I am led to imagine will be the case. From all accounts the Muskingum river inclines more to the eastward than is laid down in Captain Hutchins' map; if so, the tract reserved for the late army will be very valuable. The commercial situation of the land at the mouth of the Ohio, is fine indeed. It is a great misfortune that it is so subject to inundation. I beg leave to refer you to Mr. Tardiveau for more particular intelligence on this subject. It is my opinion that a million of acres adjoining the other million on the Muskingum, would take in excellent land, and comprehend a very valuable tract of country.

I have the honor to be, &c.,

JOS. HARMAR.

The Honorable Major-General KNOX, Secretary at War.

From same to Dr. Wistar.

FORT HARMAR, at the Mouth of the Muskingum, Jan. 21, 1788.

DEAR SIR — I have been favored with your friendly letter of the 12th of September last. Some of the large bones which you request to be procured, I believe are yet to be found at the Big Bone Lick, about thirty-five miles below the Great Miami river. I am very sorry indeed that your letter did not reach me whilst at the Rapids of the Ohio. In November last I came up the river with the two companies, and had your letter been received in time I should have made a point of halting at the Lick, which is only two miles from the Ohio, and have searched for the bones, and if any were still remaining, should with great pleasure have forwarded them to Fort Pitt and from thence to Philadelphia. We have had remarkable hard weather at this post since the new year set in. I shall make the necessary inquiry next spring or summer, and if there is a possibility of procuring these bones, they shall be sent on for your friend in London, agreeably to your wish. Permit me to return you my most grateful acknowledgments for the friendship and civilities experienced from you when I had the pleasure of seeing you in London. I am extremely obliged to you for the European news which you have been pleased to transmit me.

Believe me to be, dear sir, with great esteem,

Yours sincerely,

JOS. HARMAR.

Doctor CASPAR WISTAR, Jr., at Philadelphia.

Same to Lieutenant Ernest.

FORT HARMAR, January 22, 1788.

SIR — I have the pleasure to acknowledge the receipt of your letter of the 2d ultimo, by John Siddon, who was taken prisoner on the Wabash last summer. You inform that he was under obligation to pay the Moravian Indian who brought him into Fort Pitt, fifteen dollars, a shirt, a blanket and stroud; and that you had sent the Indian home with a promise of something being obtained for him, whenever the matter was represented to me. As yet the soldier has not been mustered, but the paymaster shall be made acquainted with the circumstances, in order that when a settlement is made, the Indian may be satisfied. I am much obliged to you for the Pittsburgh newspapers which you were pleased to send on, and am, with esteem,

Your humble servant,

JOS. HARMAR.

Lieutenant ERNEST, commanding officer at Fort Pitt.

Same to Lieutenant Ford.

FORT HARMAR, January 29, 1788.

DEAR SIR—Early in the spring I expect Fort M'Intosh will be evacuated. You will be ordered with your party to Fort Pitt, to take command there. When the evacuation takes place I shall give you particular orders on the subject. The Killikenick which you were kind enough to send me, was very acceptable.

I am, dear sir, your humble servant.

JOS. HARMAR.

Lieutenant FORD, commanding officer at Fort M'Intosh.

Same to General Knox.

FORT HARMAR, March 9, 1788.

SIR — Mr. David Zeisberger, Missionary of the Moravian Indians, has written to me requesting an exchange of the corn at M'Intosh for an equivalent in powder, linen, &c., which request I shall grant, as we are in want of the corn for the public horses. The distance those Indians are from M'Intosh, prevents their bringing it from thence. On the 14th ultimo I received a message from Captain Pipe, the chief of the Delawares, who was hunting about fifty miles from hence, up the Muskingum, with thirty or forty of his nation. I answered his message, and on the 28th detached Ensign M'Dowell, with a party of a sergeant and fifteen privates, to view his situation, and sent him a message and a string of wampum—the messages are inclosed. On the 5th instant Ensign M'Dowell, with his party, returned, after having been treated with the utmost friendship and hospitality by the Indians at their hunting encampment. Yesterday old Captain Pipe, with seven of his young men, arrived at the garrison, and are now with me. Their object is to dispose of their skins to the contractor. He is a manly old fellow, and much more of a gentleman than the generality of these frontier people.

I have the honor to be, &c.,

JOS. HARMAR.

The Honorable Major-General KNOX, Secretary at War.

Same to same.

FORT PITT, April 26, 1788.

SIR—I am now upon my tour to Venango, and shall ascend the Allegheny to-morrow, in order to visit Captain Heart's post. I left Muskingum on the 6th instant, and on the 7th met General Putnam and part of the Ohio Company. Be assured, sir, that every assistance and protection that is in our power, shall be rendered to this company. I make not the least doubt but a flourishing settlement will soon take place, as they are industrious, and quite a different set of people from these frontier men. I waited with great impatience for the arrival of General Putnam, and it would have afforded me peculiar pleasure to have been personally present with him, but Major Doughty, who commands during my absence, will (agreeably to your letter of instructions) give them every necessary assistance. Nicholson, the interpreter and messenger, who resides at this place, returned from Sandusky on the 17th instant. His intelligence is that the Indians will be late in assembling to the treaty, and that it is their determination to insist peremptorily on the Ohio river as the boundary. I do not think that full faith and credit is to be given to his intelligenee. Be pleased to receive the inclosed monthly return of the regiment, dated the 1st instant; also a profile of north view of Captain Heart's works. I have directed Captain Heart to make out a map of the country from Venango to Lake Erie, which I shall shortly have the honor of transmitting to you.

I have the honor, &c.,

JOS. HARMAR.

Same to Captain Heart.

FORT PITT, May 20, 1788.

SIR—By Sergeant Huntley I had the pleasure of receiving your letter and the map inscribed to the Secretary at War, which shall be forwarded to him. The bearer, Captain Beatty, now visits your post in order to pay the men under your immediate command. On his return you will please transmit me all the Indian intelligence which you can collect, as we do not know what the result of this grand treaty may be. I cannot too strongly impress upon you the necessity of the utmost vigilance in order to guard against surprise. You are out of all manner of support, and your dependence must be entirely upon yourself. The cranberries were very acceptable; I am much obliged to you for them. Be pleased to present my compliments to Lieutenant Frothingham.

I am, sir, &c.,

Jos. Harmar.

Captain Heart, commanding officer at Fort Franklin.

P. S. — Inclosed I send you the plats of my donation lands, likewise a plat of Captain Irwin's land, which I wish you to endeavor to find out and let me know the quality.

Same to Doctor M'Dowell.

Fort Pitt, May 21, 1788.

Dear Sir—I have received your letter of the 20th of May, inclosing your commission and a letter for Captain Beatty. He left this place yesterday for Venango, but will be here again next Sunday; your letter shall be delivered to him. Be assured, sir, that I wish you all possible happiness a civil life can afford, and am,

Your very humble servant,

Jos. Harmar.

Doctor John M'Dowell.

Same to Dr. Wistar.

Fort Harmar, June 9, 1788.

Dear Sir—The bearer, Captain Armstrong, will deliver to you several bones of the huge, unknown animal, with an explanation of them. I am very sorry that it was out of the power of the officer to procure some thigh bones, but I shall endeavor, at some future period, to send you them.

I am, my dear sir, with great esteem and regard,

Your very humble servant,

Jos. Harmar.

Doctor Caspar Wistar, Jr., Philadelphia.

Same to General Mifflin.

Fort Harmar, June 9, 1788.

My dear General — Your very agreeable letter of the 9th of May, was handed to me by Colonel Olney. Ensign Spear, on his return from

Post Vincennes, was fired upon by some vagabond Wabash Indians. He lost only two men. Mr. Melcher was on board the boat. The fire was returned from the troops; they fired two rounds instantly, but the savages have great advantage over boats ascending the river. I sincerely hope that the new government will shortly be adopted, and that the next treaty (provided the present intended one has not the desired effect,) may be held with the savages with fifteen hundred or two thousand troops. Mr. Melcher brought with him from Post Vincennes a Piankeshaw bow and quiver of arrows, also a Piankeshaw pipe, which he begged me to present to you. The bearer, Captain Armstrong, takes with him a grinder of the huge unknown beast, supposed by some to be the elephant. Mr. Jefferson in his Notes calls it the mammoth; likewise a petrifaction of the honey comb, or wasp's nest, I know not which. These are the only curiosities which I can at present offer to you. Captain Armstrong will deliver you two venison hams and some pecan nuts, the produce of the Wabash, which I beg you to accept. My best wishes attend Mrs. Mifflin and your worthy family.

I have the honor to be, my dear General,

Your obliged friend and humble servant,

JOS. HARMAR.

Same to Mr. Ross.

FORT HARMAR, June 14, 1788.

DEAR SIR — I had the pleasure of receiving your letter of the 5th of June, relative to one Jacob Countz, a Dutchman, who, you inform me, had deserted your part of the country with a view of defrauding his creditors. The fellow resides on the island a little above the garrison. Instantly upon the receipt of your letter I sent a file of men for him and brought him to the garrison. In presence of Mr. Duncan, he has promised to be honest and pay his just debts. Captain Beatty is now paying the troops; it is more than probable that this Countz will receive some money. I shall be happy to have it in my power to make him do justice to his creditors.

I am, dear sir, with esteem, &c.,

JOS. HARMAR.

JAMES ROSS, Esq., at Pittsburgh.

Same to General Knox.

FORT HARMAR, June 14, 1788.

Respecting the dispute of rank between Captains Ziegler and Ferguson, Major Doughty and myself are both clearly and decidedly of opinion that

Captain Ferguson is the senior officer. The case of Ensign Denny and Ensign Spear was exactly similar. I am surprised that Captain Ziegler should trouble the State of Pennsylvania about it. You were pleased to decide in favor of Ensign Spear, which was conclusive. If Captain Ziegler, through his efforts with the State, should obtain rank of Captain Ferguson, certainly Ensign Denny, upon the same principle, is senior to Ensign Spear. It is my ardent wish that the new government may speedily be adopted, and that all these State affairs may cease. We may then hope for order and regularity.

Same to Captain Heart.

FORT HARMAR, June 21, 1788.

SIR — Your letter of the 19th of May, was handed to me at Fort Pitt by the Indian chief, Shundaushuawan. I directed him to remain at Fort Pitt until the arrival of General Butler, and then to inform him of several of the white people having moved into their lands in the Genessee country, and having built houses, &c. From what I can learn, these people are not countenanced in their proceedings, either by the States of New York or Massachusetts. Be pleased to present my compliments to Lieutenant Frothingham. I am obliged to him for the east view of this garrison, which he was kind enough to inclose to me. In my last letter I mentioned that the utmost vigilance was necessary at your post, in order to guard against surprise, as you are out of supporting distance, and more especially as the time of the men expires so soon. I am convinced that it is unnecessary to repeat these instructions. I hope to be able to reinforce you soon.

I am, sir, with much esteem, &c.,

JOS. HARMAR.

Same to Mr. Muhlenberg.

FORT HARMAR, June 30, 1788.

DEAR SIR — I had the honor to address council on the 24th of April, from Fort Pitt, upon the subject of the Treasurer of Pennsylvania's three drafts on the County Treasurers of Westmoreland, Washington and Fayette, for monies for the recruiting service, and to inform your honorable body that there was a likelihood of obtaining nothing but the paper currency for them, and at the same time praying that some other arrangements might speedily be made in order to obtain specie, as paper would not answer the purpose; since which I have to acknowledge the receipt of two letters from the honorable the Vice President in council the one dated the 18th of April, the other the 16th of May last. The former inclosed our State commissions; the latter, I observe, desires that the final determination on the rank of ensigns Denny and Spear, may remain suspended until I have an opportunity to lay their several pretensions before the board. Respecting the dispute of rank between these gentlemen, a board of officers was convened a twelve month ago, in order to determine it. I did not choose to give my opinion at that time concerning it, but referred the proceedings to the Secretary at War, who was pleased to decide in favor of Ensign Spear, upon this principle, that Ensign Denny could not by virtue of his one year's service (which was considered as militia rank from the act of Congress of the 3d of June, 1784,) take rank of Ensign Spear, whose rank was derived from continental service. In consequence of this decision of the Secretary at War, orders have long since been issued by me, at this post, announcing Ensign Spear as the senior officer. I have been informed that Captain Ziegler is contesting rank with Captain Ferguson. The same principle which decides the rank of Ensign Denny and Ensign Spear, I presume, should operate in the case of Captain Ferguson and Captain Ziegler. The query is, whether the one year's service was militia or continental rank? If council should be of opinion that the one year's service was militia rank, Captain Ferguson is undoubtedly senior to Captain Ziegler. As the right of finally judging upon this case rests with your honorable body, I beg leave to offer the following observation. Captain Ferguson is now absent at Post Vincennes, and perhaps has not in council one friend to advocate his cause. He is an officer of distinguished and superior abilities in the artillery department. The consequence will be, that if Captain Ziegler obtains rank of him, he will instantly resign, which will be a loss, not only to the State of Pennsylvania, but the States in general. I question very much, whether an officer of equal abilities of his grade and in his line, can be furnished by any State in the Union. Doctor John M'Dowell has resigned his commission on the 1st instant. The surgeon's mate, Richard Allison, is fully qualified, I believe, to succeed him. There will be a vacancy now for a surgeon's mate from our State. Doctor Scott, the surgeon's mate of the Jersey quota, begs me to recommend a friend of his, Mr. John F. Carmichael, (a native of Pennsylvania). I have no knowledge of the young gentleman, but from Doctor Scott's representation, I beg leave to recommend him to fill the vacancy, provided the honorable council thinks it proper, and has no other person in view.

I have the honor to be, &c.,

Jos. Harmar.

The Honorable Peter Muhlenberg, Esq.,
Vice President in Council, Pennsylvania.

Same to Major Wyllys.

FORT HARMAR, July 16, 1788.

DEAR MAJOR—By this conveyance Ensign Denny sends both for you and Major Hamtramck, your proportion of stationery. I never conceived Sullivan's letter to be of such an alarming nature as the Secretary at War imagined it. Lieutenant Armstrong's report fully convinces me that the matter was highly blown, and that no mutinous designs are in agitation, either in the country called the State of Franklin, the Cumberland settlements, or the district of Kentucky. If Sullivan should set his foot in the Western Territory, endeavor to have him apprehended, but no where else.

JOS. HARMAR.

Major WYLLYS, Commanding officer at the Rapids of Ohio.

Same to Captain Heart.

FORT HARMAR, July 28, 1788.

SIR—The view of the works on French creek, also a map inscribed to President Franklin, have been received. Corporal Morgan delivered the public boat which was built at your post. The boards with which she was loaded, being part public and part private property, were received by Ensign Denny, who acts as quarter-master during the absence of Lieutenant Pratt.

JOS. HARMAR.

Same to Captain Ziegler.

FORT HARMAR, August 7, 1788.

DEAR SIR—I have received your several letters from Philadelphia and one from Carlisle. I expect this will find you at Fort Pitt. The Six Nations are on their way by water to the treaty, which is to be held at this post. I am informed that several vagabonds in the neighborhood of Wheeling, mean to fire upon these Indians on their passage down the Ohio to this post. Such a step might be attended with ruinous consequences. You are hereby ordered to take the said Indians under your protection and safely escort them to this garrison. Treat them kindly, and if any of these lawless rascals should presume to fire upon them, you are ordered to land and attack them in return, for their insolence and defiance of the supreme authority.

I am, dear sir, &c.,

JOS. HARMAR.

Captain DAVID ZIEGLER, at Fort Pitt.

Same to Lieutenant Ernest.

FORT HARMAR, October 8, 1788.

DEAR SIR—Be pleased to deliver to Major Kirkpatrick the inclosed two bank notes, of twenty dollars each, and tell the generous Major, that he may shortly expect a final settlement. Permit me to congratulate you upon your nuptials. I wish you and Mrs. Ernest[1] (in which Mrs. Harmar joins me,) every happiness the marriage state can afford.

I am, dear sir, &c.

JOS. HARMAR.

Lieutenant ERNEST, commanding officer at Fort Pitt.

Same to Major Hamtramck.

FORT HARMAR, October 13, 1788.

DEAR MAJOR—You will act properly in seizing and confining the Gross Tete, or any other villains who were accessory to the murder committed at Sullivan's Station. I observe by your letter of the 12th of August, the severe stroke which the party under Lieutenant Peters has received. The intelligence has been transmitted to the War Office. The new government I hope will soon operate, and expect in the course of the next year we shall not tamely suffer the subjects of the United States to be murdered by these perfidious savages. The savages are, in my opinion, hatching a great deal of mischief. I have detached a captain's command, with Captain Hutchins, the geographer, for his protection to the mouth of the Scioto, in order to survey the exterior lines of Messrs. Cutler and Sargent's purchase, which weakens this garrison considerably, at the present moment more especially. Let your fort be named *Fort Knox.*

I am, dear sir, &c.,

JOS. HARMAR.

Major HAMTRAMCK, commanding at Vincennes.

Same to Major Wyllys.

FORT HARMAR, December 9, 1788.

DEAR MAJOR—I have the pleasure to acknowledge the receipt of your two letters of the 1st and 13th ultimo. I am sorry to observe your ill state of health, and that of your garrison. The Falls is certainly a very unhealthy position; I wish you to make the proper inquiry concerning the route to Chota, and transmit it to me. I have directed Ensign Denny to furnish you with as many camp kettles, knapsacks and haversacks as we

---

[1] Judge William Wilkins' sister.

can spare. It is a mortifying affair that you were obliged to call upon the militia for the cattle escort. It is my wish that not a single officer of the regiment may ever have the mortifying disgrace of being subjected to militia command, but suppose in the present case you found it unavoidable. I wish you to be made fully acquainted with the proceedings of the convention and the politics of Kentucky, and transmit me the intelligence. There is a Mr. Conolly now at Louisville, very likely for no good purposes; you know his base character. It will be well to keep a watchful eye over him. The Governor has written to you upon the occasion. We are at length likely to have a treaty, as the Indians are on their way and near at hand to this post. Please transmit the rolls to Captain Beatty; through the wilderness I think will be the safest and most expeditious conveyance. Captain Ashton's men are to be mustered from the expiration of their old enlistments, which will make their time of service the regular six years.

Mrs. Harmar desires her compliments may be presented to you and the officers of the garrison, and believe me to be with very great esteem and regard,

Your most obedient servant,

JOS. HARMAR.

Major WYLLYS, commanding officer at Fort Steuben,
at the Rapids of the Ohio.

Same to General Mifflin.

FORT HARMAR, December 12, 1788.

MY DEAR GENERAL—It affords me singular happiness to hear of your appointment to the presidency of the State. Permit me most sincerely to congratulate you upon the occasion. Your introductory letter in favor of Captain Bartlet, has been received. I understand that he is somewhere up the river with his family, and does not mean to visit our quarter until spring; upon his arrival every attention in my power shall be paid him. As for the news, we are at length likely to have a treaty. Brant has been using all his influence to prevent the savages holding it at this post, but a number of nations are now near at hand, and are expected in the course of two or three days. Brant has decamped and drawn off as many as he could, but notwithstanding, his influence is not so universal as was imagined. It is a difficult matter for our yellow brethren to enter into a general confederacy and to preserve it. They are much divided in their councils. The bearer, Captain Ferguson, is a very worthy officer; suffer me to recommend him to your notice. Be pleased to present my most affectionate regard to Mrs. Mifflin and Mrs. Talbot, in which Mrs. Harmar joins me.

And believe me to be, most sincerely, &c.,

JOS. HARMAR.

His Excellency THOMAS MIFFLIN, Esq.,
President of the State of Pennsylvania.

Same to General Knox.

FORT HARMAR, December 15, 1788.

SIR—Lieutenant Kersey was at the Great Kanahwa (eighty-nine measured miles from this garrison) on the 1st instant; the party all well. I have not heard of the party under Ensign M'Dowell, but am in hopes that he has not been interrupted. My calculation is, that before Christmas the two exterior lines of Messrs. Cutler and Sargent's purchase will be completed. The geographer is at present sick at Fort Pitt. If he was able to come down and take the latitude of the northern corner of the tenth township of the seventh range, Mr. Ludlow, who is a smart active young fellow, could run the northern boundary; the purchase money could then be paid, that business finished, and in the spring the next affair would be, to take up Judge Symmes' purchase. Several chiefs of the different nations arrived at this post the day before yesterday. The inhabitants of Kentucky, I am informed, have it in contemplation to declare themselves not only independent of the State of Virginia, but of the United States altogether. I have written to Major Wyllys to make me acquainted with their politics, and to watch closely the conduct of a certain Mr. Conolly, who has hired a house at the Falls, and from his base character, can certainly be planning no good for the United States.

I have the honor, &c.,

JOS. HARMAR.

The Honorable Major-General KNOX, Secretary at War, New York.

Same to Lieutenant Frothingham.

FORT HARMAR, December 15, 1788.

SIR—I have directed Ensign Denny to send you by this conveyance, one thousand white wampum. I must impress upon you in the strongest terms the absolute necessity of the utmost vigilance at Fort Franklin, in order to guard against surprise. I observe that great harmony still subsists between the troops and the Senecas who are hunting in the vicinity of your garrison; but all our yellow brethren seem to be perfidious; I would have you, therefore, never to be off your guard.

I am, sir, &c.,

Jos. Harmar.

Lieutenant Ebenezer Frothingham, commanding officer at Fort Franklin.

Same to Captain John Irwin, at Fort Pitt.

Fort Harmar, January 20, 1789.

Dear Sir—I owe Major Kirkpatrick three half-johannes, which I wish you to pay as soon as you can make it convenient.

I am, dear sir, yours sincerely,

Jos. Harmar.

Captain John Irwin, at Fort Pitt.

Same to Major Wyllys.

Fort Harmar, January 22, 1789.

Dear Major—It is not improbable but that two companies will be ordered to be stationed at the mouth of the Great Miami, not only as a better cover for Kentucky, but also to afford protection to Judge Symmes in his intended settlement there. It appears to me that there is an absolute necessity for a party to be stationed at the Rapids, their sole object should be to furnish escorts, &c., to supply Major Hamtramck with provisions. If the two companies should be ordered to take post at or near the mouth of the Great Miami, provisions can be conveniently laid in and forwarded from Limestone by Lieutenant Schuyler.

I am, dear Major, &c.

Jos. Harmar.

Same to David Duncan.

Fort Harmar, February 25, 1789.

Let me know, by the first opportunity, whether you will purchase my black horse or not. I paid twenty-five pounds, specie, for him. There is a balance due from me to Captain O'Hara; if it does not suit you to take the horse, perhaps you can arrange the business with him. If he take him and credit me with the above sum of £24, it will answer the same end.

Your obedient servant,

Jos. Harmar.

Same to Nicholas Way.

FORT HARMAR, at the mouth of the Muskingum river,
March 12th, 1789.

DEAR SIR—I have the pleasure to acknowledge the receipt of your introductory letter, in favor of Captain Israel Gilpin and his family. They halted but an hour or two at this garrison, being bound for the district of Kentucky. It will give me peculiar pleasure to afford, not only them but any other gentlemen whom you may please to recommend to my notice, every protection and countenance in my power.

Your observations respecting the proper names to be given to towns, rivers, islands, &c., in the settlement of the western country, I think to be very just. The original Indian names are generally expressive of some peculiar and distinguishing quality or circumstance, and I am clearly of opinion with you that they ought to be adopted in preference to our copying names from England and other parts of Europe.

I am, dear sir, with very great esteem,

Your friend and humble servant,

JOS. HARMAR.

Doctor NICHOLAS WAY, at Wilmington, State of Delaware.

Same to Honorable James White.

FORT HARMAR, March 22, 1789.

MY DEAR SIR—I had the honor of receiving your letter from Limestone, and have, agreeably to your request, sent down your bridle (which my servant forgot to deliver) to Mr. Lacassagne.

We have nothing new in this quarter. A vast deal of industry is displayed by our New England brethren, in their settlement on the opposite shore. They will soon be in a very flourishing condition, especially as they expect a number of emigrators from their several States, to join them in the course of the ensuing summer

With very great esteem and regard,

JOS. HARMAR.

To the Honorable JAMES WHITE, Member of Congress at New York.

Same to Lieutenant Ernest.

FORT HARMAR, April 27, 1789.

DEAR SIR—The clergyman, Mr. Story, at last arrived with my dispatches; perhaps he might have been a little dilatory in the delivery of them; but he appears to me, to be a gentleman of liberal sentiments, and I shall notice him accordingly.

I observe that the post rider makes a practice of bringing small matters for the people in Pittsburgh, under twelve pounds weight. If I should have occasion to employ him, I will write to you to be so good as to attend to it. The garden which you have laid out, commanding a view of the three rivers, must be beautiful indeed by your description. You need be under very little apprehension of a removal, as I shall always want an officer stationed at Fort Pitt. Be pleased to acquaint Mr. Devereux Smith that his runaway servant, whom he wrote to me about, was apprehended at this garrison, and Lieutenant Pratt sent him up the river a few days since, in Mr. Wilkins' canoe.

I am, &c.

Jos. Harmar.

Lieutenant Matthew Ernest, commanding officer at Fort Pitt.

Same to Major Doughty.

Fort Harmar, April 28, 1789.

Dear Major—I am hourly expecting the arrival of Mr. Hackenwelder, the Moravian Missionary, at which time I shall afford another subaltern's command to Major Sargent, for his protection, as he has the surveying of the lands up the Muskingum, granted by Congress to the Moravian Indians. The new government, I suppose, engages the whole attention of all ranks and degrees. I sincerely hope that by this time General Washington has the reins and has set the wheels in motion. All is peace and quietness in this quarter, at least nothing has come to my knowledge to the contrary. The New England gentlemen are extremely industrious; Campus Martius is nearly completed. Gay circles of ladies, balls, &c., which I have neither time nor inclination to frequent, these are the changes which in three years this wilderness has undergone. Mrs. Harmar presents you her best respects.

I am, &c.,

Jos. Harmar.

Major John Doughty, commandant of artillery at New York.

Same to Mr. Hillegas.

Fort Harmar, April 30, 1789.

Dear Sir—I had the pleasure of receiving your letter by Captain Bradford, and now send you some more of the buffalo wool, of a superior quality to the former. In the months of February and March, is the time the wool is in proper season. I am apprehensive what was at first sent will not answer your purpose. But few buffalo are killed in the vicinity of the Muskingum. When I was in your office at Philadelphia, if I recollect right, you gave me a detail of the Rhode Island hero's exploits with the Prussian General; some part of them I have forgotten; when you have a leisure moment, I will thank you to relate the matter to me, as I wish to laugh a little upon the occasion.

I am, &c.,

JOS. HARMAR.

MICHAEL HILLEGAS, Continental Treasurer at New York.

Same to Lieutenant Spear.

FORT HARMAR, May 25, 1789.

SIR — You will continue to transmit me all the Indian intelligence which may come to your knowledge, and let not the least occurrence worthy of notice escape your attention. It is unnecessary for me to remind you that the utmost vigilance is always necessary at your post, in order to guard against surprise. Respecting your rank, as I mentioned to you in my former letter, I have used every exertion in my power in your behalf, but council have determined the matter against you, as you will see by the inclosed copy of their proceedings, which came to hand a few days since, inclosing a State commission of a Lieutenancy for Mr. Denny.

I am, sir, with esteem, &c.,

JOS. HARMAR.

Lieutenant EDWARD SPEAR, commanding officer at the Falls of Beaver.

Same to General Howell.

FORT HARMAR, August 31, 1789.

MY DEAR SIR — It afforded me singular satisfaction when I heard of your being appointed to your present office; permit your friend sincerely to congratulate you upon the occasion. You have been so obliging as to forward me the Federal Gazette which Beatty has subscribed for, which demands my thanks. Be kind enough to continue forwarding that paper, as I think it a very useful one. I have had it in contemplation, amidst the general joy, to address our illustrious President, in behalf of the regiment, but so much time has elapsed that it is more than probable an address now would rather be out of season. This I am very confident of, that every officer, one and all of us, entertain the highest love and veneration for his character, and pray heaven to prosper his administration.

Mrs. Harmar desires to be affectionately remembered to you, and accept my best wishes for your health and happiness.

Believe me to be, &c.,

Jos. Harmar.

Joseph Howell, Jr., Esq., Paymaster-General at New York.

Same to Lieutenant Ernest.

Fort Harmar, September 12, 1789.

Dear Sir—I am very glad to hear of the birth of your son, and congratulate you thereupon. I consent to your having granted Mr. Turnbull permission to run a fence for the conveniency of his pasture on the Allegheny river, but take care and suffer no further encroachments. Messrs. Craig and Turnbull have been long trying, at the War Office, to obtain the sole possession of the area and the buildings (I believe) of Fort Pitt, but without success.

With great esteem, &c., J. H.

Same to General Knox.

Fort Harmar, September 12, 1789.

Dear Sir — Major Doughty informs me in his letter dated the 21st ultimo, that he arrived at the Little Miami on the 16th, and after reconnoitring for three days from thence to the Big Miami, for an eligible situation whereon to erect the works for head-quarters, he had at length determined to fix upon a spot opposite Licking river, which he represents as high and healthy, abounding with never failing springs, &c., and the most proper position he could find for the purpose.

Same to Captain Irwin.

Fort Harmar, September 21, 1789.

Dear Sir — I have received your letter of the 1st of August, and am really sorry to find that Captain Christie disappointed you in not honoring your draft for the two hundred dollars specie; the delay on this occasion has been no loss to me; therefore your looking on yourself bound to make restitution is needless. Upon the whole, unless you meant to reside here with your family, I believe it is full as well for you not to have a concern in the purchase.

If there should be an addition to the present establishment, you may be assured, sir, it will afford me peculiar pleasure to be in any degree instrumental in procuring you a commission, or serving you all in my power. Your merits as an officer are well known to me, and I am certain the President of the United States has not forgotten you. One thing is to be observed, that the officers serving on the present establishment ought, in my opinion, to be advanced first and I shall exert all my influence in their favor; but if an addition takes place, as it certainly must in a short time, you may depend on my interest to serve you as far as I think compatible with the good of the regiment, and so as not to prejudice the feelings of the officers now in the service.

Be pleased to present my compliments to Mrs. Irwin and your sister, and believe me to be

Your friend and humble servant,

JOS. HARMAR.

Captain JOHN IRWIN, at Pittsburgh.
(Favored by Mr. Vigo.)

Same to Colonel Francis Johnston.

FORT HARMAR, September 22, 1789.

MY DEAR SIR — The bearer, Mr. Vigo, is a gentleman from Post Vincennes, a friend of mine; he has always behaved with the utmost attention to the officers and troops stationed in that quarter; permit me to recommend him to your notice. Any civilities you may show him, shall be looked upon as given to your humble servant. He will present you with a head of a curious fish, from Mr. Armstrong.

Mrs. Harmar desires her best respects may be offered to Mrs. Johnston and yourself. I wish you would write me frequently, and do not attribute it to negligence if you do not receive frequent answers, as without flattery (which I detest), there is no person for whom I have a greater esteem. I am shortly going to make my head-quarters down opposite Licking river.

Adieu,

JOS. HARMAR.

Colonel FRANCIS JOHNSTON, Philadelphia.

Same to General Butler.

FORT HARMAR, September 28, 1789.

DEAR SIR—I received your friendly letter of the 15th instant, by Captain Heart, wherein I observe that Pittsburgh is your present place of residence. Your humble servant is a bird of passage. Sometime the latter end of next month, or beginning of November, I shall move down the river, bag and baggage (leaving Ziegler's and Heart's companies at this post for the protection of our New England brethren), and shall fix my head-quarters opposite Licking river. I am in hourly expectation of the Governor.

Mrs. Harmar and myself beg to be affectionately remembered to Mrs. Butler, yourself and family. I hope that game leg of yours is perfectly recovered. The tea sent by Lieutenant Humphrey was very good; will you be pleased to send him my compliments, with thanks for the same. Don't forget to write to me, and believe me to be,

Your friend and humble servant,

JOS. HARMAR.

General RICHARD BUTLER, at Pittsburgh.

Same to Thomas Mifflin, Esq., Philadelphia.

FORT HARMAR, November 9, 1789.

MY DEAR GENERAL—It would afford me great happiness if you could steal three or four months from the Atlantic, and spend them with me. I am now on the wing, expecting to move down the Ohio in a few days, and to fix head-quarters opposite the mouth of the Licking river, about three hundred miles below this garrison, where I should be proud of being honored with your company. Venison, two or three inches deep cut of fat, turkeys at one pence per pound, buffalo in abundance, and cat-fish of one hundred pounds weight, are stories that are by no means exaggerated. I am going to a country where there is a much greater plenty of game than there is here at present. Our New England brethren are a very industrious set of people. With the protection afforded them by the troops (which they acknowledge with great gratitude), they have converted the wilderness into a fine state of cultivation. Their settlement bids fair to be very flourishing. Cornfields, gardens, &c., now appear in places which were lately the habitation of wild beasts. Such are the glorious effects of industry.

The bearer, Lieutenant Denny, is my adjutant; his long and faithful services claim my warmest regard for him; permit me to introduce him to your civilities. Will you be so kind as to offer my respects to Mentges and Fullerton? Craig I shall shortly write to.

Believe me to be, with the greatest esteem and affection,

Your Excellency's obliged friend and humble servant,

JOS. HARMAR.

16

Lieutenant Denny to General Harmar.

PITTSBURGH, November 22, 1789.

DEAR GENERAL—We did not arrive here until the 19th, owing to bad oars, indifferent oarsmen, and meeting two smart floods; however, we got safe, and had the pleasure to find Major Wyllys, Captain Beatty, Captain Mercer, Lieutenant Peters, Ensign Sedam and Doctor Allison in town. They arrived two days before us. The Governor is expected in town to-morrow or next day. His boat is here waiting for him, and Mr. William St. Clair, who came from Detroit to Fort Harmar last winter, accompanies him down the river. I have endeavored to impress Mr. Elliott with a just idea of the condition of the posts below with respect to provisions. He says he feels more concerned than we possibly can. He goes down himself in a few days.

I am very sorry, indeed, that I have to inform you of the loss of one of the most serviceable members of the Western Territory, General Parsons. He left the old Moravian town up Beaver early on the 17th, on board a canoe, accompanied only by one man. Sent his horses down by land. About one o'clock that day, as we entered the mouth of the creek we met the wreck of a canoe, with a good deal of her cargo drifting down, all separately. Part of the loading we took up. When we got to the block-house, Mr. M'Dowell told us they had taken up a piece of the canoe, a bundle of skins, and had seen a pair of saddle-bags, which were well known to be the judge's, and the same evening the man arrived with the horses, and told us he left the judge early that morning about twenty-five miles up the creek, that he intended to dine that day with Mr. M'Dowell at the block-house, and the man knew the property which we took up to be part of what was in General Parson's canoe, leaves no doubt of his being lost in attempting the Falls of Beaver. The canoe was very much shattered, and bottom uppermost, when we met her. Mr. M'Dowell has made search on both sides the creek, above and below the falls, but can make no further discovery, more than finding part of the canoe at the foot of a remarkably dangerous fall in the creek, which strengthens the belief that there the old gentleman met his fate.

I shall be glad to be affectionately remembered to Mrs. Harmar, while I remain, &c.,

E. DENNY.

General Harmar to Lieut. Ernest.

FORT HARMAR, November 27, 1789.

DEAR SIR—My last letter was dated the 10th instant, and forwarded by Lieutenant Denny, since which I have the pleasure to acknowledge the receipt of your several letters.

The three fellows of Captain Mercer's party whom you sent on by Sergeant Hays, received a proper flagellation at this post, for the robberies committed by them at Pittsburgh; they have every appearance of villains. You had better inform Captain Beatty that you paid $25.06 to release Johnson, the recruit, from the hands of the constable, in order that the stoppages may be made for you. The five muskets, five bayonets and belts, five cartridge boxes and belts, and Mrs. Harmar's saddle, together with my large Kentucky boat, were all safely delivered by Sergeant Hays.

Respecting the office of Pay-master to the regiment, I make not the least doubt that you will have a great majority of votes for it, now Beatty is promoted; this you may depend upon, you shall have all my interest and influence upon the occasion, as I am certain there is no officer in either of the corps equally qualified with yourself to fill it.

I believe I am in arrears to Captain Irwin, if he has paid Major Kilpatrick the three half-johannes which I owed him; if so, give my compliments to Captain Beatty, and tell him to reimburse Captain Irwin and charge the same to my account. Will you be pleased to present my compliments also to Major Wyllys and the other officers at Fort Pitt.

I am, dear sir, with great esteem, your humble servant,

JOS. HARMAR.

Lieut. MATT. ERNEST, comm. officer at Fort Pitt.

Same to the Committee of the Ohio Company, &c.

HEAD-QUARTERS, FORT WASHINGTON, January 8, 1790.

GENTLEMEN—I received your polite address, and thank you for your affectionate wishes for my welfare. Be assured, gentlemen, that I left Muskingum with regret. It always gave me pleasure to advance the interests of the Ohio Company, and although absent from you at present, the time may come when I shall again be with you. That your settlement may continue rapidly to increase and flourish, and you, gentlemen, experience every degree of prosperity and happiness, is the sincere and ardent wish of one who is, with the greatest esteem and affection,

Your most obedient and very humble servant,

JOS. HARMAR.

To Colonel SPROAT, Colonel MEIGS, Rev. Dr. STORY, Mr. C. GREENE, Mr. PAUL FEARING, Commodore WHIPPLE, General TUPPER, Mr. WOODBRIDGE, Major SERGEANT, Mr. PARSONS, and Colonel SHEPARD—addressors in behalf of the Ohio Company, and the inhabitants of the settlement at Marietta.

Same to General Knox.

HEAD-QUARTERS, FORT WASHINGTON, January 14, 1790.

SIR—I have the honor to acknowledge the receipt of your letter of the 29th October last, to which I shall now particularly reply.

The Governor of the Western Territory arrived at this post on the 2d instant, and departed from hence on the 5th for the Illinois country. I furnished him, agreeably to his request, with an escort of fifty chosen men, under the immediate command of Lieut. Doyle. Major Wyllys accompanies him on this tour. I did not leave the Muskingum until the 24th ult., being detained so long waiting for his and the Pay-master's arrival there. We were four days upon our passage. The distance from thence to this garrison, (which is directly opposite the mouth of Licking river,) is about three hundred miles. Major Doughty is left to command at Fort Harmar.

This will be one of the most solid, substantial wooden fortresses, when finished, of any in the Western Territory. It is built of hewn timber, a perfect square, two stories high, with four block-houses at the angles. I am particularly indebted to Captain Ferguson and Lieutenant Pratt, for their indefatigable industry and attention in forwarding the work thus far. The plan is Major Doughty's. On account of its superior excellence, I have thought proper to honor it with the name of *Fort Washington.* The public ought to be benefited by the sale of these buildings whenever we evacuate them, although they will cost them but little.

About forty or fifty Kentucky boats have begun, and will complete it. Limestone is the grand mart of Kentucky; whenever boats arrive there they are scarcely of any value to the owners; they are frequently set adrift in order to make room for the arrival of others. I have contracted for the above number for the moderate price of from one to two dollars each; thus much for the plank work. All other expenses (wagon hire, nails, and some glass excepted,) are to be charged to the labor of the troops. The lime we have burned ourselves, and the stone is at hand. Be pleased to receive the inclosed plan of the fort. The distance between the Little and Great Miami is twenty-eight measured miles. Near the Little Miami there is a settlement called Columbia; here (seven miles distant from Columbia), there is another named Losanteville, but lately changed to Cincinnati, and Judge Symmes himself resides at the other, about fifteen miles from hence, called the Miami City, at the north bend of the Ohio river. They are, in general, but small cabins, and the inhabitants of the poorer class of people.

It is very probable that the Creek nation, under Mr. M'Gillivray, may be troublesome on the frontiers of Georgia, &c., during the ensuing summer, and especially as you inform me that the commissioners who were appointed to hold a treaty with them, returned from the Omee river unsuccessful.

I observe that the Governor of the Western Territory is empowered by the President of the United States, in case the hostilities of the Indians should render the measure inevitable, to call on the nearest counties of Pennsylvania and Virginia, for militia—not exceeding, in the whole, fifteen hundred—to act in conjunction with the federal troops, in such operations, offensive and defensive, as the said Governor and the commanding officer of the troops, conjointly, shall judge necessary for the public service, and protection of the inhabitants and posts. You may rest assured, sir, that in all these cases, the most perfect harmony will ever subsist between the Governor and myself.

By this time it is presumed Congress is convened, and that instead of a temporary, a permanent establishment of the troops will be made.

Lieutenant Armstrong, I see, has been writing to the War Office about brevet rank. He is a valuable officer, but instead of troubling you upon the occasion, it is my opinion he should have represented his grievances, if any there were, unto his commanding officer.

By the latest advices from Major Hamtramck he writes me that he had manœuvred in such a manner as to divide the Weea Indians, and that eighty of their warriors had come into Post Vincennes, and put themselves under the protection of the United States. This may be considered as a very favorable circumstance, provided these yellow gentry adhere to their allegiance.

The difficulty of forwarding my dispatches from this post to the War Office, is great. Up the river, from here to Fort Pitt, is about five hundren miles; it is too fatiguing to be monthly sending a boat against the stream for the purpose, unless an extraordinary occasion should require it. I am therefore making arrangements to send my letters to Danville, in Kentucky, from thence to be forwarded through the wilderness and deposited in the post-office at Richmond, which I believe to be the most expeditious conveyance.

I have the honor to be, &c.,

JOS. HARMAR.

The Honorable Major-General KNOX, Secretary at War, New York.

Same to Ensign Jeffers.

HEAD-QUARTERS, FORT WASHINGTON, February 1, 1790.

SIR—I have the pleasure to acknowledge the receipt of your letters dated the 5th October, the 6th November, the 1st December and 2d January last, with the several inclosures. You will continue to send me regular monthly returns, dated on the first day of each month, of your command; also, of military and quarter-master stores, inspection returns, and quantity of provisions on hand, so that I may know the exact state of your garrison. I have been informed that the men, before Captain H. was ordered from Fort Franklin, were almost continually employed on fatigue, and principally for his own private emolument. That they were more of farmers than soldiers, was very evident upon their arrival at Fort Harmar—they were chiefly naked. Such conduct is a disgrace to the regiment, and any officer acting in like manner in future, shall be called to a severe account for it. I do not believe you will countenance such matters; I mention it to let you know that such unmilitary proceedings will always meet with my greatest displeasure. The plan of the fort which you have forwarded to me, I suppose to be a true representation of it as it now stands. In case of danger, you have not men sufficient to defend it. The block-house should be your principal defense. You will do well, therefore, to contract the works as much as possible.

I would have you, by all means, to cultivate a good understanding with the Cornplanter, in order to counteract the designs of Brant and his adherents. I believe him to be a friend of the United States. Give my compliments to him, and tell him I am very glad to hear that he is well, and to keep fast hold of the chain of friendship.

I would have you to use every means in your power to conciliate the minds of the Indians in your quarter, and to impress them with the majesty of the United States, and their sincere and friendly disposition toward them; at the same time, you must use the utmost precaution to avoid surprise. The savages may make the greatest professions of friendship, and be deceitful at last; therefore, never be off your guard with them.

If you should hear anything further of the intelligence given you by Half-Town, the Seneca chief, who informed you that there was great talk of the Mohawks going to war against the Muskingum people the ensuing spring, you will instantly give me information of it.

I cannot conclude this letter without repeating to you, and strongly enjoining upon you, the strict observance of economy to be used in all your departments, and the utmost vigilance and discipline to be exercised with your command.

I am, sir, &c.,

JOS. HARMAR.

Ensign JOHN JEFFERS, commanding officer at Fort Franklin, on French Creek.

Same to Mr. Jonathan Williams.

HEAD-QUARTERS, FORT WASHINGTON, February 25, 1790.

DEAR SIR—I had the pleasure of receiving a friendly line from you, by Captain Ferguson, and can well remember the gay moments we passed together in France, particularly the civilities received from you at the Palace at St. Germain en Laye, where I dined with you in company with Mr. Barclay and Colonel Franks. Here we are delightfully situated on the most beautiful river in the world, *La Belle Riviere*, opposite the mouth of Licking, in Kentucky. You'll wonder at this, when you call to mind the handsome meanders of the Seine at the foot of your old quarters. Society, unless what the military affords, is entirely out of the question. Buffalo, venison, turkeys, and fish of an enormous size (when the season arrives), we have in the greatest abundance. If ever Miss-*Fortune*, the slippery jade, should direct your course to the westward, it will give me great pleasure to regale you with some of our dainties. You shall have a hearty, soldierly welcome.

Believe me, &c.,

JOS. HARMAR.

MR. JONATHAN WILLIAMS, Merchant, Philadelphia.
(To the care of Dr. Franklin.)

P. S.—If you see Franks, give my compliments to him, and tell him I received his introductory letter in favor of Mr. Mitchell.

Same to Daniel Clymer

HEAD-QUARTERS, FORT WASHINGTON, March 1, 1790.

MY DEAR SIR—Captain Pratt handed me a few lines from you, dated at Reading. I should be happy to see you here. We can afford you buffalo and venison in abundance.

C——, I find, keeps manœuvring a little after the old manner. Sometime or other he must certainly get his *quietus.* It is surprising to me how he escapes from the numerous *fracases* he is engaged in. I am informed that Shannon at Easton had liked to have gutted him with a knife in a dispute they had together. He is a clever fellow, notwithstanding all his foibles.

We are most beautifully situated where we are at present, on the handsome river Ohio, and directly opposite Licking in Kentucky.

I have heard of no news or disturbance lately from our yellow brethren. From Fort Pitt you can easily glide down the current to see me; it is about five hundred miles. This month I expect we shall have great plenty of fish; such as pike, perch, bass, buffalo, sturgeon and cat; the latter of an enormous size. What would you think of being regaled with one of one hundred weight? There are some actually caught of that weight.

The bearer, Lieutenant Kingsbury, is an officer of mine, and is intrusted with several private letters of consequence for Philadelphia. He strikes off from Reading to Easton. Will you be pleased to notice him? I shall direct him to leave the letters in your care, which I beg may be safely forwarded by you.

I am, dear sir, &c.,

JOS. HARMAR.

DANIEL CLYMER, Esq., at Reading, Pennsylvania.

Same to Governor Huntingdon.

HEAD-QUARTERS, FORT WASHINGTON, March 2, 1790.

SIR—Lieutenant Pratt handed me a few lines from your Excellency, in which I observe his conduct, whilst employed on the recruiting service in the State of Connecticut, was such as to meet entire approbation. Although I have not the honor of being personally acquainted with your Excellency, I beg leave to address you on the following subject:

It is more than probable that an augmentation of the regular troops will take place (indeed I believe the measure will be found absolutely necessary), in which case suffer me to mention Major Wyllys as a very honest, brave, deserving officer, and in every point of view adequate to the command of a regiment. I am induced to offer his recommendation, not from any solicitation of the major's, but as he is now absent in the Illinois country, and there may be some candidates at home who are upon the courtier establishment, I cannot refrain (from the esteem I have for his character,) expressing my wishes to your Excellency upon this occasion.

The officers at present in service, forming the Connecticut quota, have conducted themselves with military propriety, and greatly to my satisfaction. I should be happy to see them advanced also, when vacancies take place or more troops are raised.

I have the honor to be, &c.,

JOS. HARMAR.

His Excellency SAMUEL HUNTINGDON, Esq.,
Governor of the State of Connecticut, at Norwich.

Same to Richard Graham.

HEAD-QUARTERS, FORT WASHINGTON, March 6, 1790.

DEAR SIR—I had the pleasure of receiving a few lines from you, dated at Dumfries the 12th last September. I shall be happy to see you at our new quarters. We have no particular news. The savages lately murdered some people at a small station about fourteen miles above Limestone, and will continue their carnages and depredations until government raise a proper force to sweep them off the face of the earth. I have detached Major Wyllys to accompany Governor St. Clair, who has set out for the Illinois country, there to regulate civil affairs.

Mrs. Harmar joins in respectful compliments to you.

Believe me, &c.,

JOS. HARMAR.

Mr. RICHARD GRAHAM, Merchant, Dumfries.

P. S.—Will you be pleased to present my regards to General Gates? I hope he enjoys his health.

Same to John Cleves Symmes.

HEAD-QUARTERS, FORT WASHINGTON, March 7, 1790.

DEAR SIR—I shall want about an acre of land, or perhaps a little more, near the garrison, on the east side of it, for the purpose of making a garden. I suppose, by applying to Mr. Ludlow, he will be able to stake off three or four lots accordingly. I wish you to give him the necessary directions.

I designed to have dispatched Lieutenant Kingsbury for the eastward long before this time, but have been prevented for want of a boat, by which delay I find it will be impracticable to procure the certificates in time for the two sections of land intended to be purchased from you, in what is called the College Township. As it is out of my power to comply with your last proposals relative to furnishing the certificates, I am nevertheless willing to agree with your first proposals, which were to pay you 2 \ 6 specie per acre for the said two sections. The money shall be ready for you whenever you please to call for it, as also for the lots for the garden. An allowance for advancing the ready money ought, in my opinion, to be made. I shall expect your answer on the return of Mr. Ludlow.

I have the honor to be, &c.,

JOS. HARMAR.

The Honorable JOHN CLEVES SYMMES, Esq., one of the Judges of the Western Territory, at North Bend.

Same to General Knox.

FORT WASHINGTON, March 24, 1790.

SIR—I had the honor to address you last on the 20th ultimo, a duplicate whereof is now inclosed.

The Indians still continue to murder and plunder the inhabitants; especially the boats going up and down the Ohio river. About the middle of this month they broke up Kenton's station, a small settlement fifteen miles above Limestone, killing and capturing the whole of the people, supposed to be ten or twelve in number. Buckner Thruston, Esq., has just arrived here, who informs me of a capital stroke of plunder which they made from the boats, one of which he was on board, a small distance above the Scioto river. This gentleman is a member of the Virginia Legislature, and has given me the inclosed written report of the attack, by which you will please to observe that the property captured by the savages was estimated at £4,000. He supposes them to have been Shawanees. No calculation will answer but raising a sufficient force to effectually chastise the whole of those nations who are known to be hostile.

Ensign Francis Luse has given me his resignation, and I now inclose his commission, which I hope you will be pleased to accept. I have allowed him to be run upon the rolls until the first of May next, as he is considerably embarrassed in his circumstances. Permit me to recommend cadet John Morgan to fill the vacancy, unless there is a probability of promotion for him in the corps of artillery, in which case, and not otherwise, I would beg leave particularly to recommend Mr. David Britt to fill the vacancy occasioned by the resignation of Mr. Luse, or the first vacancy which may happen in future. Mr. Britt was a former partner of Messrs. Turnbull, Marmie & Co.; has served as a cadet for some time in the different grades, from a private sentinel to a non-commissioned officer. He has also been of great service to me in many other instances, and is, in my opinion, deservedly entitled to preferment.

I have received no intelligence, as yet, of Major Doughty, but have detached Lieutenant Armstrong to undertake the business recommended in your secret letters. No written orders have been given him upon that subject. Be pleased to receive the inclosed monthly returns of the regiment, dated the 1st February and the 1st of March.

I have the honor to be, &c.,

JOS. HARMAR.

Same to William Govett.

FORT WASHINGTON, April 4, 1790.

DEAR SIR—I have altered my mind respecting purchasing the certificates to pay Judge Symmes for land. You will therefore pay no attention to that matter, as I have declared off the intended purchase.

I am hourly expecting the arrival of Lieutenant Denny, by whom I shall hope to hear from you.

I am, dear sir, &c.,

JOS. HARMAR.

Same to Captain Ziegler.

FORT WASHINGTON, April 5, 1790.

DEAR SIR—I have received your several letters of the 18th February, and the 6th, 24th, 26th and 27th ult.

You did right in sending two men with the contractor's boat, as the Indians begin already to be very troublesome on the river near the Scioto.

The clothing, sheet iron, cartridges and flints all arrived safe. The remainder of the clothing I shall be expecting when Lieutenant Denny arrives.

Mrs. Harmar joins me in respectful compliments to Mrs. Ziegler and Mrs. Heart. Give my compliments to all our New England acquaintances. I wish their settlement may prosper. We have a delightful situation here, and an excellent garrison; no danger, as there is with you, of an inundation.

I am, dear sir, &c.,

JOS. HARMAR.

Captain DAVID ZIEGLER, commanding officer at Fort Harmar.

Same to Doctor Wistar.

FORT WASHINGTON, April 5, 1790.

DEAR SIR—It is a long time ago since I received your very agreeable letter, acknowledging the receipt of the bones by Captain Armstrong; you will please to receive by this conveyance a few more. We are at present stationed opposite the mouth of the Licking river, not above twenty miles, by land, from the Big Bone Lick creek. I intend shortly to let Dr. Allison, the surgeon of the regiment, proceed to that place and stay there for about a week. Upon his return I am in hopes to be able to send you a proper collection of the bones, and worthy of your acceptance, as the Doctor is curious in those matters.

The savages begin already to be very troublesome with the boats descending the Ohio river; nothing will cure them but an effectual chastisement. I beg you to accept my thanks for your obliging letter and shall be happy in hearing from you frequently.

I am, dear sir, with very great esteem, &c.,

JOS. HARMAR.

Same to Wm. Govett.

FORT WASHINGTON, June 8, 1790.

DEAR SIR—I have to acknowledge the receipt of your letter by Lieutenant Denny, dated the 23d January, inclosing your account current.

Mr. Leiper's Encyclopedia would not have answered us. I want the most elegant edition that can be procured. The thermometer will do.

The ground rent on Market street lot must be settled with the University on the best terms you can. I have already written to Colonel Craig concerning my small plantation; consult with him upon the occasion.

I observe the rent for the Market street house is too much in arrears. It is very likely the old lady will shortly be able to pay it; therefore it is not my wish to distress her.

As to selling the Germantown ground rent and purchasing the ground rent on Market street lot, I leave it entirely to your own judgment, how to act for me in this respect.

The Indians have been, and still are troublesome. I am in full hopes that the new government will give me the materials to work with, and the next year be prepared for a general war with them.

Mrs. Harmar writes to Mrs. Govett by this conveyance.

I am, dear sir, &c.,

JOS. HARMAR.

Same to Joseph Howell, Jr.

FORT WASHINGTON, June 9, 1790.

DEAR SIR—I wrote to you on the 28th January last, and inclosed it in my letter to the War Office. I am surprised it has not been received. I now have to acknowledge your several letters of the 2d, 17th and 31st January, and the 28th March, and am extremely obliged to you for your care and attention in forwarding me the newspapers. They all came safe and regularly to hand.

Captain Beatty is just now on the wing for Muskingum, and from thence to the falls of Beaver and Venango, making a final settlement as he goes along, up to the first of the present year.

I have written to General Knox, why I thought it most advisable for him to draw the third instalment, and be done with the business before he leaves the country. He will be with you early in September. Lieutenant Ernest is his successor. There has been a Major J—— here, for the avowed design of speculating upon the necessities of the soldiers and some others, but I have prevented them. It is, in my opinion, a most dishonorable traffic; by God, my hands are clear of it, and if I find that any officer is concerned in it, he shall be called to a strict and severe account for such unmilitary proceedings. The Indians are exceedingly troublesome. I know of nothing that will cure the disorder, but government raising an army to effectually chastise them—all treaties are in vain.

Mrs. Harmar and my little flock are well. She desires to be affectionately remembered to you. Do not forget writing to me; it will afford me great happiness to hear constantly from you.

Believe me, yours truly,

Jos. Harmar.

Joseph Howell, Jr., Esq., Pay-master General, at New York.

Same to Lieutenant Matthew Ernest.

Head-Quarters, Fort Washington, June 9, 1790.

Dear Sir — My last letter was dated the 5th of February, and forwarded by Lieutenant Kingsbury, which I observe you have received; I now have to acknowledge the receipt of your several letters, dated the 22d and 26th of February, the 20th and 25th of March, and the 13th of May, with the different dispatches. The deeds, patents, &c., belonging to me, I left with you by Mr. Denny, I wish you to take particular care of and keep them safe. You may inform Ephraim Douglas, Esq., that I have long since returned all the drafts to council, amongst which was one for one hundred dollars drawn upon him, consequently that business is at an end. I have no objections to your having lent the arms to Messrs. Wilkins and Blaine, provided they are returned in good order. Mr. Parker delivered to me the six old muskets which you lent him. The chief part of the cartridge paper has arrived at head-quarters, the remainder was left at Fort Harmar.

All the officers at this post (agreeably to the list inclosed) are unanimous in their votes for you as Pay-master, and I take it for granted that there will not be above three or four votes for Lieutenant Frothingham. You are therefore to consider yourself as the new Pay-master to the regiment, and as soon as possible you are to repair to New York, and there to use all your address to prevent old times taking place; I mean so much arrearages being due to the corps. Captain Beatty draws all his instalments as he goes on, and settles with the troops up to the first of the present year. It will therefore be your duty to look out sharp for the pay, &c., due from the 1st of January, 1790. As I said before, you must use all your address; indeed, all the graces of Lord Chesterfield will be necessary upon this occasion.[1]

---

[1] Ernest was one of the most polished and gentlemanly persons in the army.

I cannot conclude my letter without assuring you that I am very well pleased with your attention and accuracy in forwarding my several dispatches. For the news I refer you to Captain Beatty.

I am, sir, with very great esteem, your most humble servant,

JOS. HARMAR.

Lieutenant MATTHEW ERNEST, commanding officer at Fort Pitt.

P. S.—Tell the contractors that we have not had an ounce of meat for some time, and that the flour and whiskey are just out.

List of Officers at Fort Washington, June 9th, 1790.

1. General Harmar,
2. Captain Ferguson,
3. Captain Strong,
4. Captain M'Curdy,
5. Captain Beatty,
6. Lieutenant Armstrong,
7. Lieutenant Kerney,
8. Lieutenant Forde,
9. Lieutenant Pratt,
10. Lieutenant Denny,
11. Ensign Sedam,
12. Ensign Hartshorn,
13. Ensign Thompson,
14. Doctor Allison.

Same to same.

FORT WASHINGTON, August 13, 1790.

DEAR SIR—My last letter to you was dated on the 9th June, and forwarded by Captain Beatty; since which I have the pleasure to acknowledge the receipt of your letters of the 10th and 27th June, with the different dispatches, letters, &c., which, together with my private stores, all arrived safe, and in good order. In my letter by Beatty, you will observe that the officers at this post gave an unanimous vote for you as the new Pay-master of the regiment; in consequence of which I ordered you to proceed for New York, to use all your address to receive and bring on our pay, subsistence, &c., from the first of the present year; but since writing that letter, the late Act of Congress for regulating the military establishment, has come forward, which totally changes the face of affairs, and renders those orders of no effect. You are therefore not to go to New York. It is more than probable that you will be elected Pay-master to the battalion of artillery, in which case Major Doughty will give you the necessary orders.

Lieutenant Denny left with you sundry deeds, patents, &c., &c., of lands belonging to me in Westmoreland county. I gave Major Huffnagle a power of attorney to transact that business for me; it is revoked, but it has not yet been returned. Let me beg you either to undertake this business yourself, or if it is inconvenient, be pleased to inform me of some gentleman in Pittsburgh or its vicinity, who is willing to receive a power of attorney for this purpose, and will pay proper attention to my interest. I have thought of young Mr. Woods, but know not whether he would be inclined to undertake it. The lands are certainly valuable.

The old public stores have not yet arrived at head-quarters from Fort Pitt.

As for news, all hopes of peace with the savages in this quarter and on the Wabash, are at an end. We are preparing to carry on an expedition against them this fall, in conjunction with the Kentucky militia.

I am, dear sir, &c.,

JOS. HARMAR.

P. S.—I am much obliged to you for forwarding the bones to Doctor Wistar.

Same to Rufus Putnam.

FORT WASHINGTON, September 2, 1790.

SIR—I have had the pleasure of receiving your letter of the 22d June last, wherein you are pleased to make me an offer, and my friends also, to become adventurers in as many shares as we may choose, in company with you, in the Scioto speculation. I am much obliged to you for the offer, but matters are so circumstanced with me at present that I must decline accepting it. You may be assured, sir, that I shall afford the European emigrants every assistance and protection in my power, consistent with my duty, and agreeably to the orders I may receive upon that head.

Be pleased to make my most respectful compliments to all my friends at Marietta, and believe me to be, with much esteem,

Sir, your very, &c.,

JOS. HARMAR.

The Honorable RUFUS PUTNAM, at Marietta.

Same to Major Hamtramck.

FORT WASHINGTON, September 3, 1790.

DEAR SIR—The information you gave me, that a plan was certainly on foot to assemble a number of nations at the Miami village (as soon as the corn will be ripe), in order to pay me a visit, I am obliged to you for; perhaps we may be beforehand with them. If you should be so fortunate as to make a successful stroke, either at the Ouiatanon, Vermilion or

L'Anguille, circumstances may render it necessary that you should instantly return to the post instead of remaining in the country, which I shall leave to your own judgment; but at all events, endeavor to let me hear from you verbally, by a trusty Frenchman or some other person. You acted very right in dismissing those scoundrels, the Pottawattamies and Weeas, who came into you with their usual professions of peace, without giving them any goods. I suppose they came for nothing but in expectation of receiving some presents. The substance of Mr. Tardiveau's letter which you inclose me, I observe is a request to you to send him a detachment of troops from Post Vincennes for the security of the Illinois country. This is utterly impracticable at present, and we must have more troops before it can be any way practicable in future. I hope you have perfectly recovered your health. Major Sargent left me yesterday; he writes to you by this conveyance. It will be proper that you take into the field with you, a brass three-pounder, and I place the fullest confidence in your abilities, as what we are going to undertake is a serious affair. I take it for granted that there is not the least relaxation from your former rigid discipline. If any officer should prove refractory, arrest him instantly. You will find that I shall always effectually support you in maintaining the strictest subordination. I am indeed very sorry to hear of the distressing situation you have been in with respect to provisions, but by this time Mr. Elliott will certainly have forwarded a sufficiency; say two months' provisions for five hundred men. I have not yet heard from the Pennsylvania militia, nor received any late accounts from Kentucky; but report says they are determined to turn out spiritedly upon the occasion.

I am, &c., JOS. HARMAR.

Major J. F. HAMTRAMCK, commanding officer at Fort Knox, Post Vincennes.

P. S. — We have heard that you have entered the matrimonial state. Mrs. Harmar and myself wish you every happiness in it. You will please to present our kind compliments to Mrs. Hamtramck, and accept them yourself likewise.

Same to General Mifflin.

FORT WASHINTON, September 4, 1790.

MY DEAR GENERAL—I did myself the honor to write you a few lines by Lieutenant Kingsbury, since which Lieutenant Denny has handed me your letter of the 23d January. I am much obliged to you for the attention paid in delivering Lieutenant Denny orders for the several sums stated by me to be due to him and other officers for recruiting services for which they have received payment. The official letter from the Secretary at Council, giving me proper credit for the returned orders on the treasurers of Westmoreland, Fayette and Washington, has been also received, which is very satisfactory, as it settles all public accounts which the State of Pennsylvania had against me. I am preparing for an expedition against the savages, to go forward the first of next month. Our regular force is but small; there is a prospect of being joined by a considerable body of militia, who I hope will stick to the text, and not leave me in the lurch.

Believe me dear General, &c.,

JOS. HARMAR.

His Excellency THOMAS MIFFLIN, at Philadelphia.

Lieutenant Denny to General Harmar.

PHILADELPHIA, March 9, 1791.

DEAR GENERAL—The great people here have at length determined to carry on another campaign against the savages upon a more extensive plan than the last. In the meantime they have thought it necessary to order a temporary expedition, entirely of militia, for the purpose of amusing the Indians and to prevent them from committing any further depredations on the frontiers. Mr. Brown, of Congress, is furnished with ten thousand dollars for this business. G. K. took up so much time in forming his report for Congress, and both houses debated so long upon it, that I am doubtful whether men can be enlisted for the grand object and marched over the mountains in season; the encouragement will not be sufficient, though six dollars bounty is to be given. I was in hopes that when these military arrangements were all settled, that G. K. would dispatch me for head-quarters, but I am now afraid he means to detain me to recruit. Armstrong has received his instructions and began this day—Beatty and myself are yet waiting in suspense. I wish most sincerely to be with you, for I am perfectly sick of the court and all courtiers.

Captain Beatty writes to you by this conveyance, and incloses the military establishment, by which you will find that Major ——— is appointed Lieut.-Col. commanding of the second regiment. Some reasons which will operate very forcibly upon him, make me think that it is uncertain whether he will accept or not. Some people are troubled with the *cannon fever*, and if I was not much mistaken, he was very subject to it—a feather bed would be a fitter place than the field. The Governor being appointed to command the army this summer, I hope you will be reconciled. I am very confident that no other man would be submitted to; but the long friendship which has subsisted between you both, and his commission expiring at the end of the campaign, as I am informed it does, will make it more easy. Believe me, he has been a sound friend when you greatly stood in need of one, and

I am, dear General, your obedient

E. DENNY.

Brigadier-General HARMAR,
Head-Quarters, Ohio river.

Same to same.

PITTSBURGH, June 1, 1792.

DEAR SIR—We have alarms here hourly. The savages begin to show themselves. The settlements north of the old Pennsylvania road are all abandoned and the people fled across the Monongahela. Myers' and M'-Nair's, and along there, are frontiers. Several circumstances seem to combine to frighten the people here and cause them to dread a stroke. They have a Frenchman confined in jail, suspected for being a spy; indeed he has acknowledged that he was sent to gain information of the strength of the town, and had his orders from Colonel Butler, of Niagara. He has also confessed that two men of this place were concerned with him, one of them a *confidential character* in public service, the other is Tom Girty. You may have seen by the papers, that Jeffers had a kind of independent command of friendly Indians and rifle men. We heard yesterday from Venango that several of these friendly Indians had in a formal manner delivered up to Captain Cass, the commandant there, their rifles, and had declared that they intended joining against us. This circumstance is not very favorable. You will suppose that I have very early hark'd in with the people, but it was always my opinion that fifty bold fellows might set the town on fire and retire without any loss, and I am very certain it could now be done with ease. As to the soldiers here, though there are fifty, I would not give them their half gill a day for all their services, unless it is that perhaps the appearance of them may deter the enemy from making an attempt; for should an attack be made, the utmost they could do would be to defend the stockade fort where they are quartered. The militia are really tolerably well employed. A strong guard mounts every evening, from which there are constant patrols all night; besides they are frequently out on scouts for one, two and three days at a stretch. The people wonder the soldiers don't come out. The present protection appears not to be sufficient. The State troops are under no subordination, and it is a question whether they render as much service as they might. Should you see Governor Mifflin, please to offer my respects. My kind compliments to Mrs. Harmar, and believe me,

Yours, &c.,

E. DENNY.

General HARMAR, Philadelphia.

General Harmar to Peter Audrain.

PHILADELPHIA, July 12, 1792.

DEAR SIR — I have had the pleasure to receive your letter of the 22d ultimo, per post. The gentleman whom General Gibson informed you that he dined in company with at my house, was Monsieur Peyroux, the commandant at St. Genevieve. He does not leave this city for sometime; but when he does, it will afford me peculiar happiness to be in any way instrumental in serving you; your name shall therefore be mentioned to him, and I will give him an introductory letter to you before he sets out for Pittsburgh.

I shall remember you to the French Ambassador when I see him. Be pleased to present my best respects to all our good friends in Pittsburgh, and believe me to be, with great esteem,

Yours, &c.,

JOS. HARMAR.

Mr. PETER AUDRAIN, Merchant, Pittsburgh.

Same to Ebenezer Denny.

PHILADELPHIA, September 6, 1792.

DEAR SIR—Your two letters of the 1st June and the 30th July, have been duly received, by which I am happy to learn your success in trade. The loss of Hardin and Trueman I sincerely regret, particularly the former. Murdering of flags does not seem to indicate a speedy peace with the savages. I have conversed with Major Asheton relative to the settlement at Presqu' Isle, but we are not yet sufficiently informed on that subject. I am rather inclined to think that I shall not become an adventurer in it.

I shall not forget to remember you to Governor Mifflin, and hope something may turn up to your advantage through his means. You wish to know the price of stocks. They tell me six per cents bring 22f. cash. Mrs. H. sends her compliments to you. Our friend Ernest will deliver you this letter; and believe me to be,

Your friend and humble servant,

JOS. HARMAR.

Mr. EBENEZER DENNY, Pittsburgh.

E. Denny to General Harmar.

PITTSBURGH, January 5, 1793.

DEAR SIR — I have just time to write a few lines by a very particular and one of my most intimate friends at this place, John Woods, Esq. Any civilities which may be shown him will lay me under new obligations. He has a short letter from me to Governor Mifflin on the subject of militia appointments. I hope that you will be the adjutant-general. Respects to Mrs. Harmar, and believe me, dear sir,

Your faithful,

E. DENNY.

General Harmar to E. Denny.

PHILADELPHIA, February 8, 1793.

DEAR SIR—I have the pleasure to acknowledge the receipt of your two letters, the one dated the 22d December last, the other on the 5th ultimo. I am very sorry for the loss of Stephen,[1] as by all accounts he was a faithful, honest lad. As for the Population Society, and the Presqu' Isle plan, I have no great opinion of it, and therefore choose to decline it altogether. You may depend upon it, what influence I have with the Governor shall be exerted to serve you upon the militia establishment. Mrs. Harmar sends you her respectful compliments.

I am, dear sir, with very great esteem and regard,

Your affectionate friend,

JOS. HARMAR.

E. Denny to General Harmar.

PITTSBURGH, February 22, 1793.

DEAR SIR—I feel myself much obliged by your flattering assurances. The militia establishment—I hope it may please you and be the cause of a visit to this country; it will add to your health and enable you to attend personally to your private concerns. My affectionate respects to Mrs. Harmar, and believe me to be, dear sir,

With the highest esteem and regard, &c.,

E. DENNY.

General HARMAR, Philadelphia.

General Harmar to Governor Howell.

PHILADELPHIA, August 20, 1793.

DEAR SIR—With great pleasure I received your friendly letter of the

[1] Major Denny's servant during his Indian campaigns.

9th instant. To hear from an old soldier, for whom I have a particular regard, was highly gratifying to me. I live in a small house in Eighth street; when you arrive in this city, I shall do myself the honor to wait upon you and give you soldierly fare. Sorry I am indeed, that it is out of my power at present to accept of your polite invitation to visit you at Trenton — being so much busied with the militia business prevents it. You are desirous of having one thousand copies of the Baron Steuben's Manœuvres, printed on good paper, with well executed plates, procured at a reasonable rate, to be bound with your militia law. I have made the necessary inquiry, and inclose you the proposals of Mr. Cist, a printer here, which, if they meet with your approbation, shall be cheerfully attended to on my part. The edition has had the sanction of the War Office, consequently must suppose it to be *correct*. You will be pleased to receive the inclosed militia law of this State — the plates have been struck, but are not annexed to the instructions; perhaps you would wish to go to no more expense than they have done, if so, let me know.

I have the honor to be, dear sir, with every sentiment of friendship and regard,

Yours, &c.,

JOS. HARMAR.

His Excellency RICHARD HOWELL, Esq.,
Governor of the State of New Jersey.

Same to Ebenezer Denny.

PHILADELPHIA, November 23, 1793.

DEAR SIR — It was not until the 20th instant that I had the pleasure of receiving your two letters of the 13th September and 11th October last. That the treaty did not succeed, does not at all surprise me; I never was of the opinion that it would. If General Wayne should be unsuccessful with his army (which I sincerely hope may not be the case), the frontier settlements on the Ohio must be left in a wretched exposed situation. The consequence would be dreadful indeed. It is to be lamented that government has not long since established a post at Presqu' Isle, as it is most undoubtedly a very eligible position to prevent an intercourse between the Six Nations and the western Indians, and at the same time secure their trade and friendship, and encourage settlements upon the lands of the State on Lake Erie. I have conversed with the Governor, and showed him your letters upon this subject, but his reply was, that to establish a post there is an object that should come under the notice of the general government; therefore, my friend, your expectations of a command there are fruitless, which I am sorry for.

The direful contagion which has been so long prevalent in this city, has now entirely ceased. You may venture to come down with perfect safety. It is supposed that from the 1st August to the 10th November, about five thousand persons have died, but certainly not altogether with this malignant disorder. If Colonel Neville should resign his brigade-inspectorship, it is probable you may fill that office; but *kissing goes by favor*. I can promise nothing, only that, by the Lord, you shall have my interest for it. Mrs. Harmar joins me in congratulating you on your matrimonial connexion, and believe me to be, dear sir, with great esteem and regard,

Your friend, &c.,

JOS. HARMAR.

Governor Mifflin to Captain E. Denny.

PHILADELPHIA, March 1, 1794.

SIR—Inclosed you will receive a copy of an Act of the General Assembly, entitled "An act for more effectually securing the trade, peace and safety of the port of Philadelphia, and defending the western frontiers of the Commonwealth;" a commission by which you are appointed captain of the Allegheny company; a sketch of the appointments and arrangements of all the companies directed to be raised, and a copy of an act, entitled "An act for laying out a town at Presqu' Isle." You will be pleased, sir, to take all lawful measures, under the instructions of the brigade-inspector of the county, and with the aid of the officers of your company, for engaging, during the term, and for the pay prescribed by the act for the defense of our frontiers, four sergeants, four corporals, one drummer and fifer, or two buglers, and sixty-five rank and file, or privates. In making your enlistments, you will stipulate with the men, that, if the state of the war on the frontiers shall, in my judgment, require their continuance in the service of the Commonwealth, after the expiration of the term of eight months mentioned in the law, they shall continue accordingly until the meeting of the Legislature next ensuing the expiration of the last term, for any shorter period that I may direct. From the sketch of the appointments and arrangements of the several companies, you will perceive that you are called on to command the detachment which is made, in order to carry into effect the act entitled "An act for laying out the town of Presqu' Isle;" and the importance of the object, as well as the difficulties that may attend its accomplishment, will evince the confidence that is reposed in your zeal, spirit and prudence. In the discharge of your trust, I am persuaded you will pay a due respect to the design and spirit of the laws I have communicated to you; and therefore, I shall content myself with suggesting the following general regulations:

1st. Messrs. Irvine, Ellicott and Gallatin, the commissioners who are employed to lay out the town at Presqu' Isle, will probably be engaged in that duty early in the month of May next. It will be necessary, therefore, that before that time arrangements should be made for establishing some post for protection and defense in the neighborhood of Presqu' Isle; and the commissioners have thought that a spot at Le Bœuf will be the most eligible and convenient for their undertaking. The lieutenant who is detached from the artillery company, will transport thither, under the convoy of his detachment, a competent supply of provisions, cannon, arms, ammunition and camp equipage. Of these articles, an officer in the nature of quarter-master will have the immediate custody; but they are, nevertheless, to be considered as being under your superintending care and disposition, to be preserved with the greatest caution; not to be used but in cases of necessity, and to be accounted for by you, to any person who may be appointed to succeed you in command, or who may be authorized to receive the same when the purposes of the post shall be attained You will be pleased to strengthen the detachment of artillery by a party of infantry under your command, whenever they advance from Pittsburgh; and this party should consist, I think, of not less than a sergeant and fifteen men, or if circumstances will admit, of an officer and twenty men.

2d. As the object of the detachment under your command is to carry the act for establishing a town at Presqu' Isle into effect, you shall deem it your duty to comply with every lawful request of the commissioners; in stationing the men in such numbers and at such places, as they shall from time to time think requisite to insure their safety and defense, and generally in aiding and facilitating their measures by all means in your power.

3d. The Legislature having made provision for surveying and opening the roads, one from Reading and the other from French creek to Presqu' Isle, it is obvious that the establishment of the town is intimately connected with those objects; and therefore you should deem it your duty to grant all the aid and protection to the respective commissioners and contractors employed in surveying and opening these roads, that is compatible with a due attention to the particular charge which is confided to you.

4th. In the present state of our northern frontier, you will deem it a duty peculiarly incumbent upon you, to avoid giving any occasion of offense to the peaceable Indians or to the British garrisons which are in that quarter. You will endeavor, in case any intercourse should necessarily or accidentally take place with them, to conciliate and cultivate a good and friendly understanding; and you are, above all things, to remember that the objects of your appointment are strictly those of protection and defense, and that any act of aggression or hostility committed against any person or persons in amity with the United States, or committed against any person or persons whomsoever, out of the jurisdiction of Pennsylvania, will be unauthorized and punished according to law.

5th. For the purposes of information, you will keep a journal of your proceedings, and maintain a regular correspondence as well with the commissioners appointed to lay out the town of Presqu' Isle as with the brigade-inspector of Allegheny county; and when any matter of public importance shall occur, you will, with all possible dispatch, communicate the same to me.

To these regulations it is perhaps unnecessary to add that it is expected that you will give the strictest attention to the health, order and discipline of the detachment under your command; and in all things so act as to justify the confidence which your country has reposed in you.

THOMAS MIFFLIN.

To EBENEZER DENNY, Esq.,
Captain of the Allegheny company, &c.

Captain Denny to Governor Mifflin.

PITTSBURGH, April 25, 1794.

SIR — I had the honor of writing to you by the last post, mentioning the necessity we were under of calling out a few militia in order to take advantage of the rivers while up. I then could not calculate with any certainty what time the detachments from other counties would arrive; however, the greatest part of them came in time to join the volunteers. They marched on Monday last and encamped the first night twenty-one miles from here, on the route to Fort Franklin, and in all probability would reach that place yesterday. Ensign Mehaffy, from Westmoreland, had the direction of the State troops, two sergeants, two corporals and forty-three privates; the volunteers consisted of a captain, lieutenant, thirty men; total, one captain, one lieutenant, one ensign and seventy-seven men. They will go no farther than Le Bœuf.

I have not such confidence in the Six Nations as to think they will favor the establishment; and a small party subject to the power of a few ill-disposed Indians, would be more liable to be stopped by them; not that I think they will offer any violence immediately, but I think they will throw some objections in the way; perhaps desire the business postponed for a while. We have certain information that the chiefs were lately assembled in council at the mouth of Buffalo. Their meetings there have always been influenced by British agents, and I should not be surprised to find them return with a wish to prevent the settlement at Presqu' Isle. I have received letters from the inspectors of Washington and Westmoreland counties, informing me of the orders they had from you, telling me that whatever reinforcements we required might be depended on. Doctor Wilkins is gone in company with the party to Le Bœuf. I have requested him, and directed Mehaffy, to write to me by every opportunity; and should anything material be discovered, to send off an express.

I am, with respect, &c.,

EBENEZER DENNY, *Captain*

Same to same.

PITTSBURGH, May 2, 1794.

SIR — I had the honor to address you on the 25th ultimo, since which nothing material has happened. The party sent forward to establish a post of protection and defense at Le Bœuf, consisted of a captain, lieutenant and thirty volunteers, and an ensign and forty-seven of the State troops; they were at Fort Franklin on the 24th, as expected. A very seasonable rain, which fell while they were on the march to this post, will (provided the way is open) enable the contractor to push all the provisions and stores up the creek without loss of time. We are not without apprehensions that this council-holding between the chiefs of the Six Nations and the British, at the mouth of Buffalo creek, may terminate unfavorably to our establishment. The Cornplanter is not with them; but I am told that he has ordered away the traders who had stores in his town. Before our detachment proceeds farther than Mead's settlement, the disposition of the Indians will be known; and in case any opposition is offered, the party will halt and secure themselves and the stores until a sufficient reinforcement joins them. I depend upon Doctor Wilkins' and Ensign Mehaffy's earliest notice. Lieutenant Murphy and Ensign Patterson have been about three weeks away endeavoring to find men for the Allegheny company. Patterson has been tolerably successful; Murphy I have not heard from; he is in Fayette county. They must both be here in a few days now. No doubt but you have been informed of the death of Lieutenant Hazlewood; his men will reach this perhaps in six days.

I acknowledge the honor of your letter of the 25th April. The delays which took place in sending on the men from the other counties, the inspector took pains to account for, and I am in hopes there will be no ill consequences. The inspectors are all desirous to promote the establishment of Presqu' Isle, and have informed me of their orders from the Governor.

E. DENNY.

Same to same.

FORT FRANKLIN, June 14, 1794.

SIR — I have the honor of acknowledging your two letters, dated the 9th and 11th instant; after receiving the first, we concluded it would be best to proceed on our march. We arrived here the day before yesterday; all well. The account of Ransom's people being killed was too true, but by what nation of Indians is yet doubtful. Mr. Ellicott and Mr. Wilkins have written and sent two runners for the Cornplanter, and they have requested me to wait the return of the express; when they arrive you will be informed of the success of the message. I am suspicious the old fellow will not show himself. The fact is, that the Indians about here, from twenty downward, for some time past have been exceedingly insolent, treating the officers, the fort and every person about it, with the utmost contempt; but since our arrival they have altered their tune, so say Lieutenant Polhemus and Doctor M'Cray. We have written to Le Bœuf and gave the officer there a caution. The day after to-morrow the runner is to be back. Van Horn and Bales, the two men who brought your last letter, saw one Indian at the plain, about twenty miles this side of Pittsburgh, and the trace of six or seven.

June 16th. — Yours inclosing a copy of Polhemus' came yesterday. The Cornplanter's nephew arrived from the towns about the same time. He delivered a long speech from his uncle to Lieutenant Polhemus. Upon summing up the whole, we have not a shadow of doubt but that a plan was formed to destroy all the posts and settlements in this quarter. It was all done upon the strength or prospect of a war between the British and ———; *that* subsiding, the other, I am in hopes, has also. There is no doubt but the English will urge them to join the western Indians, and have done every thing possible, and perhaps a few may; but I rather think that unless we have a war with them, we'll have none with the Six Nations generally.

The Cornplanter has gone to another council at Buffalo; he set out the same time the nephew started for this place, and will return in about ten days. He says he is very sorry for the mischief done lately, and is extremely concerned at the account given of their going to take up the hatchet; says they are bad men who reported it; that it's a lie, and insists upon knowing whom the information came from. It is evident that a stroke was meditated, but now perhaps dropped. Every apology which he can possibly make won't be sufficient to clear him of the imputation of a traitor. Some of the nation say that the English have bought O'-Beal. We shall spend two days to come, in helping Mr. Polhemus to put his garrison in some state of defense; for should anything happen it, we should fare the worse above.

I have the honor, &c.,

E. Denny.

Same to Major-General Gibson.

Fort Le Bœuf, June 27, 1794.

Dear Sir—Inclosed you will receive a copy of a message brought me by a deputation of chiefs and warriors sent for that purpose, from the Six Nations, and also our reply. You will perceive by the message that the Indians are disposed to have us pushed back; and if we don't leave the country they are to consider us as no friends. I don't apprehend much danger here as long as we can keep our men together; but at present, a number of the people who were on before me are ill with the flux; and the working parties which we are necessarily obliged to have at some distance, together with two escorts, one sent to Franklin with pack horses, the other somewhere between here and Cussewago, with boats, reduces our force considerably. Doctor Wilkins[1] has made a requisition for ten or twelve men to be sent to Pitt, to guard a drove of cattle on to this place. From the present appearances it would be very improper to detach so many men from my command; I am, therefore, here under the necessity of begging a few militia for that purpose; they will be wanted about the first week in the next month. Indeed, at this particular juncture, I don't think a company would be too many to assist us in having the supplies brought forward. The people of Cussewago wished for a guard of my men; I could not spare them yet; the consequences, I am afraid, will be a total evacuation of that settlement. If you should think proper to send on a company, a part posted at Mead's will answer a double purpose; there the contractor has a deposit, and it serves our people as an intermediate post between Franklin and this place, which ought to be by all means, supported. You promised you would not neglect us.

E. Denny.

---

1 Since better known as General John Wilkins.

Same to Governor Mifflin.

FORT LE BŒUF, June 29, 1794.

The route from Franklin to Le Bœuf, by way of Cussewago, is not less than sixty miles. The first part may be made good, but the other will be very difficult. A straight road from Franklin to Le Bœuf won't exceed forty-five miles; but it is yet uncertain what kind of road this country will afford.

We would be much better of a surgeon; many of the men who were on here, are lying bad with the flux. However, we are doing every thing possible to get them on foot. Constant salt provisions, and not the least attention paid to cleanliness, has caused it to spread. Our fresh meat, with the little knowledge we have of medicine, has already had a good effect. The evening of our arrival here I received the inclosed letter from Israel Chapin, superintendent for the Six Nations. The next day, by the time mentioned, he and the Indians arrived. They expected to meet us at Presqu' Isle. They came from the mouth of Buffalo there, in a row boat. Next morning we met and received their message, a copy of which, together with our reply, is also inclosed. William Johnson, who is mentioned in the message, is a British agent; he acted slily as prompter to the chiefs. They denied having sold their country; told us that the paper (deed) which they signed at Fort Harmar, was thought by them *then* to be nothing but a treaty of peace, and that the goods which were delivered them they considered as presents. Money, they say, they received none. The line which they had marked upon their map began at O'Beal's town, and in a direct line crossed French creek just below Mead's, and on the head of Cuyahoga; from thence to the Muskingum, and down the Ohio and to its mouth, and up the Mississippi, leaving a small square for a trading house at the mouths of the rivers, and one where Clarksville now is. The fellows were very inquisitive to know if any surveyors were out, and told us to stop every person going toward the lake. They will expect an answer from our great council.

I would just remark, that in case of a war, it will be very difficult keeping either horses or cattle about the place, and impossible to get any supplies, being so near their towns, unless we have three times the number of men which we now have, and establish several intermediate posts. I have the honor to inclose a return of the troops, and am with perfect respect, sir,

Your most obedient servant,

E. DENNY.

General Harmar to Governor Mifflin.

December 26, 1796.

DEAR GOVERNOR—Be pleased to receive the inclosed letter from Captain Denny. He informs me that there is reason to expect several new counties will be laid off to the westward of Pittsburgh, this winter, in which case he has solicited my influence to interest myself with you in his behalf. The commission of prothonotary, with the recorder's office attached, would answer his wishes. If those new counties should be laid off, I beg leave in a particular manner, to recommend Captain Denny, as a man of honor and probity, and capable of filling such an office. Your Excellency will add to the numerous obligations already conferred upon me, by taking Captain Denny's application under your earliest notice, and securing one of those offices for him.

I have the honor to be, &c.,

JOS. HARMAR.

Same to Ebenezer Denny.

HARMAR'S RETREAT, December 27, 1796.

DEAR SIR—I have been favored with yours of the 5th instant, wherein I observe it is your wish to be appointed prothonotary and recorder to one of the new counties expected to be laid off this winter, to the west of Pittsburgh. An inflammation on my leg has confined me at home for this sometime past, which has prevented my visiting Philadelphia as usual; but immediately upon the receipt of yours, I wrote a letter to the Governor in your behalf, a copy whereof I now inclose you. In a few days I shall be able to repair to the city, when you may depend upon it, your application shall receive personally all the support in my power to give it, and sincerely hope it may be attended with the desired success. Let me know whether I shall send you a power of attorney to transact the business respecting my lands in Westmoreland. As you are well acquainted with those landed matters, I wish very much that you would undertake it, and pray do not let any of my lands be sold for payment of the taxes. By the next conveyance I shall send you a particular description of all of them. Mrs. Harmar joins me in best respects to Mrs. Denny and yourself, and believe me to be, with true regard,

Your friend and humble servant,

JOS. HARMAR.

Captain Denny to General Harmar.

PITTSBURGH, May 5, 1797.

DEAR SIR—I was happy to hear of your recovery. Our friend Ernest is about to leave us, with his family, for Detroit; we in a particular manner will feel the loss; but it must be so. The difficulty of living at this place on account of the very high price of provisions, will oblige a number to remove. Instance, butter 2 / 6 current; indifferent beef 9d., and bacon 1 / 6, and every other article nearly in proportion, and all for cash, and a scarcity of the whole. This extraordinary change can easily be accounted for—but there is no remedy; time will perhaps regulate things, at present there is nothing to be done.

Governor St. Clair has been for some time past at his place not expected to live, but I have heard to-day that he is recovering once more. Mrs. Denny joins me in best respects to Mrs. Harmar and yourself, and believe me to be, with affectionate regard,

Yours, &c.,

E. DENNY.

General HARMAR, near Philadelphia.

Same to same.

PITTSBURGH, December 14, 1797.

DEAR SIR—Several candidates for office in the new counties have started up lately. Robert Galbraith, States Attorney here, and George Thompson, one of our associate judges, are both aiming for what I applied for last winter. John Woods, Senator, has told me that his influence is promised to them — he would serve me, but they must be served first. Esquire Wallace and Captain Herron, our Representatives, are my particular friends—Wallace will interest himself more than the other two. He is equally the friend of Thompson, at least I think he would be glad to serve us both. I should like very well if Thompson could be provided for along with myself. We regard his family, and he stands in as much need as I do.

Yours, &c.,

E. DENNY.

Same to same.

PITTSBURGH, December 20, 1799.

DEAR SIR — I was sorry to hear by Mrs. Harmar's letter of the 8th, that your indisposition rendered you unable to write. I am not certain if you have any land in this county other than your State donation, and that is not taxable. There are several tracts near a creek called Puckety, which empties into the Allegheny river eighteen miles above this, in Plum township, that has been returned for several years past in your name, but since I have been commissioner, have entered them in the name of Jenkins' heirs; I think they are a part of Mr. Kenley's division of the estate; but you must know best. I wish you would inform me; at any rate, while I am in office there shall be none sold that you can have any possible claim to. What lies in Westmoreland county, or the Western Territory, is entirely out of our reach.

I did expect to see you this fall, but was obliged to be abroad the months of August and September last, after which found it necessary to be at home. Ernest was in from Detroit in July. Mrs. Denny accompanied him back. They rode to Presqu' Isle, got on board a sloop and had a passage of twenty-seven days — stormy weather in August. They were beat back to Presqu' Isle twice, and and over to the English shore, where they got shelter. I left home a month after they did, was at Presqu' Isle in four days and a half. There was no vessel for Detroit; shipped myself for Fort Erie, got down in a day and a night; engaged a passage to Detroit in a British sloop ready to sail in two days; in the meantime procured a horse, rode eighteen miles down Niagara river to the Falls, where I spent part of one day. Returned back to Fort Erie the evening of the second day; got on board that night, weighed anchor and had a pleasant passage in five days up to Detroit. I intended coming off in the first vessel, but Ernest and Mrs. D. had been there but a few days before me. Colonel Strong commands there. He and the old woman are so fat you would scarcely know either — rolling about in *nothing*. We were treated very politely by the old couple. I was much disappointed in the place. It is filthy beyond measure—calculated to accommodate a few traders. A square of about three hundred by four hundred yards divided by narrow street, one only that a cart can turn about in, and the lots no larger than sufficient for a tolerable house to stand on. One or two houses excepted, they resemble the buildings at Vincennes — pickets round the whole. There is a small regular work back of the town, but it is lost to appearance, and covers only the side next itself. It seems to have been designed for a retreat for the commanding officer. They say there is a covered way to it from what is called the citadel. This last place is nothing more than the barracks and small parade within the town square, separated from the dwellings by pickets. There is a great quantity of goods taken to Detroit yearly, but no trade there — it is made a place of deposit; deputy traders, who go out into the Indian country, are fitted off from thence. The plan answered the first intention. The traders jammed up together, in order to fence in the whole and keep out drunken Indians The place is crowded at present, and not an inch of ground to extend their buildings. I staid ten days. We got on board a vessel bound to Fort Eric (where the goods are stored that come round the Falls). The captain promised to touch at Presqu' Isle and land us. The first day we dropped down the river and came to anchor at a new town the British are building at its mouth, eighteen miles below Detroit. We had time to go ashore a while. They are making this place very strong; it commands the river. When the wind sprung up we got under way and into the lake with daylight, and next evening before sunset we were ashore at Presqu' Isle—about twenty-four hours pleasant sailing.

It is rare that both shores of Lake Erie can be seen at the same time. Land lies very low, and is not discovered until within four or five leagues. Our shore is high, and the bank for the most part is ninety feet. The land rises gradually for five miles back. The British, in a few years, will have their shore settled from one end to the other. They give the land to people who are sick of a democratic government. A great many Germans have settled there from Pennsylvania. Upper Canada is now very strong. The inhabitants like the government; no taxes but for repairing roads and bridges.

But this "report" is so lengthy, that I think I see you throw it to Charles or Eliza. [Here a piece of the letter is torn off.] I wanted to let Mrs. H. know what sailors, &c., we are.

I must inform you, further, that Colonel Hamtramck has been here since September. You know he married again; his wife is at Fort Wayne. He is about as broad as he is long. Our Colonels, as they were advanced in the army, seemed to have been better furnished; they look like men who have received an additional allowance; they are both much the shape and figure of Pratt. I saw Kingsbury this summer on his way to Connecticut. He was very anxious to see you, but he was afraid to go to Philadelphia. He had been disappointed in a furlough, and thought if he made his appearance he would be ordered off somewhere. He had leave of absence from General Wilkinson, whom he left at Natchez. He looked well—much better than ever he did before. He was one of your officers that I thought could be depended on—never promised more than he intended, and always ready when ordered. I think him an honest fellow.

In all that I have said, I have not made one complaint. I am determined to make the best of what offers—rough or smooth—and say nothing; except mob government, I can't but dislike; I shall always hate disorder. How a man brought up in an army can join in the democratic hue and cry and be Jacobin, is the most astonishing thing to me in the world; and yet I am told there are many of our old officers such. It is wonderful. I will do my own duty punctually, let me be in what station I may; must take thought how I place myself. I wish it was in my power to see you soon. You have my prayers, and Mrs. Denny joins me in our best and most affectionate respects to Mrs. H. and yourself.

Yours, &c.,

E. DENNY.

General HARMAR, near Philadelphia.

APPENDIX No. II.

VOCABULARY OF WORDS IN USE WITH THE DELAWARE AND SHAWANEE INDIANS.

FORT M'INTOSH, January, 1785.

One. Guttee.
Two. Nechshaa.
Three. Nochhaa.
Four. Nevaa.
Five. Paaleenough
Six. Gutdosh.
Seven. Neshaush.
Eight. Haush.
Nine. Peechkung
Ten. Tellen.

Answer. Nauhcoomel.
Ashes. Tenday poonk
Army. Magy napy nagay.
Away. Magyktallinohway.
Angry. Maanumksee.
After. Ohhtengue.
Abuse. Mamhaylachhky.
Above. Hoqruongg.
Acquaintance. Keneehnateena.
Active. Longseet lenew.
Adopt. Laabhalteen.
Advice. Cataamecoomel.
Afraid. Weeshaso.
Affront. Daaheehook.
All. Weamay.
Alive. Leahelleahy.
Allow. Quanaleinaneenolama.
Alone. Nahopanee.

Bottle. Seekhockhock.
Beggar. Wayheenowayt.
Begone. Allemohakeoky.
Believe. Colamheetole.
Begin. Lapeechoceelahtoo.
Behind. Oahtengk.
Bird. Tcholenze.
Bite. Sapalake.
Bitter. Wissacone.
Black. Seakcay.
Bleed. Moocooelhasey.
Blend. Capengoat.
Blood. Mhoak.
Bold. Hchamenseet.
Buck. Paluppy.
Beaver. Thomaagru.
Bear. Mochguee.
Bag. Hempsee notich.
Belt. Calaman beeson.
Big. Hengue.
Blanket. Auchqueon.
Binding. Helaames.
Brother. Neemat.
Bridle. Rechgalundom.
Brotch. Anechkomman.
Bread. Auchbone.

Buffalo. Serelea.
Bed. Ahpeeinah.
Bad. Tacoo-willet, or Metehick.
Brag. Nehnochqehelachemo.
Build. Weekhail.
Bullet. Tackalonne.
By-and-by. Peahho.

Cow. Ockshamways.
Cat. Poosheis.
Coat. Shauchuqueon.
Child. Meemendat.
Corn. Musquem.
Cold weather. Tayheekk.
Cold. Taayh.
Camps. Weekhaten.
Carry. Naoindayt.
Church. Paadamoecaan.
Churl. Ahootong.
Civil. Tahowsing.
Clean. Cahsheehieck.
Comb. Tcheeamookan.
Comrade. Neetes.
Coarse. Cauhjeck.
Cry. Laback.
Cruel. Nemowhahelyhent.

Doe. Nonsheto.
Dog. Myckhanee.
Delaware. Ellenopey.
Don't. Cottchee.

Eyes. Nishking.
Ear. Netaamket.

Fox. Oqwes.
Father. Nouche.
Feet. Zeetla.
Fire. Tenndaa.
Farewell, brother. Congomallneemot tally mesko.
Fatigued. Noeeqehella.

Gorget. Ocanque.
Good. Wellett.
Give me. Meebil.
Grog. Behauseck.
Go with me. Weejaywee.
Good night. Colacquunhomane.
Great deal. Hhealea.
Get well. Theykell.
Great. Ahaylemoosete.
Goose. Cahauck.

Horse. Nahaaniungas.
Hat. Alluquep.
Hunt. Dallie.
Hard. Cheetoneck.
High. Hoqueong.
How many. Cechhanoe.
Hut. Wigwam
Hot sun. Shealonday.
Handkerchief. Acuntpepey.
Hair. Nemeelauch.
Have you tobacco. Cosshatymay.
Have you cellecaneck. Cokellicanchy.
Have you got. Coulhotoonhots.
Hill. Tchewaung.

I don't know. Tackatane.
I can't understand. Tackoopendy.
I am hungry. Gadapewee.
I wan't drink of water. Gadusomembech.
I will. Mouch.
I don't care. Quanacetch
I want. Gaatatamen.
I love. Doughogay.
I love you. Keyhtaholal.
I'll go with you. Gaughquecheywel.
I'll give you. Peehhocoomelunn.
I must sleep with you. Quebemell.
I'll pay you. Teannhoolan.
I know you. Kanenoale.
I agree with you. Colameellewayen.
I'm glad. Nolelindum.
I'll go. Tallymesko.
Jewsharp. Tatumwaick.

Knife. Sheekcon.
Kettle. Hoose.

Legs. Negataa.
Leggings. Kaakune.
Little. Cochittee.
Lead. Alunze.

Looking glass Cheechanqwe.

Man. Lennew.
Muskrat. Thomusqwes.
Mink. Venengus.
Moccasin. Chippoucko.
Mouth. Doone.
Meet. Veuse.
Moon. Wessking.
Moon rising. Poocanee keesho.
Me. Nee.
Make. Moneeto.
Maybe. Tompsey.

No. Tackoo.
Nopone. Smoke.
Nose. Negeeon.
Not good. Meat heek.
New. Keyshoo.
Night. Peeiskea.

Otter. Connumoch.
One moon. Coodequishoche.

Powder. Nunguee.
Pretty. Willesso.
Pipe. Hobocan.
Pipe stem. Setaughqwe.
Powder-horn. Shemmoo.

Quill. Mesqwin.

Run. Tchamaheil.
River. Sepoo.
Road. Tomaughcon.
Rain. Sugelane.
Ring. Shapulenguhun
Raccoon. Naahoanum.
Rifle. Tutattabaala.

Sister. Neelum.
Smoke. Nopone.
Salt. Seekki.
Snake. Hauchgaske.
Sleep. Caaweele.
Sun setting. Allmeisseegoan.
Sun rising. Cogeinggwahela.
Sober. Leppoati.
Sit down. Lalamatahpee.
Stool. Lehailamatahpenk.
Snow. Veeney.
Spring. Toopayh.
Stone. Auhsson.

Turkey. Chickaanum.
Tomahawk. Temmeheck.
To-morrow. Alaapi.
To-night. Pecheek.
Thimble. Echawessech.
Thighs. Bome.
Too much. Sawmeihheilto.
Tobacco. Kooshaatie.
Teeth. Nepetauch.
Table. Hindaleepwinke.
Tree. Heetock
Tall tree. Quinoxetheitock.
This is. Uuneind.
Town. Hooteeneyg.
Trap. Ceilaheekan.

Very bad. Machelesso.

Woman. Ochqwe.
Wolf. Tummaa.
Water. Beegh.
What do you want. Keekukatatum.
Wood. Tauchhan.
Warm weather. Neepen.
Will you make. Hleilpeil-moneeto.
Warm. Casheita.
What. Kaycoo.
Will you. Hleilpeil.
Where is your. Tahatchkey.
Where. Taanee.
When. Chingy.
When will you. Chingy hotch.

Yes. Coohan.
You. Keygh.
You are foolish Cepechhaw.
You and me. Theyhlonee.
You make. Theyh moneeto.
You drink. Meynell.
You not good. Keyhtacoo-willet.
You. Loosse.

I am not angry, you are a good man. Taakoo maanunhsee shekee lenew.

You are no good man, I am angry. Taakoo woolasee lenew maanuncaksee.

Let me brother smoke. Peetat neemot nopone.

Sit down, brother. Lalamatahpee nee mot.

Will you sleep with me. Gaaitatam.

Did you see him. Wenoussee.

Alone by myself. Nahoohaunee.

Have you tobacco. Cosshatymay.

Have you cellicaneck. Cokellicaneckey.

I know you. Kanenoale.

I agree with you. Colameelewayen.

We are free. Canechelapyehara.

Me no angry, you good men. Nee taacoo menunksee keigh willet lenew.

THE foregoing glossary was made by Major Denny at Fort M'Intosh, when the Delawares were there at the treaty. What follows he got subsequently at Fort Finney, mostly from a Shawanee woman called "the Grenadier Squaw."

FORT FINNEY, January, 1786.

One. Necootey.
Two. Neesway.
Three. Nethway.
Four. Neaway.
Five. Nalanway.
Six. Necotwathway.
Seven. Neeswathway.
Eight. Ethwaasicthey
Nine. Chakethway.
Ten. Matathway.
Eleven. Matathway kete-necootey.
Twelve. Matathway kete-neesway.
Twenty. Neiswapataky.

Answer. Keelakayhaachama.
Ashes. Peckway.
Army. Noatshettepey.
Away. Hellechallay.
Angry. Weacoway.
Alone. Nonseeka.
After. Metanakee.
Abuse. Nelskeemaqua.
Above. Spemekay.

Active. Newaytepay.
Adopt. Lapwawa.
Advice. Necokeahkeema.
Afraid. Coopaney.
Affront. Ackquisseka.
All. Chaiokey.
Alive. Lonowaywe.
Allow. Kepahee.
Advance. Netah.
Always. Mosakee.
Among. Keelaway.
Apple. Missimena.
Arm. Whootseweeka.
Ask. Notootawee.
Aunt. Nethequeatha.
Awake. Amomoh.

Bottle. Weesakaqua.
Beggar. Cottooway.
Begone. Aleckhallee.
Believe. Tepahtoawa.
Begin. Sepoonanoo.
Behind. Wetanakee.

Bird. Weeskelotha.
Bite. Nathepoqua.
Bitter. Wethacanwee.
Black. Cuttaywah.
Bleed. Nemscowee.
Blood. Mesque.
Blind. Nallawaskee.
Bold. Wanasketha.
Back. Pauhcomekee.
Bear. Mouhqua.
Beaver. Amahqua.
Before. Nekanee.
Bag. Petauga.
Belt. Metsquathapay.
Big. Mesaway.
Blanket. Acqueway.
Banding. Awekepetsqua.
Brother. Nechenenah.
Bridle. Nethayketonaypetseca.
Brotch. Sockhoway.
Bread. Tackhawn.
Buffalo. Mathuetha.
Bed. Tahnepakee.
Bad. Mattawessah.
Build. Osetolay.
By-and-by. Paluchahee.
Bring. Peatolah.
Bashful. Nettaqueathy.
Beard. Takawa.
Boil. Welaatay.
Bone. Oohcanee.
Bow. Lenahqua.
Boy. Meskeelawethetha.
Buckle. Monethepay.
Button. Thakhoway.
Buck. Sicapee.
Bull. Keecalthey.

Cow. Soseewa.
Cat. Poosetha.
Coat. Neepcetenaco.
Child. Theemahee.
Cold. Wepee.
Camp. Kesepay.
Carry. Nemeloo.
Churl. Esanee.
Civil. Meloonahee.
Clean. Wothepeah.
Comb. Thequa.
Comrade. Neecanah.
Curse. Matseweehewa
Cry. Maawa.
Cruel. Tepeloo.
Cabin. Sackeweekewa.
Calf. Macooteletha.
Chimney. Tawetay.
Circle. Cayahwecoo
Come. Weheapealo.
Coarse. Kepuckenewee.
Cock. Napayay.
Corn. Tommey.
Cup. Tepheca.
Cross. Ausetethekee.
Canoe. Sokeasea.

Doe. Nosescuttey.
Dog. Wessee.
Delaware. Lenappee.
Don't. Tekee.
Dance. Menelaypee.
Danger. Metseka.
Dark. Pepeketsa.
Drunk. Weenetho.
Daughter. Tanaytha.
Dead. Nepowa.
Deaf. Corkeapesea.
Dear. Ketaqueulemela
Dirty. Ceaawe.
Drink. Menello.
Devil. Matchemanetto.
Door. Squatah.
Dream. Tappoem.
Dress. Waawesah.
Drive. Kahkelay.
Deer. Pesicthey.
Day. Kesakee.

Eagle. Wapalaneathy.
Ear. Towacoh.
Eyes. Seekseco.
Enough. Howay.

Fox. Ocutseethy.
Father. Nothaw.
Feet. Othechey.
Fire. Scootay.

Fatigue. Locatothy.
Face. Heesayke.
False. Mattetepoanee.
Fear. Coopanee.
Feast. Sewethenepee.
Feather. Mequanaa.
Fetch. Peatolah.
Fire. Scootah.
Fish. Noameatha.
Fat. Pemee.
Flying. Onethay.
Forgive. Tekekeecomecawaylatah.
Fork. Nosetchualaya.
Fort. Wahkahoway.
Free. Otepayleta.
Frost. Thocatena.
Fry. Thothecatay.
Full. Quekamee.
Fawn. Macootelathey.
Farewell. Nepaukeche.
Flour. Locana.
Fowls. Cockalamothekay.
Friend. Neekanauh

Gorget. Coselamelouhqua.
Give. Meeleloh.
Good. Wessah.
Grog. Skepecothy.
Go. Puckechey.
Great. Mesaway.
Goose. Lekaw.
Going. Paukeche.
Gold. Othawa monee
Gone. Paukechey.
Grease. Pemee.
Green. Skeporscotto.
Ground. Assiskay.
Gun. Takewa.

Horse. Messawah.
Hunt. Halaway.
Hat. Petaukho.
Hard. Sepenwee.
High. Spemekea.
House. Wigwame.
Hot. Keesetay.
Handkerchief. Peltreway.
Hair. Weletha.
Hay. Pathea.
Hand. Olechey.
Hominy. Methequiatay.
Hawk. Peleethay.
Head. Weesay.
Heart. Teakee.
Help. Notamaweelo.
Hen. Queyatha.
Here. Youmoh.
Hero. Nehohto.
Hide. Keeketoloh.
Hole. Wasalacatwee.
He. Weela.
Horn. Petalwa.

Ice. Mequamah.
Impudent. Matta wessa.
Iron. Coopelayque.
Island. Menethe.
Itch. Pessepaupyea.
Indeed. Tepeloo.

Knife. Manethey.
Kettle. Cohqua.
Kind. Wessa.
King. Okeemaa.

Legs. Ocatchey.
Leggings. Mattatawalee.
Little. Matsquathay.
Lead. Awloolay.
Looking-glass. Wapatnooway.
Labor. Peatetheloo.
Lace. Moneewaykeptseca.
Lady. Wyakiquawa.
Lie. Nonhauchemaw.
Light. Watheyaw.
Linen. Popseahkee.
Long. Keenawaway.
Loss. Newaneto.
Love. Auhqualechekee.
Louse. Wopequa.

Man. Lenay.
Muskrat. Wesasqua.
Mink. Thepanalewetaw.
Moccasins. Mockeethena.
Mouth. Tonee.

Moon. Tepekekeeswa.
Me. Neela.
Make. Hosetopway.
Merry. Lamelewekechelesso.
Milk. Meleneyawpo.
Mountain. Watschekee.
Mamma. Nekkaen.
Mile. Quapekee.
Much. Metchey.
Meridian (12 o'clock). Lawahqua.
Maybe. Quahqua.

No. Matta.
Nose. Potsasey.
New. Oskenway.
Night. Tapahkay.
Name. Eseththo.
Needle. Saponeka.
Nobly. Wessa.
Noise. Wawonessetamekay.
Now. Enookay.

Offer. Ketatewa.

Paint. Welamoh.
Pain. Nekekeetethe.
Peace. Meloonehee.
Powder. Mockcottay.
Pipe. Ohquakay.
Pretty. Welethee.

Quart. Tepneeka.
Quick. Wetapee.
Quiet. Welonahee.

Ribbon. Pepakethakay.
Run (a water). Theepewithe.
River. Theepay.
Road. Meaway.
Rain. Kemewaney.
Ring. Kelechepethoway.
Red. Mesquaway.
Rough. Caassaw.
Raccoon. Othepottee.
Rifle. Pemahiatake.
Rum. Withocapay.
Rich. Pawaywa.

Saddle. Poppeeaway.
Sister. Theemathayquy, or, tootemat.
Smoke. Lewata.
Salt. Nepepemay.
Snake. Monetto.
Sleep. Nepaywah.
Sugar. Thenamesay.
Sober. Quatethe.
Seat. Opetakewaypay.
Snow. Cooney.
Stone. Seegriana.
Sun. Keesothy.
Scarlet. Masquaway.
Scold. Skeemah.
Shot. Pepquan.
Sing. Makamoola.
Silk. Silkee.
Stop. Neepawelo.
Strong. Wesecatewee.
Sick. Auhkaylookay.
Steal. Keemotwa.
Soap. Ketheneka.
Soldier. Saymacanekee.
Sorry. Matchelepo.
Stab. Possepoh.
Star. Alaqua.
Strike. Pehetahweelo.
Sweat. Weesatho.
Sweet. Weecanwee.
Swim. Lolopatheway.
Squirrel. Huneyqa.
Shirt. Papeeseauk.
Sunrise. Peatockwithama.
Sunset. Pucksemo.
Silver. Monee.
Sword. Keeskeca.
Swan. Wapethee.
Speak. Callaweelo.

Turkey. Paleawa.
Tomahawk. Teckhawk.
To-morrow. Wapakey.
To-night. Tapakey.
Thimble. Ketchetanekay.
Thighs. Cheequa.
Too much. Pothemeachy.
Tobacco. Athemah.
Teeth. Wepetalah.

Tree. Metahqua.
Town. Otayway.
Thank. Neeaway.
Talk. Hauchemou.

Very good. Allame wissah.
Very bad. Matta wissah.

Ugly. Mattawelethee.
Uncle. Neseetha.
Undress. Leekeeloh.
Understand. Notaway.

Woman. Auhquawan.
Water. Nepay.
Wood. Tahcoh.
Where. Tahne way.
When. Tanaway lawqua.
White. Wahcanaquah.
Woods. Peleskee.
Wampum. Pettawakay.
Warriors. Nenoptookey.
Wonder. Kanhaw.

You. Keela.
Young. Mianee.
Yesterday. Olagau.
Yes. Skeahla, or, aughaw.

I'm glad to see you. Awassolepo neneaway, or, newalah.
I'm glad. Nowassolepo.
I'm sorry. Wallamelawessalepo.
I'm going to hunt. Neehalaway.
I have been hunting. Neetapalawee
Will you hunt. Hakeypahalaway.
I want. Nowesaweletah.
I don't care. Callapache.
I am merry. Lamelewekechelesso.
I am poor. Ketemaneela.
I love you. Nenasewelemelay.
You love. Kenasewelemay.
I give. Nemeela.
I want to see you. Negwalemela.
I want drink. Naweesamenay.
I am hungry. Neetsqualaway.
I am full. Tepholoh.
I'll dance. Neehmeneelah.

I don't know. Kooque.
I think. Teacetay.
Young brother, or child. Theemakee.
Daylight. Allanawesauspanee.
This night. Tapaykay.
Fine day. Allamawissekesekey.
Very good. Allamewisso, or, wessah.
Great foot. Wanatethay.
Sit down. Lematapeloo.
Farewell. Nepaukechey.
Come back. Keewaylo.
You're healthy. Keewaconele.
Your health. Keewacomelay.
Bad weather. Matcheykeesek.
Will you go and hunt. Hakeepahalaway.
Stay a good while. Natame.
Great ways. Pelloway.
Not far. Mochachenehee.
Put wood on. Potawelote otahco.
Cut wood. Monthelo.
How many. Keathway.
Have none. Matalaqay.
Great many. Metcheay.
You love. Kenasewelemay.
You give. Keemeela.
My wife. Neewa.
Will you. Ketela.
Will you have. Okaymomay.
Have you got. Hockepoona.
My son. Nequatho.
My daughter. Ottanetha.
Where's your wife. Tanakaywa.
Will you smoke. Ockeepotetho.
Come with me. Wetemeloh.
You must. Papeach.
Come here. Peaalah.
Great many. Metchay
Great deal. Metchay.
Shut the door. Keephanso.
Very drunk. Alamawanetho.
Maybe. Queque.
You understand. Keelanotaway.
You lie. Keenanhotchemoh.
You say. Kee hotchemoh.
He says. Wela hotchemoh.
I want. Netuckawatah.
What you want. Wehewayketuckawatah.

NOTES.

"*The flag.*" (p. 10.)

To be assured that I was not wrong in my recollections of what was said by my father, in relation to the flag at Yorktown, I wrote to General Jesup on the subject, knowing that if there was any person living who could correct me, he was the one. General Jesup was not only the son-in-law of Major William Croghan, who served in the staff of Steuben, but he was also a connexion of Colonel Richard C. Anderson, an aid-de-camp of Lafayette. From General Jesup's very high rank in the army early in life, long before the death of these old officers, his intimate friends, I was sure that he must have conversed with them on a subject so much to his taste. The General was absent in Kentucky, and did not get my note until after the Memoir had been stereotyped. The following is his answer:

"WASHINGTON CITY, July 13, 1859.

"MY DEAR SIR—Absence from the city prevented my receiving your letter of the 18th of last month until yesterday, and my reply may therefore be too late for the object you had in view; but late as it is, I will endeavor to give you the anecdote which you requested in regard to the Revolutionary Generals, Baron Steuben and the Marquis Lafayette, at the siege of Yorktown, the surrender of which closed the Revolutionary War.

"Baron Steuben, inspector-general of the army, commanded in the trenches at Yorktown when the flag was received from Lord Cornwallis, commanding the British forces, proposing a capitulation. The proposition was sent to General Washington; commissioners were appointed to arrange the terms of surrender, and were engaged in discussing them, when General Lafayette, whose tour it was next to command in the trenches, marched with his division to relieve the Baron. The latter refused to be relieved, urging that having received the flag, the rules of European warfare secured him the right to retain the command until the negotiation should terminate either by the renewal of hostilities or the surrender of the place. General Lafayette appealed to Washington, who, after consulting Count Rochambeau, commander of the French auxiliary force, and other foreign officers, informed him the Baron was entitled to the command, and must retain it until the matters then under discussion should be decided.

"I had this anecdote from my father-in-law, the late Major William Croghan, of Kentucky, who at one period of the Revolution served in the staff of Baron Steuben, and from the late Colonel Richard Anderson, of the same State, who during the campaign in Virginia, which terminated with the surrender of Lord Cornwallis, was an aid of Lafayette.

With great regard, I remain, my dear sir,

Yours, truly,

TH. S. JESUP.

"Dr. WM. H. DENNY, Pittsburgh, Pa."

"*Tired rider.*" (p. 18.)

The late Mr. William Meredith, many years ago, entertaining at dinner a large party of gentlemen, (among whom I remember his brother-in-law, David C. Ogden,) by way of kindly noticing myself, who, except his son William, was much the youngest person present, took occasion to mention to his guests the first time that he had ever seen my father. "We were," said he, "several of us, young Philadelphians, supping, by invitation, with General Harmar, at his country seat on the Schuylkill. A servant informed our host that there was a gentleman on horseback who wished to see him. The General went out and immediately returned, bringing in a young stranger, who seemed pale, thin, and very much travel-worn and exhausted. He was an officer from the army, and gave us the first news of St. Clair's defeat."

"*The first glass works.*" (p. 24.)

The first glass works of Pittsburgh was erected by Messrs. O'Hara and Craig, in 1797, under the superintendence of Peter William Eichbaum, a German; for at this early period, in those enterprising establishments, the undertakers were obliged to seek for skill and experience amongst our European emigrants. The stone building was standing four or five years ago; its site below Jones' Ferry, on the Monongahela, nearly opposite the Point, is now occupied by other houses for the manufacture of glass. This first establishment made green glass. In a note of General O'Hara, found among his papers after his death, in his own handwriting, is the following remark: "To-day we made the first bottle at the cost of thirty thousand dollars." Ever since, during a period of sixty years, with intervals of depression in common with every other business, the glass manufacture has not ceased to flourish and enrich those engaged in it, until now it even claims to be the leading staple of the "Iron City."

"*Lafleur,*" (p. 24.)

The glass blower, concerned with Denny and Beelen in the glass works at the lower end of the present town of Manchester, was drowned in the Ohio not far above the site of that place. As this poor Frenchman established the first factory there, indeed the first on that side of the river, Lafleur would have been a more appropriate name than Manchester — especially as there has never been a cotton factory in it—and would have given one example of a departure from that servile practice of adopting in our own country very inappropriate European names for our new and flourishing towns.

"*Denny & Beelen.*" (p. 24.)

In getting ready for the preface the desultory sketch or "Memoir," (which at first was intended to be written leisurely as a note for this appendix,) we omitted to mention that the late William B. Foster was, in 1806, a partner of Ebenezer Denny. Mr. Foster subsequently in the war in 1814, got great credit for patriotic personal sacrifices in the service as military storekeeper.

"*Branch Bank of Pennsylvania.*" (p. 25.)

In 1806 or 7, General Moreau and his aid-de-camp, Rapatelle, were at Pittsburgh, on their way to New Orleans. They were out of money. The gentlemen to whom they had letters, O'Hara, Woods and Neville, would have cheerfully supplied their wants; but General Moreau would not permit his aid-de-camp to apply to them. In this embarrassment, Rapatelle consulted an old fellow countrymen, formerly a wealthy planter in St. Domingo, who, from the wreck of a large fortune, kept a shop in Pittsburgh, for thirty years the tenant and next neighbor of Major Denny. Rouaud said, "Here is a receipt for Bologna sausages. Pork in this market is three cents a pound, less than half its price in France or Italy. Venison, which you can substitute for jackass meat, is only three and a half cents. *Allez! vous etes jeune et fort, travaillez!*" Rapatelle rolled up his sleeves—the buffalo packs of the Missouri Fur Company were cleared from the corner of the cellar (since famous for its whiskey), to make room for a chopping bench. Putting a white shirt over his Paris black coat, the gallant cavalier, with a cleaver in each hand, worked as if he really was the son of a butcher. Only one night there was a cessation of the eternal pounding; it was on the occasion of a ball at Spencer's tavern, corner of Second and Market streets, in the very room in which these types are being set. With the exception of that occasion, "the Count" worked every night at his sausages. When he had completed a wagon load he sent them to Baltimore, and drew on the house to which he consigned them. The Branch Bank discounted the bill, and the proceeds enabled the noble exiles to resume those wanderings which terminated at Leipsic and Montmartre.

"*Doctor Carmichael*" (p. 28.)

Went to Natchez, became wealthy, revisited his friends in Pittsburgh after many years—returned to Mississippi, and died a bachelor.

"*Colonel Monroe*," (p. 58.)

Mentioned by Mr. Denny as his companion in one of the voyages down the Ohio, like a true and practical statesman, was even then awake to the importance of opening the navigation to the Gulf. His services subsequently in aiding to accomplish that object by the purchase of Louisiana, were recognized in public addresses by the population on the banks of the great river, when, thirty years after, they received him as the President of the United States.

"*Captain Ercureus Beatty*." (p. 84.)

On leaving the service Pay-master Beatty settled at Trenton, New Jersey, and married the widow of Major William Ferguson, a distinguished artillery officer of the Revolution, who was killed at St. Clair's defeat.

"*Richard Butler*." (p. 166.)

It is probable that in the action of the 4th of November, 1791, Richard Butler was not more severely wounded than his brother Major Thomas Butler, who was brought away with great difficulty and hazard by his younger brother Edward.

The five Butlers at the close of the Revolutionary War held the following grades: Richard and William were colonels, Thomas a captain, and Pierce and Edward lieutenants. Thomas commanded at Fort Fayette, during the Whiskey Insurrection; and although distinguished in that responsible command, was quite as well known subsequently for disobeying the order to cut off queues.

"*Colonel George Gibson*," (p. 173.)

Mortally wounded at St. Clair's defeat, was the father of General George Gibson of the War Department, and of the late Chief Justice of Pennsylvania. He was the brother of General John Gibson (commonly called by his *nom de guerre*—"Horsehead,") the well-known Indian interpreter in Dunmore's war. Colonel George Gibson, besides being a gallant soldier, was an accomplished gentleman, a man of wit and fine imagination. Had *he*, instead of his brother, been at the treaty of Camp Charlotte, and present at the "delivery" of Logan's speech, that posthumous leaf from the plants of Sir William Johnston, might have been imputed to him.

"*General Irvine*." (p. 181.)

William Irvine was one of the best of the five Revolutionary colonels (of Irish birth) who resided in that nursery of brave officers, Carlisle, and Cumberland county. His descendants reside at Brokenstraw, in Warren county, Pennsylvania.

"*Lieutenant Murphy.*" (p. 187.)

In August, 1849, three years before the death of this famous Indian hunter, I went into Armstrong county to see him, having heard my father say that "Samuel Murphy was the best soldier he ever knew;" which in his sense of the word implied truthfulness, honor, intelligence, as well as courage. I thought it possible Murphy might have been in Lord Dunmore's Expedition—probably its only survivor. He was living, where he had settled more than seventy years before, twelve miles below Kittanning, on the "Indian side" of the Allegheny, on his own tract of river bottom, which he had plowed for half a century, and often with a loaded rifle on his shoulder. I was taken by his two maiden daughters to the original cabin, a rod or two detached from the present family dwelling, where he sat on a chair in the middle of the puncheon floor, with his hat on, in his Sunday suit, which hung loosely upon him. It was evident that the noble and gigantic form was wasting away with age.

He said to his daughters who introduced me: "Is it Harmar?" After a minutes silence he remarked, "We encamped at Presqu' Isle the night your brother Harmar was born." As he spoke of that expedition I adverted to the accident on their return descending the Allegheny—when my father fell out from the bow of his perogue, and as the current swept him astern was caught by Murphy and lifted on board with one hand whilst he steered with the other. He quietly corrected me and said, "I was not steering—your father thought one of the men could steer better—I was amidships." For a man ninety-two years old his memory was most faithful—at least of occurrences in early and middle life. He was born in Frederick county, Virginia, in 1756, at a place called Bullskins: came to Fort Pitt the first time in 1772, to get a saddle which had been lent to Doctor Conolly. "It was then," said he, "that I first met your father; and passed the night with him at Turtle creek, on his return from Fort Pitt—at 'Granny Myers',' and not at Hannahstown, on his way going out, as you suppose. I knew him too well to think that he would have mentioned to me that he was a bearer of public dispatches, until after he had executed his mission and delivered his message." Murphy said that he accompanied the Earl of Dunmore's expedition as far as it proceeded. He described the Earl as "a large, full, red faced man—looked as if he lived high;" "was near him, when on foot among the men he came to the Hocking. Saw him step into the water and wade the river with the unconcern of an Indian—rejecting the offer of a young sergeant to carry him over."

Murphy did not recollect Logan; "though," he said, "I must have seen him, as he was among the Indians in the neighborhood. He said he was not present at any reading of the speech at the Scioto treaty. But it was next day the talk of the camp, that Logan boasted he had killed many white men—had taken his revenge."

Murphy said, "I was well acquainted with John Gibson, served under him when he was colonel of the thirteenth regiment—have seen his Indian wife, Betty. I do not recollect his character for veracity."

On my way from Freeport and on the high bluff or river hill, overlooking "Murphy's Bend," I stopped and left my vehicle at John Craig's. Craig was in his ninety-seventh year. He told me that he was five years older than his neighbor Murphy. His mind and memory were nearly gone. He had belonged to what was called "the flying camp"—had been taken prisoner by the Indians, and confined in the same guard house on an island sixty miles above Montreal to which Murphy had been carried by Simon Girty when he was checkmated on the Bear Grass. Craig used to tell the story that one quiet morning Murphy jumped to the ceiling of the guard room and gave the war-whoop. The British sentinel on duty had just said to him that if he would not mention it he would tell him something that would make him glad; on the promise being given, he whispered to him slowly — "Cornwallis is taken!"

"*Major Hamtramck.*" (p. 217.)

This excellent officer died, I believe, at Detroit where Major Denny, on his visit to that place, found him in command. Jesse B. Thomas, at one time a Senator from Illinois, married his widow.

"*Lieutenant Matthew Ernest.*" (p. 224.)

A mysterious fate subsequently attended this officer, whose position as commandant at Fort Pitt made him a frequent correspondent of General Harmar. He was commissioned in the New York militia, then by the President of Congress; and finally appointed by Washington, lieutenant of artillery. After his resignation he settled in Detroit; was collector and inspector of revenue in 1805, when that town was burnt. In the fall of that year he left home for Washington, thence went to New York; from which city several letters from him were received by his family at their residence, "Spring Wells." In the last he said he would leave in a few days "*for his home.*" Since then nothing has ever been heard of him.

"*Captain John Irwin,*" (p. 227.)

Whose residence was then in Pittsburgh; a gallant and severely wounded officer of the Revolution, whose descendants are now residents of Pittsburgh.

Indian Vocabulary. (p. 274.)

The original of the glossary here given is in the handwriting of Major Denny, and was got from the Indians assembled at the treaties — probably the Delaware dialect at Fort M'Intosh, and the Shawanee at Fort Finney. An interesting acquisition at the time was the Delaware Indian spelling book sent to General Harmar by David Zeisberger, Missionary of the Moravian Indians, from his residence on the river Huron.

Recollecting that the late Secretary of the Treasury, William M. Meredith, then a very young man, was sitting next to me at the table, when his father related the incident referred to in a preceding note, I wrote to a friend and correspondent in Philadelphia to ask Mr. Meredith if he remembered what was said. The following is the note in reply, and the answer of Mr. Meredith:

Philadelphia, 15th Sept., 1859.

My dear Dr. Denny—I acknowledged, last week, your letter of the 2d inst., stating what Mr. Meredith had said to me in conversation. I now have the pleasure to inclose a note from Mr. Meredith, which I only got last evening, too late to send by last night's mail.

Always, my dear sir,
Very truly yours,
Benjamin Rush.

Dr. Denny.

Mr. Meredith to Mr. Rush.

Philadelphia, 12th Sept., 1859

My dear Sir—I have read Dr. Denny's note to you, which I herewith return. I have frequently heard my father speak of having been, with other friends, at General Harmar's on the evening during which Major Denny arrived, bringing the first intelligence of St. Clair's defeat. General Harmar did not live at Norristown, but at his country seat in the suburbs of Philadelphia. Major Denny was the bearer of General St. Clair's dispatches, and my understanding was, that after delivering them to the commander-in-chief, he rode straight to General Harmar's, of whom he was an intimate friend, and had been, I think, his aid-de-camp.

My lamented friend, Harmar Denny, was named after him. Of course I need not speak of their relation to each other, as Dr. Denny must be familiar with it. My father always spoke with great feeling of the profound impression made upon himself (then a youth of nineteen) and the other guests, by the sudden entrance of Major Denny, travel-stained, worn and exhausted, and by his earnest and soldier-like narration of the battle, defeat and massacre, and description of the sufferings to which the inhabitants of the frontier were thereby exposed.

I am, with great esteem,
Very faithfully yours,
W. M. Meredith.

B. Rush, Esq.